Critical Reading and Writing for Postgraduates

SAGE Study Skills

Critical Reading and Writing for Postgraduates

Mike Wallace
& Alison Wray

3rd Edition

SAGE

Los Angeles | London | New Delhi
Singapore | Washington DC | Melbourne

SAGE

Los Angeles | London | New Delhi
Singapore | Washington DC | Melbourne

SAGE Publications Ltd
1 Oliver's Yard
55 City Road
London EC1Y 1SP

SAGE Publications Inc.
2455 Teller Road
Thousand Oaks, California 91320

SAGE Publications India Pvt Ltd
B 1/I 1 Mohan Cooperative Industrial Area
Mathura Road
New Delhi 110 044

SAGE Publications Asia-Pacific Pte Ltd
3 Church Street
#10-04 Samsung Hub
Singapore 049483

Editor: Marianne Lagrange
Editorial assistant: Rob Patterson
Production editor: Tom Bedford
Copyeditor: Elaine Leek
Marketing manager: Catherine Slinn
Cover design: Stephanie Guyaz
Typeset by: C&M Digitals (P) Ltd, Chennai, India
Printed and bound by CPI Group (UK) Ltd,
Croydon, CR0 4YY

First edition published 2006, reprinted 2006, 2007, 2008
Second edition published 2011, reprinted 2014
This third edition published 2016

Library of Congress Control Number: 2015951090

British Library Cataloguing in Publication data

A catalogue record for this book is available from the British Library

ISBN 978-1-4129-6181-3
ISBN 978-1-4129-6182-0 (pbk)

Contents

List of Figures and Tables

Figures

Tables

Author Biographies

Mike Wallace is a Professor of Public Management at Cardiff Business School, Cardiff University. From 2009 to 2012 he was the Economic and Social Research Council's Strategic Adviser for Researcher Development. His research on managing change in the public services is reported in many books and academic journals. He is co-author, with Eric Hoyle, of the 2005 book *Educational Leadership: Ambiguity, Professionals, and Managerialism* (SAGE), and lead editor, with Michael Fertig and Eugene Schneller, of the 2007 book *Managing Change in the Public Services* (Blackwell). His teaching at Cardiff centres on postgraduate research methods training.

Alison Wray is a Research Professor of Language and Communication at Cardiff University. Her research concerns the modelling of lexical storage and processing, particularly in relation to formulaic phrases, and it has been applied to language learning, evolution of language and language disability. Her two monographs *Formulaic Language and the Lexicon* (Cambridge University Press, 2002) and *Formulaic Language: Pushing the Boundaries* (Oxford University Press, 2008) are internationally acclaimed. Her current research is into dementia communication. She has a longstanding commitment to researcher training, including the developing of academic expertise. She is lead author of the popular undergraduate research methods textbook *Projects in Linguistics* (Hodder, 2012).

Between 2010 and 2014 Mike and Alison collaborated on a Researcher Development Initiative Award funded by the Economic and Social Research Council, examining the nature and development of expertise in social science research. A training resource booklet based on this research can be found at www.restore.ac.uk/researchexpertise/

Acknowledgements

We are grateful to the postgraduate students at Cardiff University and the University of Bath who helped us develop the materials in the first edition of this book, and to the many academics, whether participating in our workshops or directly approached, for feedback informing the second and third editions. The ideas of the late Ray Bolam were a key influence on our thinking about mental map components and structuring a dissertation. The late Louise Poulson kindly gave us permission to draw on material (co-authored with Mike Wallace) that previously appeared in Chapters 1 and 2 and Appendix 2 of:

Wallace, M. and Poulson, L. (eds) (2003) *Learning to Read Critically in Educational Leadership and Management*. London: SAGE.

Goodwin, A. and Stables, A. (eds) (2004) *Learning to Read Critically in Language and Literacy Education*. London: SAGE.

Poulson, L. and Wallace, M. (eds) (2004) *Learning to Read Critically in Teaching and Learning*. London: SAGE.

Thanks also to John Staczek and Equinox Publishing Ltd for permission to reproduce in abridged form the material in Appendix 1, and to SAGE Publications Ltd and the British Educational Leadership, Management and Administration Society (BELMAS) for permission to reproduce the material in Appendix 2. The full references are:

Wray, A. and Staczek, J. (2005) 'One word or two? Psycholinguistic and sociolinguistic interpretations of meaning in a civil court case', *International Journal of Speech, Language and the Law* 12(1): 1–18, published by The University of Birmingham Press © 2005. Reproduced with the permission of Equinox Publishing Ltd.

Wallace, M. (2001) 'Sharing leadership of schools through teamwork: a justifiable risk?', *Educational Management, Administration and Leadership* 29(2): 153–67. Published by the British Educational Leadership, Management and Administration Society (BELMAS) © 2001. Reproduced with the permission of SAGE Publications Ltd.

How to Use This Book

The book is aimed primarily at postgraduate students in the social sciences, embarked on work requiring an engagement with the published (and unpublished) literature, including coursework essays, masters dissertations, doctoral dissertations or theses, and related research papers and oral presentations. But critical reading and self-critical writing are highly transferable skills, crucial to effective professional academic publications, presentations and research grant proposals. So the book will also be useful to early-career academics who wish to enhance the quality of their research writing by reading the literature more critically and by honing their skills as self-critical writers.

The book design makes it suitable for self-directed learning, for use as a class textbook in a research methods module and as a handbook from which supervisor and student can work side by side. In addition, peer mentors within the academic profession may find a role for it in supporting their less experienced colleagues. The text is supplemented by online self-study materials (see https://study.sagepub.com/wallaceandwray3e). They include exercises and illustrations of our approach to the in-depth critical analysis of individual texts, and electronic versions of forms for analysing texts and checking the development of the overall argument in a dissertation.

Our structured approach to learning critical reading and self-critical writing skills is underpinned by two core ideas. The first is the recognition of academic discourse as a two-way constructively critical process of enquiry where:

- as a critical reader, one evaluates the attempts of others to communicate with and convince their target audience by means of developing a sufficiently strong argument; and
- as a writer, one develops one's own argument, making it as strong and as clear as possible, so as to communicate with and convince one's target audience.

The product of critical reading is, typically, a written account of what has been read. Assessors take such accounts as the basis for judging an individual's ability to engage critically with the literature in the field of enquiry. Successful writers, therefore, are those who can apply their critical reading faculties equally to the research literature and to their own commentaries upon it. The techniques we introduce will make it easier to respond effectively and positively to constructive feedback on assessed work, and to emulate the good practice (and avoid the worst practice) observed in published materials.

The second core idea is that arguments combine two major components: the *conclusion*, a set of claims or assertions about some aspect of the social world or how to interpret it, plus the *warranting*, backing for these claims based on some form of evidence. For a conclusion to convince a sceptical audience, it must be adequately warranted by sufficient and appropriate evidence to justify its acceptance. Sources of such evidence include research findings, professional experience, the definition of a theoretical idea, or guidelines on research ethics.

The book is structured in three parts, which cover:

- Getting started on critical reading and self-critical writing.
- Developing a mental map for navigating the literature, analysing individual texts in depth and writing critical reviews of them.
- Structuring critical reviews of the literature for a dissertation, and applying the structure to research papers and oral presentations.

Parts and chapters	**Insights and techniques**	**Target written product**
Part One (Chapters 1–6) Becoming a Critical Reader and Self-Critical Writer	Critical reading for self-critical writing Critical choice of texts to read Developing an argument Critically reading an abstract Critical Synopsis Questions Critical Synopsis of a text	Critical Summary (one text) Comparative Critical Summary (several texts)
Part Two (Chapters 7–13) Developing an In-Depth Analysis	Mental map Critical Analysis Questions Critical Analysis of a text	Critical Review (one text) Comparative Critical Review (several texts)
Part Three (Chapters 14–18) Putting Your Critical Reviews to Work	Structuring a Critical Literature Review via Critical Analyses and Critical Synopses Integrating Critical Literature Reviews into the structure of different types of dissertation Integrating a Critical Literature Review into the structure of a research paper and as underpinning for an oral presentation	Self-contained Critical Literature Reviews Dissertation incorporating several Critical Literature Reviews Research papers and oral presentations underpinned by a Critical Literature Review

The material in the book is designed to build up skills and confidence gradually as the reader works sequentially through each chapter and the associated exercises, many of which are suitable for classroom activities or as a basis for assessed Critical Review assignments. In the two most central exercises, readers are invited to analyse and review two abridged academic journal articles, supported by worked examples, as a preparation for writing their own reviews of texts that they have chosen.

We chose these two articles because they raise contrasting generic issues for critical readers during critical analysis, while also exemplifying aspects of how ideas are managed. The main focus of the article in Part One, by Wray and Staczek (2005, see Appendix 1), is a conceptual model of how different people might process the same linguistic material in different ways. The exemplification comes from a court case that assessed the intended and received meaning of the American dialect term 'coonass', which the plaintiff found racially offensive. Wray and Staczek's interest lies in applying their theoretical model to this real-life case, as a means of accounting for what happened, without engaging directly with the substantive issues of the case. Through this paper, Wray and Staczek exemplify for readers how to engage critically with two sides of an argument, while maintaining a distance from their personal views about the substantive issue. This is an important academic skill.

The article in Part Two, by Wallace (2001, see Appendix 2), also focuses on the link between theory and empirical evidence. However, whereas Wray and Staczek apply a general model of language processing to illuminate an empirical case, Wallace derives a model from empirical cases of teamwork within senior management teams in UK schools. Also, whereas Wray and Staczek adopt a relatively impartial standpoint towards the substantive issue, Wallace adopts an explicitly value-laden approach. Wallace exemplifies for readers how an author's own views can be appropriately expressed within an academic paper, to make a normative argument and offer proposals about what should be done.

The book offers practical tools for tackling particular critical reading and reviewing tasks, including forms to complete when analysing texts, checklists to prompt thinking and structures for planning reviews. Blank versions of these forms can be downloaded from the SAGE website (https://study.sagepub.com/wallaceandwray3e).

The guidance material in each part develops a progressively more sophisticated engagement with texts and the target written product. Attention is paid to both single-text analysis and the integration, in a review, of comments on several texts. From first steps into critical reading and self-critical writing, through incorporating multiple literature reviews into a dissertation, to harnessing literature for research reports or oral presentations, the text explains and exemplifies in logical stages these necessary skills of sound academic practice.

In this third edition we have made three significant modifications. We have introduced a technique for developing critical thinking skills by interrogating the abstract of a paper. We have revised and clarified the mental map in Part Two. And we have supplemented our guidance on incorporating critical literature reviews into a dissertation, to take account of cumulative, thematic and inductive styles of research.

Companion Website

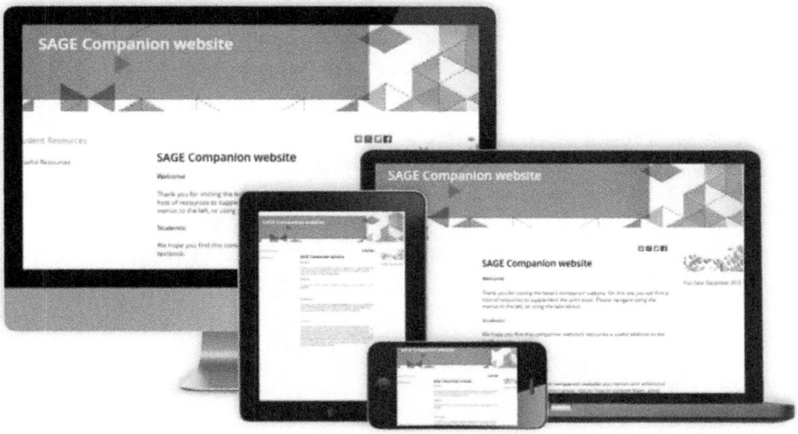

Critical Reading and Writing for Postgraduates is supported by a wealth of free online resources to aid study, which are available at https://study.sagepub.com/wallaceandwray3e

- **Watch and learn!** Author videos featuring discussions of key concepts to foster understanding and facilitate learning
- **Critical analysis templates and examples** will give you the confidence to critically analyse a piece of academic text and incorporate this into your own writing

Part One

Becoming a Critical Reader and Self-Critical Writer

1

What it Means to be Critical

Keywords

academic traditions; critical reading; discernment; scepticism; self-critical writing

You may already be a more critical reader than you realize. Take a look at this fictional advertisement and think about how you would respond to it.

WHY DO IT THE HARD WAY when you can be rich NOW!!!

It took me five years to make my first million. I made my second million in six weeks. Now I just can't stop making money. I own four luxury villas on three continents, five top-of-the-range sports cars and my own helicopter. Most important of all, the financial security of my family is ensured.

Now I want to share my good fortune with you. By following my simple instructions you too can be a millionaire within just a few months. There is no risk and it just can't fail. I have already helped hundreds of people attain their dream of a new life. They are so grateful to me – no longer do they worry about domestic bills, healthcare or their children's education. Their future is certain. And yours can be too.

Just call me on the number below, and I will send you my introductory pack *free of charge*. It will explain to you how my failsafe method can bring you guaranteed wealth and happiness. Call now, and let your life change forever for the better.

The advertisement promises to make you a millionaire. Would you call the phone number? If not – or if you are not sure whether you would – why is that?

The introductory pack is free. Your financial worries could soon be over. What would stop you picking up the phone?

The fact is that we do not necessarily take everything we read at face value, nor should we. Our life experiences make us suspicious of advertisements like this. We might ask: 'Are you as rich as you claim? Why do you want to help people you have never met? Is your method legal and ethical? Is there really no risk? Would I just end up making you richer, at my own expense? If your method is so wonderful, why have I never heard of it before? What will you do with my personal details once I give them to you? How much will the phone call cost?'

These are all critical questions. They indicate that you can see more in a text than is presented on the surface. You are looking for a hidden agenda, the author's real purpose. You are relating what you read to what you already know about the world. It is a sad reflection upon that world, perhaps, but we rarely expect to get something for nothing and we sometimes expect that people will try to trick us.

Learning to be critical in academic enquiry

Academic writing is generally much more benign. We do not expect authors to be lying or trying to swindle us. But there may still be hidden layers to an academic text. A critical approach to the reading of a journal article or book is therefore essential if we are to assess the value of the work it reports. Certain expectations underpin the way in which academic writing operates. The most fundamental expectation is that any claim will be backed up by reasons based on some form of evidence. So, the reader asks at every point: 'Have you given me sufficient grounds for accepting your claim?' Such a question need not imply that authors are untruthful. In most fields of enquiry it is not a matter of truth, but of viewpoints, interpretation and significance. As readers we are attempting to find common ground between our own understandings and beliefs, and those of the authors. That can be done only by thinking about the extent to which the claims and supporting evidence in a text – which satisfied the authors – also satisfy us.

Since each person has different knowledge and experience, it is sensible for the reader to adopt a critical frame of mind that maintains a distance from, and friendly scepticism towards, what authors say. In reading an academic article, we might keep in our mind these sceptical provisos:

- The authors mean to be honest, but may have been misled by the evidence into saying something that I consider untrue.
- The authors mean to be logical, but may have developed a line of reasoning that contains a flaw.

- The authors mean to be impartial, but may have incorporated into the account some assumptions that I do not share.
- The authors mean to tell me something new, but may not have taken into account other information that I possess.

Reasonable scepticism means being open-minded and willing to be convinced, but only if authors can adequately back their claims. It entails striking a balance between what one expects and what one accepts. No study can achieve everything. The critical reader is not put off by the limitations of a study, but will expect authors to interpret their investigation in a way that takes account of those limitations. Accomplished authors will clearly signal to the reader the basis for their conclusions and the confidence they have in any generalizations they make.

Most novice critical readers take a while to learn how to interpret authors' signals, and to work out how to respond to them. Often, part of the learning process is that one goes too far towards one or both extremes – uncritical acceptance or overcritical rejection of authors' claims – before finding a happy medium. Learning the knack of reasonable scepticism is, of course, particularly challenging because published material does vary in its rigour and reliability.

To assess your current ability to evaluate what you read, consider the short (fictional) extract below from a paper by someone we have called Browning. What questions might you, as a critical reader, ask of the author in relation to the claims made? The account refers to a study where some children were taught to read using the *phonics* method (sounding out words on the basis of the component letters) and others were taught using the *whole word* method (learning to recognize and pronounce complete words).

> In the reading test, the five children who were taught to read using phonics performed better overall than the five children taught using the whole word method. This shows that the phonics method is a better choice for schools.

Your questions might include:

- Is a study of just ten children sufficient to draw such a strong conclusion?
- What does 'performed better overall' signify? Did some children taught using the whole word method perform *better* than some children taught using phonics? If so, what does this mean for the results?
- Were the differences between the two groups sufficiently great for us to be satisfied that they would occur in a re-run of the experiment with different subjects?
- How were the two teaching programmes administered, and might there have been 'leakage' of whole word teaching into the phonics teaching and vice versa?
- What was the reading test actually testing, and might it have been unintentionally biased to favour the children taught using phonics?

- What care was taken to check how parental involvement at home might have influenced what and how the children learned?
- Were the two sets of five children matched for intelligence, age, gender or other factors?
- Is it reasonable to infer that what works well in a small experimental study will work well in school environments?
- How does Browning envisage phonics being used in schools? Would there still be a place for the whole word method?

Some such questions asked of a short, decontextualized extract like this will almost certainly be answered elsewhere in the text. That is where to look first. But other questions may remain unaddressed, leaving you to seek your own answers or to consider the risk entailed in accepting the report without answering them. Suppose the text is central to your study for an essay, so that you want to comment on it in detail. Then you will need to include some account of the weaknesses that your critical questions raise, as a balance to your description of what the authors are claiming. Here is an indication of how, in an essay, you might comment on a published text that is useful, but not perfect.

> Browning (2005) found that children taught to read using phonics did better in a reading test than children taught using the whole word method. However, the study was small, the test rather limited, and the subjects were not tightly matched either for age or gender. An examination of Browning's test scores reveals that, although the mean score of the phonics group was higher, two of the highest scorers in the test were whole word learners. Since this indicates that the whole word method is effective for some learners at least, Browning is perhaps too quick to propose that 'the phonics method is a better choice for schools' (p. 89).

Your critical reading of others' work will usually be in preparation for producing your own written text. This marriage of reading and writing has many benefits. First, you will develop a sense of what is and is not a robust piece of research – essential when you come to plan your own empirical investigation (for a dissertation, say). Second, you will soon begin identifying where the existing research has left a gap that your investigation can fill. Third, the attention you pay to different authors' texts will naturally affect the quality of your own writing. You will soon:

- demand of yourself evidence to back up your claims;
- be alert to the possibility of making an illogical jump in your reasoning;
- become sensitive to your own assumptions and how they might affect your claims; and
- realize the importance of checking the literature thoroughly to ensure that your understanding is sufficiently deep.

In short, you will develop a mature academic style of writing that is both fair and discerning in its accounts of others' work, and that maximizes the opportunity for others to take seriously what you have to say.

The skill of critical reading lies in assessing the extent to which authors have provided adequate justification for the claims they make. This assessment depends partly on what the authors have communicated and partly on other relevant knowledge, experience and inference that you are able to draw on.

The skill of self-critical writing lies in convincing your readers to accept your claims. You achieve their acceptance through the effective communication of adequate reasons and evidence for these claims.

Academic traditions and styles

All academic traditions require a critical engagement with the works of other scholars. However, some traditions emphasize it more than others. Depending on where you have been educated till now, you may have been encouraged to take predominantly one or another approach to what you read and write. Let us point to the opposite ends of a particular dimension in these traditions: student-centred learning versus knowledge-centred learning. Both have a role for the balanced learner, but neither should be taken to an extreme. Table 1.1 illustrates what can happen at the extremes, and how mature academics must strike a reasonable balance between their own ideas and those of others. Try using these descriptions to help you judge where your educational experience has located you on the continuum.

TABLE 1.1 Targeting an effective balance between different academic traditions

Too student-centred (values imaginative thought even if not fully grounded in established theory and knowledge)	**Target balance (appropriately reflects fair and constructively critical reading)**	**Too knowledge-centred (values traditional wisdom over the views and experience of the academic apprentice)**
Too easily dismisses the expertise of others	Assumes authors are knowledgeable, while remaining alert for possible flaws in their reasoning	Takes too much at face value
Fails to see the big picture	Juxtaposes the overall picture with the specifics of particular situations	Fails to see implications of generalized ideas for a specific context
Underestimates the task of becoming truly knowledgeable about a model or idea	Is prepared to criticize a model or idea, while retaining a sense of what authors might say in reply	Believes it is sufficient to be knowledgeable about a model or idea

Student-centred learning helps individuals gain confidence in developing their own ideas, by using existing knowledge as a stepping stone on the way to originality. In knowledge-centred learning, individuals are encouraged to become aware of existing scholarship and to value it above their own ideas as a novice. Ultimately, both traditions are aspects of the same thing: individuals make a personal effort to contribute something new to an existing bank of respected knowledge. However, the assumptions underlying each tradition do make a difference to how scholars operate. Typically, the rhetoric of the western-style tradition emphasizes the importance of the individual. Western-educated students can easily over-interpret this emphasis and forget to give sufficient importance to the work of others. In contrast, non-western-educated students may be intimidated by the sudden emphasis on what they think.

The term 'critical reading' is often associated with individuals trying to show why their own interpretation of some idea or observation is better than someone else's. It may seem, then, that someone from a student-centred learning tradition is at an advantage in learning to be a critical reader. However, students from both traditions bring something useful to the task and have pitfalls to avoid. The techniques introduced in this book bring together skills from each tradition.

Being critical as a requirement of academic study

Just what is expected in postgraduate study? Here is an example description of key skills.

> Critical thinking and creativity: managing creative processes in self and others; organising thoughts, analysis, synthesis, critical appraisal. This includes the capability to identify assumptions, evaluate statements in terms of evidence, detect false logic or reasoning, identify implicit values, define terms adequately and generalize appropriately. (Adapted from 'Skills for all Masters programmes', 2007 subject benchmark statement from the *Masters Awards in Business and Management*, Quality Assurance Agency for Higher Education (UK), www.qaa.ac.uk/en/Publications/Documents/Subject-benchmark-statement-Masters-degrees-in-business-and-management.pdf)

The critical skills here can be boiled down to the capacity to evaluate what you read and the capacity to relate what you read to other information. Applying these skills to any academic text involves looking out for its potential strengths and weaknesses.

Evaluation is important. If knowledge were simply a set of facts, we could take all that we read at face value. However, knowledge is only partly about the facts. Knowledge also entails the *interpretation* and the use of past facts to help us make predictions about future facts. It often also entails the *evaluation* of facts against certain assumed values. For instance, it was assumed in the earlier discussion about phonics and whole word reading that it is desirable for children to learn to read efficiently and effectively. If you take away that assumption, the facts will be open to different interpretations. University students are sometimes shocked to discover that facts can be interpreted in diverse ways, leading to very different predictions about what will happen in the future, or judgements about what should happen.

The critical reading of a text is rarely about questioning the facts. Mostly it is about assessing the quality of the case that has been made for interpreting and evaluating the facts in some way. Thus, the critical reader is interested in whether there is sufficient evidence to support a claim, whether there is another possible interpretation that has not been considered, and perhaps whether the authors have argued convincingly that their interpretation applies to other cases.

The critical reader can achieve this by focusing on several potential objects of scrutiny. They include:

- The evidence provided in the account.
- Whether the reasoning of the author's argument follows logically to the conclusion that has been drawn.
- Explicit or implicit indications of the author's values and assumptions.
- The match between the author's claims and those of other authors.
- The match between the author's claims or predictions and the reader's own research evidence or knowledge.

To engage thoroughly with a text, the reader ideally needs to have a clear understanding of what the authors are doing, sufficient knowledge of the field of enquiry and (where possible) reliable evidence of his or her own, or at least some reliable intuitions about the way things work in the real world. But no readers have the necessary time or expertise always to put themselves in this advantageous position. The art, then, is to know how far to go with any text. This, in turn, will depend on how central the text is to the study activity that one is involved in, and one's goals in reading it. Maintaining a sense of why you are reading a text makes evaluating it much easier.

Task-driven critical reading

It should always be possible beforehand to state why you are going to read a book or journal article. Reasons might be:

- You have been told to read it in preparation for a class.
- You are doing background reading on your subject, just to get your bearings.
- It reports a particular approach or technique that you want to see in action.
- It addresses a particular question that you want to know the answer to.
- You are looking for evidence to counterbalance something else that you have read.
- You have a particular story to tell, and you need some supporting evidence for it.

Irrespective of your reason for reading a text, it is worth having one or more questions in mind whose answers will help you progress your own work. A broad question addressed to the author such as 'What did you do, and what did you find out?' will be best answered with a straight description of the content of the paper. However, more finely tuned questions will help you focus on specific issues, while automatically providing a direct route into critical reading. For example: 'Is this author's method of investigation the best one for me to emulate in my own work? How does this author's position compare with that of another author whose work I've read? Would this author challenge the claims that I am making in my own work?'

After the initial background reading stage, you will rarely have the luxury of reading for reading's sake. There is simply too much literature out there. You will have to choose what to read and how thoroughly you read it. Your choices will be based on your best guess about what you might use the information for: usually some written task of your own. So the questions you bring to the text, as illustrated above, can guide your decisions on what to read and in how much depth.

It may seem a bad idea to decide *before* you read something what you are going to get out of it. How can you know until you have finished reading? If you start with a particular question, might you miss seeing what else the material has to offer? The danger is less than it may seem. If you are alert, you will notice other things that are relevant to your task, even if you did not expect to find them there. The single-minded approach will help you to separate out the different kinds of information you are seeking and deal with them at the right time.

Imagine you are reading a paper reporting a questionnaire study because you are seeking hints on how to design your own questionnaire. While reading, you realize that one of the results of the study has a bearing on your research. The fact that you already have a focused question regarding the study design will encourage you to make a note to return to the paper later, when you are specifically working on a data-related question. Doing so will help you avoid distracting yourself from the matter in hand so that you end up achieving neither task properly.

This disciplined strategy means that you sometimes read the same work more than once, for different purposes. It also means that any notes you make on that work will tend to be in different places, under topic headings, rather than in the form of a single, bland and unfocused summary of what the paper says.

Linking critical reading with self-critical writing

One person's writing is another person's reading. Whatever you write as a student will be read critically by your assessors. If you progress to writing for a conference presentation or publication, anonymous reviewers and then the general academic community will also be critical readers of your work. A secret of successful writing is to anticipate the expectations and potential objections of the audience of critical readers for whom you are writing. So you must develop a sense of who your readers are and what they expect. What you learn from this book about the techniques of critical reading in the academic context can be directly applied to making your own academic writing robust for other critical readers like you: intelligent, well-informed and fair-minded, ready to be convinced, but expecting high standards of scholarship and clarity in what they read.

As you work through this book, identifying effective ways of interrogating what you read, you will find that some of the techniques are familiar because you already use them. Others you will now be able to apply for the first time. If you demand certain things in what you read, it makes sense that you should supply them to your target audience in what you write. If you want clarity, then you yourself should be clear. If you need authors to be explicit about their assumptions, then you should be explicit about yours. If you want authors to provide evidence to support their claims, then you should provide evidence for your own.

No two readers want quite the same things, and you will probably never fully anticipate all of the requirements and preferences of your assessors. But you can get a long way towards that goal. How far have you progressed so far in becoming a critical reader and self-critical writer? Try the exercise in Table 1.2.

TABLE 1.2 Linking a critical approach to your reading with a self-critical approach to writing

How critical a reader and self-critical a writer are you already?

A	Rate each element of critical reading in the list below according to how much you already employ it when you read academic literature. Use a scale of 0–2 (*where 0 = rarely/never, 1 = sometimes/quite often, 2 = always*)
B	Now do the same for your own academic writing. (You may find it helpful to look at assessors' comments on your past work, to see what they have praised and criticized.)
C	Then add up the ratings separately for each column, and consider your response to our statement at the end of the exercise.

(Continued)

TABLE 1.2 *(Continued)*

How critical a reader and self-critical a writer are you already?

Element of critical reading	*Rating*	*Element of self-critical writing*	*Rating*
When I read an academic text I:	0–2	**When I write an academic text I:**	0–2
1 try to work out what the authors are aiming to achieve;		1 state clearly what I am trying to achieve;	
2 try to work out the structure of the argument;		2 create a logical structure for my account, to help me develop my argument and to help the reader to follow it;	
3 try to identify the main claims made;		3 clearly state my main claims;	
4 adopt a sceptical stance towards the authors' claims, checking that they are supported by appropriate evidence;		4 support my claims with appropriate evidence, so that a critical reader will be convinced;	
5 assess the backing for any generalizations made;		5 avoid making sweeping generalizations;	
6 check how the authors define their key terms and whether they are consistent in using them;		6 define the key terms employed in my account, and use the terms consistently;	
7 consider what underlying values may be guiding the authors and influencing their claims;		7 ensure that I am aware of how what I write reflects my values; and, where appropriate, that I make these values explicit;	
8 keep an open mind, willing to be convinced;		8 assume that my readers can be convinced, provided I can adequately support my claims;	
9 look out for instances of irrelevant or distracting material, and for the absence of necessary material;		9 sustain focus throughout my account, avoid irrelevancies and digressions, and include everything that is relevant;	
10 identify any literature sources to which the authors refer, that I may need to follow up.		10 ensure that my referencing in the text and the reference list is complete and accurate, so that my readers are in a position to check my sources.	
Total score for reading		*Total score for writing*	

The higher the scores, the further you have already progressed in becoming a critical reader and/or self-critical writer. Look back at any items you gave 0 to. Consider how you might increasingly incorporate these elements of critical reading and self-critical writing into your habitual approach to study.

In Table 1.2 we have highlighted the link between elements of critical reading and their counterparts in self-critical writing. Whatever you look for as a critical reader of literature, your assessors may also look for in your writing when judging how far it meets their assessment criteria. The elements of self-critical writing relate to meeting the needs of your readers, so that they can grasp what you are trying to communicate. But just as importantly, they enhance your capacity to make your argument convincing to your readers. This is why developing a strong sense of your audience is to your advantage. Meeting your target readers' needs and convincing them will help to ensure that your account meets the assessment criteria. During your studies, you will find it useful to refer back to this exercise occasionally, to monitor your progress in developing critical reading and self-critical writing skills.

Where now?

The next chapter considers how to select effectively from the vast array of literature available. Chapter 3 presents a way to develop your critical thinking by asking questions of journal article abstracts. Chapter 4 introduces five Critical Synopsis Questions that you can ask of a text. Chapters 5 and 6 use these insights to introduce some simple techniques for self-critical writing: presenting your own ideas in a well-supported way. Part One thus prepares you for the more detailed engagement of Parts Two and Three, where we revisit the same approach at a more advanced level.

2

Making a Critical Choice

Keywords

encyclopaedias; handbooks; Internet resources; readers; reading; research literature; textbooks

What you choose to read in preparing for your assessed written work is as important as how critically you read it. Becoming a critical reader must entail becoming a discerning selector of those texts that promise most centrally to suit your study purposes. The Internet makes it possible to access far more potentially relevant literature than you will ever have time to read. So making effective choices about what to read is the first step in critical reading.

Our chapter begins with techniques for deciding what to read. We then distinguish between different types of literature that you will come across in the course of your studies. Finally, we consider how to use the Internet effectively as a resource.

Deciding what to read

Suppose it is time to start reading for a piece of assessed work. Where do you begin? You may have been supplied with an indicative reading list and perhaps some set texts. If so, someone else has made decisions on your behalf to get you started. But there will still come a point when you have to decide what to read. The more principled you can make your choices, the better.

Strategy is paramount. Apart from planning ahead – getting to the library before the crowd for instance – it is useful to operate a two-stage process when identifying what to read. First, draw up a long-list of texts that look important. Then select those that look most central to your reading purpose (discussed below). An advantage of this approach is that you can easily compensate if an item you had targeted is not available; you can work out from your long-list what other text might fulfil the same function. Drawing up the long-list is relatively straightforward. You might:

- Use any recommended reading list for your module or subject area, including those from past years.
- Search the Internet for reading lists posted up for similar modules at other universities, and identify texts that are repeatedly recommended.
- Look up one or two important texts in the library catalogue and then do a search using their subject code to see what else has been classified as covering the same topic.
- Go to the library shelves and see what is physically stored under the same class mark as the key recommended texts.
- Note how many copies the library has of a particular text – if there are plenty, it has evidently been a recommended text at some point.
- As you begin to read, note texts that are often cited by others, and whether positively or negatively (both may be useful).
- Make a list of the three or four journals most often carrying papers that have been recommended or frequently cited, then check the back and current issues of those journals for similar papers.
- Use abstracts databases to search for papers via keywords and author names that you associate with the topic.
- Look through the catalogues of the leading academic publishers to see what has come out recently.
- Check what books have been reviewed in recent academic journals.

In this way, you can soon build up your list of *possible* reading, from which you can choose what you actually read and in how much detail.

From long-list to short-list

How should you decide which items on your long-list to prioritize? Your reading has to achieve several aims that your selection of texts must take into account. A convincing essay (or dissertation) is likely to cover some or all of the following in relation to the literature:

- An overview of what the key issues in the field are and why they are important.
- An overview of what has been done and found out, and a summary of where the field of enquiry currently stands.

- Some specific examples of the sorts of methodology, results and analysis reported by individual researchers.
- Answers to one or more specific questions that you must, or choose to, address.

No single text can support all of these agendas. You may need one set of texts to help you develop your overview, another set to help you interpret the work to date within its wider context, yet another to give you specific information about methodology and analysis, and so on. To target your reading, ensure that you short-list a variety of texts that between them will help you achieve each of your goals. But how can you tell what a particular text is most likely to be useful for? One way is by categorizing texts according to their main purpose.

Support texts

Textbooks

Most students turn to textbooks early on in their academic studies. There are two basic types. First, skills textbooks (like the one you are reading now) aim to help you learn such things as how to design a robust investigation or analyse data statistically. They are not usually problematic to use, since it is clear that they are a tool rather than a resource. Second, subject textbooks generally introduce readers to a field of academic enquiry, and are explicitly designed to support students' learning. Features of textbooks may include:

- They are relatively cheap compared with research books.
- Words like 'introduction', 'guide' or 'study' appear in the title or the series title.
- They are available in softback, and have an eye-catching cover.
- The title evidently encompasses a field or sub-field rather than a particular research agenda (e.g., *A Short History of the English Language*) or else it covers a particular skill (e.g., *Statistics in the Social Sciences*).
- The cover blurb indicates a student target readership.
- There are multiple copies in academic bookshops and libraries. Also, popular textbooks often run to more than one edition.

While textbooks are crucial for any student, they fall outside the central realm of research activity. At postgraduate level you will be expected to have more on your reference list than just textbooks. They can be an excellent place to start, but inherent limitations mean that they are usually *only* a starting place, and should be used only to gain an overview and to identify frontline texts (see below).

Subject textbooks are often so like a literature review that it is difficult for you to find something new to say. The author appears to have summarized all the important works effectively. Conclusions about the big patterns seem to follow logically, and to capture the situation well. You might also feel it is inappropriate to question the judgements of the author, who is obviously more experienced and knowledgeable. However, it is important to view the textbook author as just one interpreter of the facts. Expect that there will be other ways of interpreting the facts too, and look for those ways, both in other textbooks and by thinking things through for yourself. If you view a textbook as one commentator's interpretation, rather than a summary of some unassailable truth, it becomes possible to pitch accounts against each other and discuss the reasons for the differences.

Getting the measure of support texts

In the library, try looking up the same concept or topic in the index of several different textbooks, encyclopaedias and handbooks. To what extent do they all report the same information, make the same claims or interpret the evidence in the same way? For some topics and concepts there is general consensus. For others there is huge variation, based on differences in assumptions, scope and interpretation. Understanding the range of views can help you decide where to position yourself and recognize which of your claims will be most subject to scrutiny by those reading your work.

A second difficulty with a textbook is that it normally tells you *about* research, without you seeing the original research report. You should attempt to read for yourself anything that you judge to be of central importance. You cannot guarantee that textbook authors have interpreted research in the same way that you would do, or have focused on the aspects that are significant for you. The only way you can be sure is to read the original works. Most textbooks provide full references to their sources, and you should aim to follow them up so that you have had sight of everything you discuss. Occasionally you may have to compromise and simply identify a particular work as 'cited in' some other work – that is, admitting that you have read *about* it but not actually *read* it. But keep such references to an absolute minimum.

A third limitation of some textbooks is that, in the interests of offering the reader a clear story, authors may make strong claims that are not backed up with sufficient evidence and they may over-simplify complicated issues. This is not necessarily inappropriate, given the introductory nature of a textbook. But it can be a hazard for students, who may fail to appreciate the complexity underlying an apparently simple observation, or fail to realize that opinion is divided on a matter that is presented as fact. Again, the solution is to see the textbook as a signpost to information, rather than a fully reliable source, and to read the original works that it cites wherever possible.

Readers, handbooks and encyclopaedias

Readers are collections of classic papers on a subject. Chapters may have been written especially for the collection, or may be articles or extracts from books already published elsewhere. The editors will have selected what they consider to be the most important work for students to read. But their selection is personal and other academics may not consider it fully representative of key works in the field. If a paper in a reader has been reproduced in full, it is acceptable to reference its appearance there and not to have seen the original. However, it is a good idea to give the original date as well as the date of the reader, so that it is clear when the paper was written.

Handbooks and specialist encyclopaedias are like readers, except that the articles will normally have been specially commissioned. Leading academics will have written an overview of research, theory or methodology in their area. Such articles are immensely useful for gaining an understanding of the state-of-the-art in a field. Remember, however, that even top researchers can give only their own perspective and there are likely to be other perspectives that you should also consider.

Tell-Tale signs of over-reliance on support texts

Watch out for these signs of over-reliance on support texts in your work:

- Presenting ideas and evidence without giving their original source.
- Giving references to works without having read them yourself.
- Only referring to works described in one support text.
- Using secondary referencing, e.g., 'Jones (cited in Smith, 2009) found …'.
- Plagiarizing by presenting an identical or slightly rewritten version of the support text, as if you had done the reading and thinking.

'Frontline' texts

This book deals predominantly with the critical reading of *frontline* publications: theoretical descriptions and explanations, reports of original research, accounts of current practice, and policy statements. Such works are the direct link between you and a researcher, practitioner or policy-maker. They report what has been done, how, why, what it means and what should be done next.

Types of frontline text

A rough distinction may be made between four types of frontline text: theoretical, research, practice and policy literature. Typically, frontline texts are easily identifiable as belonging primarily to one type of literature or another, but they can also feature aspects of more than one literature type. Thus, a journal article that is mainly reporting an empirical investigation may also discuss implications for theoretical development. Here is a brief description of each type.

Theoretical literature models the way things are (or might be), by using evidence to identify patterns. The evidence may include experiments, observations, experience or ideas, and may not be work that the theorizers have conducted themselves. The patterns, once formalized into a model, may enable researchers to make predictions about what will happen in future scenarios. Such predictions are called *hypotheses* (Figure 2.1).

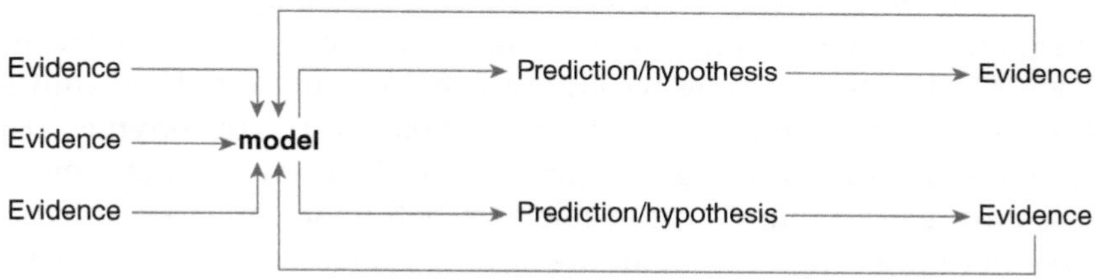

FIGURE 2.1 How theory and evidence interact through modelling

A model can help readers to deepen their understanding of the social world and to anticipate what things might be observed in the future, and under what circumstances. Theoretical literature can also be used to present the case for a viewpoint or to recommend changes. Consider a journal article putting forward a predictive model about the consumption of the earth's natural resources. The model predicts that, at current rates of consumption, some resources will be used up within 50 years. In itself, such an account is merely a statement of what the facts appear to be. However, it could be used to criticize national or international policy, to underpin recommendations for change, to influence the way people are educated, or to encourage individuals to take greater responsibility for their personal use of resources.

Research, or data-driven, literature reports findings about aspects of the social world, often relating them to a prediction or hypothesis derived from a model. Data sources include people's behaviour, talk, written texts, and artifacts such as drawings that have some meaning for them. One major difference in approaches to generating data relates to whether or not the researcher manipulates the situation. In a classic experimental design, a comparison might be made between two groups or situations that are identical except in one regard determined by the experimenter. Any difference in the outcomes is assumed to be due to that one contrast. In a classic observational design, the researcher might gather data that will indicate how a particular individual or group operates, but without intervening. Between the two lies a range of options, including:

- Observing two contrasting groups or situations that occur naturally (a natural experiment).
- Observation in which the researcher participates in the observed activity or situation (participant observation).
- Detailed observation of, or interviews with, one or more individuals or groups with the same, or contrasting, profiles (case studies).
- Individual or group interviews, whether asking a series of pre-specified questions or just pursuing looser themes.

As with theoretical literature, data-driven research may augment a general understanding about how phenomena operate. It can also be used to help explain where things are going wrong, to demonstrate a method that seems to work well (or better than some other method), to try to convince trainers or policy-makers to effect changes in present methods, or to enable individual readers to gain fresh insights into their own behaviour or practice.

Practice literature comprises accounts of how things are done, and will often be written by experienced practitioners who feel that others might benefit from an understanding of how they operate. This type of literature features most strongly in applied fields of enquiry focusing on a domain of practical activity in the social world, such as nursing. An account might, for instance, offer a personal illustration of how a nurse working for a relief agency has learned to cope with the extreme demands of over-crowded refugee camps. But the account might also be used for identifying shortcomings in existing systems, recommending practices that have been found to be effective, training others who will soon encounter similar situations or, at the personal level, influencing readers to reflect on similarities between their own situation and the one reported.

Policy literature (also featuring most strongly in applied fields) emphasizes change to improve practice, according to particular values. This type of literature is mostly produced by policy-makers, those working for them or others whose primary agenda is to influence policy-makers. For example, government ministers might publish a report drawing attention to shortcomings in present practice, proposing an alternative policy that will lead to more desirable outcomes, and outlining how it is to be implemented. A pressure group whose members do not share ministers' values might publish their own report, criticizing the government proposals and setting out their preferred alternative.

Being discerning about frontline literature

To a novice researcher, all published frontline research may look impressive. In due course, with your critical reading skills developed, you will be well equipped to evaluate the claims made. But in the short term, it is worth having a sense of some general patterns that can affect the quality of the frontline texts you consider reading.

The single most important thing to remember is that learning to do good research does not end with the completion of a dissertation. There are many more skills to acquire, ideas to understand and assumptions to challenge. The best researchers will tell you that the learning never stops. This means that research done at any stage of a career may be pushing at the boundaries of the researcher's knowledge or abilities, and could display weaknesses as a result.

A second thing to keep in mind is that research writing goes through varying amounts of revision before it is published. Papers in refereed journals will have been sent for review and will typically be accepted for publication only after substantial revisions. However, the reviewers, like any other reader, will have made their own interpretations and judgements in advising on improvements to the paper. Other researchers, including you, may come to different interpretations and judgements. So there is always scope for you to engage critically with authors' claims to knowledge. No one's claims can be beyond question.

Authors apply their own quality checks too, and a good sign can be when there are acknowledgements in the paper to the helpful comments of colleagues. This usually means the author sent the draft paper to others who have helped improve it. Similarly, multiple authorship usually means that the co-authors have all contributed to maximizing the quality of the paper. Co-authors also discuss the basic ideas and findings of their research, so that the claims made may reflect the combined knowledge of several people.

The quality of books also varies. Some edited collections are the result of selection – as when a few papers from a conference are published. Others may be the outcome of the editor's invitations to particular authors, with minimal quality checks of their texts. The quality of research monographs (books written by a single author or team, without authors' names on the individual chapters) rests largely on the expertise of the author(s). Most publishers send out monograph *proposals* for academic review, but not all have the final manuscript reviewed. Those that do will require responses to the reviewers' comments before they will accept the manuscript. Books that have undergone this process are likely to be more reliable for the reader.

Using the Internet

Opportunities and dangers

Much support and frontline literature is available in both electronic format and hard copy. Internet access enables you to use powerful search engines, directing you to myriad websites and downloadable files. However, care must be taken in using the Internet. It offers enormous opportunities to gather information but it carries certain dangers.

Beware of two major potential pitfalls. One is using Internet resources as a convenient replacement for the harder work of constructing your own text. Copying and pasting material from the Internet into your own work is regarded as cheating, or *plagiarism*, and usually carries heavy penalties. Resist any temptation to take this shortcut! Your assessors are very likely to spot what you have done and, more fundamentally, you will not learn as much as you would by doing the work yourself. Why undertake postgraduate study if you do not attempt to maximize your learning? Plagiarism is a serious problem in higher education. We recommend that you inform yourself fully about plagiarizing and scrupulously avoid it.

The question of *unreliability* is the other risk-laden aspect of Internet usage relating to critical reading. However critically you aim to read, it makes sense to favour texts that you have reasonable confidence in. The support literature and frontline publications discussed earlier have been written by people with a commitment to accuracy. All such texts have undergone some level of scrutiny by others to ensure that they live up to that commitment. The Internet, on the other hand, is an amoral, uncoordinated dissemination forum. While it includes some of the support literature and frontline publications whose reliability is ensured by the means we have just described, there are no safeguards to ensure the quality of everything else that can be posted on websites. As a result, the content of the Internet overall, and its reliability, are very variable.

Thus, you need to be critical in sorting the good material from the bad. This is not always easy, so you need techniques for ensuring that your use of the Internet only enhances, and never diminishes, the quality of your academic work. These techniques include applying all the standards of critical reading that we describe, and not assuming that the confidence with which something is said is a reliable guide to its validity.

When you are learning about a new topic, it is often difficult to evaluate the quality of an argument or of evidence. You may feel uncertain whether a claim you find on the Internet is reliable. A technique for avoiding this difficulty is to think of the Internet not as a repository of knowledge but as a catalogue. When you find something on the Internet, avoid making that the end point of your search. Use the information you have gathered to locate another kind of material in which you can have more confidence.

For instance, you might find on a web page the following claim: 'Metaphors are central to how we navigate the world (Lakoff and Johnson, 1980)'. Rather than accepting this claim without any further investigation, it would be much safer to check out who Lakoff and Johnson are, and to see if they have written an academic paper or book making the claim. (Indeed they have: Lakoff, G. and Johnson, M. (1980) *Metaphors We Live By*. Chicago: University of Chicago Press.) If so, obtain the text from the library and use that as your resource. In this instance, then, the Internet has been a springboard, much as your supervisor might be when advising you to read a particular text.

The dangers of over-reliance and unreliability can be well-illustrated in relation to one very valuable resource that should be used with care: Wikipedia, www.wikipedia.org. Whether Wikipedia is sufficiently reliable as a source of information, since anyone can contribute to it, has been much discussed. See http://en.wikipedia.org/wiki/Reliability_of_Wikipedia for Wikipedia's own article on this topic. It cites empirical studies and also indicates which aspects of its coverage are least likely to be reliable. This article indicates that perceptions of reliability depend on beliefs about the nature of 'correct information', and that it is always wiser to find an additional independent source of evidence for a claim, rather than accepting just one. Using Wikipedia as a springboard means finding out what is claimed about a topic there, and then following up the ideas using the reference list, names and keywords. It is never appropriate to copy text from Wikipedia directly into your own essay.

Internet resources for research

More resources are continually becoming available on the Internet, and you will probably be familiar with using general search engines such as Google. If you are trying to track down a copy of a published paper or conference presentation, simply typing in the title, inside inverted commas, will often lead you to an electronic version. However, researching a whole topic using a search engine, in the hope of finding relevant and reliable publications, is too hit-and-miss. Searches are usually prioritized on a commercial rather than knowledge basis. General searches may lead you to materials that are less trustworthy than the academic sources you need, so it is useful to employ more specifically academic searching methods. These include a range of major publication databases such as Web of Science, to which your university should hold a subscription. You should be able to obtain instructions from your library.

In addition, many international research libraries have now offered their resources for digitization, making available thousands of items that previously had to be viewed by travelling to that institution. The priority has been to offer materials that are rare and out of copyright. Such materials may be of more relevance for your original research than for the literature reviewing aspect of your work. However, libraries also hold many items that are more recent and that constitute part of the research literature. Usually they are still in copyright, so legal questions have arisen (yet to be fully resolved) over making these items available electronically to all. Currently, the copyright issue is resolved by displaying only sample pages from the work. Yet this can often be enough for scholars to establish whether an item is of primary importance to their research. Digitized works are searchable, and those sources collecting items from many different sites will tell you where you can find hard copies.

Major open access e-resources relevant to researchers include:

- Google Library project (http://books.google.com/googlebooks/library.html) is the largest, and contains digital versions of works from many university and national libraries. The searching facility for Google Library is Google Books, at http://books.google.com.
- Google Scholar (http://scholar.google.com) provides powerful searching of a huge number of academic journals, though often only the abstract can be read, because access is restricted to individuals and institutions with a subscription to the journal. Good university libraries usually subscribe to huge bundles of journals. So once you have identified the paper you want, it is worth checking if your university has access to it. If you cannot access it that way, try a general Google search on the title to see if there is a copy elsewhere on the Internet (e.g., the author's web page or a research network site like Researchgate, www.researchgate.net/home). Furthermore, most authors will send a copy if you email them with your request.
- Internet Archive (www.archive.org) includes texts, audio, moving images, software and archive web pages from the Library of Congress and the Smithsonian, amongst others.
- Europeana (www.europeana.eu/portal/usingeuropeana_search.html) offers access to millions of digital images, texts, sounds and videos from European museums, galleries, libraries and archives.
- Gallica (http://gallica.bnf.fr/), the digital library of the Bibliothèque Nationale Française, provides access to items from its own collection, including texts, images, musical scores, maps, manuscripts and audio material.

The texts you can access through these resources are as reliable as the hard copy equivalent you would find in the source library. All the requirements for critical reading described in this book in relation to books and journal articles apply also to electronically accessed texts.

Internet material – the good, the bad and the ugly

Likely to be very reliable:

1. Peer-reviewed journal articles that are also published in an academic journal. These should be referenced according to their paper details, rather than as an Internet resource.
2. Peer-reviewed journal articles published in genuine electronic journals. These should be referenced using their volume number and date, plus the full web address. It is possible that they will not have page numbers.
3. Already published journal articles and book chapters that have been posted, usually in PDF format, on an academic's home page. Check, however, that it is the published version. If it says 'submitted to' a journal, or 'draft', it has yet to be peer-reviewed. You could then check if it has since been published.
4. Electronically readable books written by subject experts.
5. Official materials published on a recognized institutional website, e.g., the British Museum site, or the Institute of Linguists' site. You can find out what site you are on by going to the home page.

Likely to be fairly reliable:

1. Pre-peer-reviewed material, as described in (3) above – but track down the published version if possible.
2. Lecture or research notes on the site of an academic working at a recognized institution.

Likely to be unreliable:

1. Material on the home pages of individuals.
2. Material on organization websites that is written by enthusiasts rather than experts.
3. Free-for-all post-your-views sites (unless restricted to a recognized set of academic contributors).
4. Web-logs (blogs), chatroom pontifications, etc.

Referencing Internet sources: golden rules

Internet sources are subject to two common problems. First, it may be unclear who wrote the material (and so what their credentials are for writing reliably). Second, web pages may disappear or move location, making them difficult to find in future. Therefore, it is always advisable to try tracking down a more permanent reference (to a book or journal article, for instance). Where you do have to reference an Internet source:

(Continued)

(Continued)

1. Attribute the material to a person if possible, not just a web address. Giving the URL (web address) alone is like referencing a book by describing where you found it in the library.
2. If (and only if) no author is named, give the institutional details instead. If you cannot find an author or an institution, do you really want to trust this material?
3. Give the date when it was posted or last updated, if available, otherwise the year in which you saw it.
4. Indicate the date on which you last accessed it.
5. Check that the URL you have given will indeed take someone to the exact material you are citing.

An example of how to reference an Internet source:

In the text:

... Children can be reliable witnesses, adults may not be reliable questioners (Aldridge-Waddon, 2015) ...

In the reference list:

Aldridge-Waddon, M. (2015) *Research Bite*, www.cardiff.ac.uk/english-communication-philosophy/research/themes/language-and-communication (accessed 29 October 2015).

Academic authors who aim to convince a critical reader that their work is robust will *only* reference Internet sources where:

- the material is robust and reliable;
- there is no equivalent published paper version; and
- the Internet resource has been the legitimate end of the line, not the means to finding a published paper resource.

Varying your reading strategy

Three useful reading strategies are:

- *Scanning* – looking through a text to find specific sections or keywords and phrases indicating where the information you are seeking is located.
- *Skimming* – reading quickly through those parts of a text that can give you an overview of the content.
- *Intensive reading* – carefully reading every word of a text from beginning to end.

Some students feel nervous about employing the full range of reading strategies. They fear that while scanning and skimming could save time, so more material is covered, vital information or subtle messages could be missed. So they play safe, reading everything intensively. Other students go too far in the opposite direction, failing to read any texts intensively or reflect adequately on what they read, leading to an overly descriptive written account. Or worse, they engage critically without having checked the detail or considered the implications of the claims. Such students may make sweeping statements and generalizations based on inaccurate reading.

Efficient and effective reading involves compromise between reading deeply and broadly, engaging fully with only those texts most central for your reading purpose. Skimming and scanning help you to find out which these are, enabling you to reduce the risk of missing what matters. Thus, you have the best possible chance of learning what you need to learn – without also wasting time on things you don't need to know.

What next?

Once you have identified a text as important, how are you to read it not just intensively, but also critically? That is the focus of the next chapter.

3
A First Look: Interrogating Abstracts

Keywords

abstracts; information; insight; questions

We saw in Chapter 1 that critical reading comes quite naturally when we are suspicious of the motives of the author. In academic writing, however, it can feel uncomfortable at first to ask questions. After all, the author is a published researcher and you might feel that he or she has more knowledge and expertise than you. In Chapter 4 we will show you how to get beneath the surface of a published text, to identify potential weaknesses in claims or alternative ways of interpreting evidence. Doing so successfully requires some confidence in asking questions, and this chapter introduces a technique for developing that confidence.

The technique makes use of an important design feature of the abstract typically found at the start of a published paper. We will come to what that design feature is in a moment. Abstracts are invaluable, because one of the most challenging aspects of working with the research literature is just how much of it there is. It would be impossible to read everything fully just to see if it was relevant to your needs. It follows that authors have a responsibility to ensure that the abstract carries the most useful and appropriate information for the reader. For that reason, in Chapters 17 and 18 we will look at how to write a good abstract for your own dissertation, journal article and conference presentation.

It is important to note that although we will focus in this chapter on a way of using the abstract on its own, there is no substitute for the full reading of an article once you have decided that you need to use it. The reason, as we shall see, is that there is not enough information in the abstract for it to give you all the knowledge you need, if you are planning to refer to the paper as a whole.

The aim here is to help you make a habit of 'active' reading – that is, thinking critically all the time when you are reading. As a result, you will enjoy your reading more, and find it more engaging. You are less likely to wake up at teatime and have no recollection of what you have been reading all day.

Using the abstract as a resource

The author of an academic paper provides an abstract as a service for the reader. It summarizes the paper, making it easy for the reader to gain an idea of what topics it covers, what sort of approach is taken and what the main claims are. But the abstract has a hidden value for the critical reader, precisely because it is so short.

As will become clear in the later chapters, critical reading, as defined and demonstrated in this book, revolves around asking questions of the text that are relevant to what you need to know for your own research. But it can be difficult, when reading the entire paper, to keep track of whether those questions are being adequately answered or not. Information is not necessarily given in the most convenient places, and so there is always the risk of missing something important. When you are reading a research article you can easily feel overwhelmed, wondering if in fact a certain piece of information *is* in the text and you just missed it. It would be much easier if you knew, before you started, what exactly you were looking for.

This is where the abstract comes in. When you read the full article, you generally expect that most of the information you need to know will be there somewhere. But when you read the abstract, you know that it probably *will not* all be there. After all, an abstract is typically no more than 150 words – far from long enough to explain everything. Most importantly, the abstract will typically make claims without any space to back them up.

As a result, if you ask yourself 'is this a good study?' (which is a core element of evaluating the usefulness of a paper), the abstract may not give you enough information about how the authors reached their conclusions for you to work out the answer. Even if you are asking the more basic question 'is this study relevant enough to what I need?', you may find that you cannot tell, because the abstract misses out some key aspect of the theoretical approach, data source or set of underlying assumptions and beliefs. It is this inherent absence of information that we will be using here to prompt your critical thinking.

Asking questions of an abstract

Even if you would usually feel nervous asking questions about a published paper, when you are dealing with the abstract, you know you are right in believing that they have not told you what you need to know. How could they have, in such a brief text? And, from what they *have* told you, you now know what else you need them to say. For example, as you read the abstract of a paper that uses statistics to report research, you might be asking:

- Yes, but what did you *mean* by that term?
- You have told me what sort of informants you used, but how many were they, and why did you choose *them*?
- You have told me what you wanted to find out, but why was it *interesting and important* to find it out?
- You have said that a lot of research has been done on this topic, but what are the key studies that I should be checking out?
- You have said that you found a significant difference between your two experimental groups, but what statistical test were you using?

These are the sorts of questions that you might ask someone face-to-face, if they had given you a brief overview about their work. In response, they would no doubt fill in the gaps, and you could probe further till you had all the information you needed. With a written article, the authors are not in the room with you, but you can use their full text as a potential source of answers to the questions raised by reading the abstract. Before you looked at the paper in its entirety, you could work out what answers would satisfy you, and why. So for this paper:

- ***I will expect a clear definition of that term.*** I will want to see if they are aware of the problem with defining it that I have read about in other work. If I do not find a definition, or if the definition is inadequate, I will need to work out whether that is just an oversight, or whether they have failed to appreciate the complexity of the phenomenon. If the latter, then it may not be clear what they have really found out here.
- ***I will expect a clear statement about the identity and selection of the informants.*** Because other work I have read suggests that age is an important variable relating to the feature under examination, I will be particularly looking for information about the age of the participants. If they are all young, and the authors nevertheless claim that their findings are generalizable across the entire population, I will be able to cite that other literature to cast doubt on the quality of their backing (warranting) for that claim.
- ***I will expect a clear steer from them about why they think it is interesting to extend the existing research into this new domain.*** Previous studies in other domains have claimed that the phenomenon is universal. If that is so, their study was not necessary. So I want to know why they thought this domain might be different.
- ***I will be checking their literature review for two things – relevant studies that I have not read, and that they can convince me I should go and find; and studies that I know about***

but that they do not mention. Where they have not mentioned a study that I think is important, I will be looking for clues as to why. If I conclude that they were not aware of a particular line of research that would have altered how they see things, I will be able to mention that in my critical commentary – after all, it could undermine the reliability of their claims.
- ***I will expect them to indicate what statistical test they used, and to justify it.*** Before I read the paper, I will try to figure out what stats I think they would use here, and then I can see if that is what they did. If they did not, I will try to figure out why. Perhaps I can learn from them. Or perhaps they have made a decision I have good reasons to disagree with.

How the questions help you think

The sharply focused questions that you develop by reading the abstract will, mostly, be answered in the main paper, because it was only lack of space that prevented them occurring in the abstract. However, one or two of the questions might *not* be answered. And because you are reading the article looking for answers, you are much more likely to notice when that happens. Because the questions are based on your own current knowledge and the nature of your own research project, they will be the very ones of most importance to you. Not finding the answers in the main text will, as a result, be very relevant to your narrative. It will give you the basis for a critical commentary about the paper.

A worked example

The process of critically reading an abstract is best explained through an example. Firstly, note that although we have talked about the abstract, in fact the interrogation begins even higher up the paper – with the title and the authors. You are free to ask whatever you most need to. It is an exercise in focusing on what is important for *you* in *your* study, and in developing confidence to think of questions.

Text	Reader comments
SOURCE: *Educational Researcher, 2012, vol. 41 (9): 339–351*	• This is a journal that addresses researchers of education. Why did the authors choose this audience?
TITLE: Are Minority Children Disproportionately Represented in Early Intervention and Early Childhood Special Education?	• What do they mean by 'minority'? Which country are they talking about? • What age range are they covering? • How do they define 'early intervention' and 'special education'? Do their definitions create any potential problems?

(Continued)

(Continued)

Text	**Reader comments**
AUTHORS: Paul L. Morgan,[1] George Farkas,[2] Marianne M. Hillemeier,[1] Steve Maczuga[1] [1]*Population Research Institute, The Pennsylvania State University, University Park, PA;* [2]*University of California, Irvine, CA*	• Why are there four authors? What skills does each bring? • What is the Population Research Institute? • Where in UCI does Farkas work? • What is their main purpose in writing this paper likely to be?
ABSTRACT: We investigated whether and to what extent children who are racial-ethnic minorities are disproportionately represented in early intervention and/or early childhood special education (EI/ECSE).	• Why did they think that racial-ethnic minority children might be disproportionately represented? What was their starting assumption?
We did so by analysing a large sample of 48-month-olds ($N = 7{,}950$) participating in the Early Childhood Longitudinal Study–Birth Cohort (ECLS–B), a nationally representative data set of children born in the United States in 2001.	• Is this sample size big enough for the kind of questions they want to answer? For example, how much variation might there be across different States and/or different minority groups? • Who says that the ECLS–B is nationally representative? Has anyone challenged that?
Multivariate logistic regression analyses indicate that boys (odds ratio [OR] = 1.66), children born at very low birth weight (OR = 3.98) or with congenital anomalies (OR = 2.17), and children engaging in externalizing problem behaviours (OR = 1.10) are more likely to be represented in EI/ECSE.	• What is 'odds ratio'? Are large values a stronger effect, or weaker? Have they demonstrated *cause* or just a link? • Do they define 'low birth weight' clearly? • What sorts of 'congenital anomalies' are they talking about, and where are the lines drawn? Similarly for 'externalizing problem behaviours'. Might the definitions affect the findings (e.g., if certain anomalies and behaviours are less prevalent in some ethnic groups)?
Children from low-socioeconomic-status households (OR = .48), those displaying greater numeracy or receptive language knowledge (ORs = .96 and .76, respectively), and children being raised in households where a language other than English is primarily spoken (OR = .39) are less likely to be represented in EI/ECSE. Statistical control for these and an extensive set of additional factors related to cognitive and behavioral functioning indicated that 48-month-old children who are black (OR = .24) or Asian (OR = .32) are disproportionately under-represented in EI/ECSE in the United States.	• What languages 'other than English' are they talking about? • Do they take into account large minority communities (e.g., Spanish) versus being the only kid with that language in the neighbourhood? • What were the 'additional factors'? • Are any reasons given for this disproportionate under-representation?

Welcome to critical thinking

It takes only a few minutes to generate questions by interrogating an abstract. It is something you can easily try out and develop the technique for. All you need to do is print out an abstract and annotate it by hand. Or, if you prefer, copy and paste the text into an electronic document and add comments boxes. There are no right or wrong answers when you create these questions. Simply, write down whatever comes into your head as something that you want to know and the authors have not told you. Prioritize questions that are most relevant to the study you are doing yourself – that is, questions it would be useful to know the answer to, for the sake of your own research. It is fine if you ask about things they do tell you in the main part of the paper – in fact, that is what you should generally expect will happen. Using the questions, when you read the paper you will have a good idea of what you are looking for. And if the authors do not ever answer your question, then that gives you food for thought. For example, if they never do define their main terms, you can consider whether that is a problem: are there alternative potential definitions that would impact on how their claims are interpreted? Or, if they do define their terms, are they then consistent in deploying these terms across the paper? (Authors often are not.)

Having given you this quick way into a paper using the abstract, in the next chapter we introduce the first of our main tools for engaging with a critical reading of the main paper. By the end of the chapter you will not only have an overview of how that tool works, but you will also see how it relates to the pre-questioning you do in the abstract.

4

Getting Started on Critical Reading

Keywords

arguments; claims; conclusions; critical reading; Critical Synopsis; Critical Synopsis exercise; warranting

Critical reading is a dynamic process. You cannot avoid being affected by your own expectations, prejudices and previous knowledge, which will shape your understanding of the literature you read. It is vital to realize that authors also have prejudices, assumptions and beliefs. These too will tend to influence your understanding of a text. Therefore, a key critical reading skill is identifying authors' underlying aims and agendas, so that you can take them into account in your evaluation of the text. Sometimes you will have to think carefully and 'read between the lines' to establish authors' values and aims. More often, you will easily be able to establish their purpose, provided you realize the importance of doing so.

We have already noted that critical reading for postgraduate study is task-driven: usually the task culminates in a written product for assessment. In Chapter 2, we discussed the first step in taking charge of your response to a task: making your own critical choice about what you read. Once you have done that, you need to make the texts work for you. Far from having to absorb slavishly everything the authors have written, you can *focus* your reading by asking questions of a text and looking for answers that will help you to achieve your goals. In Chapter 3 a technique for generating questions about the abstract was introduced.

In this chapter, we look at how you can identify authors' arguments and judge the adequacy of the backing they offer for their claims. We harness the skills of focusing and evaluating through five generic questions that you can ask of any text. This approach paves the way for a more detailed analysis of texts in Part Two. Finally, we show how the five questions relate to the questions generated by the abstract, as presented in Chapter 3.

Focusing through a central question and review questions

In Chapters 1 and 3 we saw that asking questions as you study a text enables you to focus your reading. The first step is to formulate a broad *central question* to underlie your entire piece of work or a substantial thematic section. A central question is expressed in general terms. It is a question about something in the social world that will almost certainly need to be answered by asking more specific questions. An essay title is often framed as a central question (e.g., 'Does perceived social status affect how pharmacists address their customers?'). An essay title that is not framed as a question (e.g., 'Discuss the impact of perceived social status on the ways in which pharmacists address their customers') can usually be reframed as a question. Doing so is a very effective tactic for finding and keeping focus in your work.

A *review question* is a more specific question that you ask of the literature. Review questions that are derived from a broader central question will ask something that directly contributes to answering the central question (e.g., 'What does research suggest are key factors determining how pharmacists would be likely to address their customers?'). However, review questions can also help with theoretical questions (e.g., 'Whose model is most relevant for investigating style shift in speakers?'). Similarly, review questions may arise in justifying the methodology of your own developing research for, say, a dissertation (e.g., 'What can I learn from published studies about how to observe interaction in shops?'). The review question, or questions, you ask of the literature will therefore vary according to your purposes and the type of text you are engaging with.

Evaluating the usefulness of what you read

Working on the assumption that not all texts will prove equally useful, how can you establish the relative merits of each one? Obviously, you want to take most notice of the works that contribute something reliable and plausible to your quest for an answer to your central question.

To determine how reliable the material in a text is, you need to identify and evaluate its *arguments*. An argument consists of a *conclusion* (comprising one or more claims that something is, or should be, the case) and its *warranting* (the justification for why the claim or claims in the conclusion should be accepted). The warranting is likely to be based on evidence from the authors' research or professional experience, or else it will draw on others' evidence, as reported in the literature.

OPINION = UNWARRANTED CONCLUSION

ARGUMENT = CONCLUSION + WARRANTING

The *conclusion* is only half of an argument. You can legitimately ask of any set of claims: 'Why should I believe this?' The other half of the argument is the *warranting*. The warranting is the reason for accepting the conclusion, including evidence for it. Demand a convincing warranting for every conclusion that you read about. Also, demand of yourself that every conclusion you draw is adequately warranted.

This conception of 'argument' is very simple, but is effective for our current purpose. In philosophy and rhetoric, 'argument' is more precisely defined, with more components. You can see how a more sophisticated approach to argument structure relates to critical reading by looking at the relevant chapters in Booth, W.C., Colomb, G.C. and Williams, J.M. (2008) *The Craft of Research* (3rd edn), Chicago: University of Chicago Press. The 'argument' definition can be applied to single sentences, paragraphs, chapters, even entire dissertations or books. It can be used to identify and evaluate what is said in the texts you read, and also to ensure your own scholarly writing is well constructed.

It is the authors' job to provide you with the best available warranting for their conclusion. Your job is to judge whether the warranting is enough to make the conclusion convincing, and so whether to accept or reject that conclusion.

Example of argument construction

The following passage comes from a report of research into the quality and extent of training experienced by researchers employed on academic projects.

> For example, one practitioner researcher commented that 'I think that my TLRP [Teaching and Learning Research Programme] experience was very, very positive. It caused me to reflect back on where I was and to accept that I am really happy

in FE [further education], that I don't want to be a lecturer in HE [higher education].' Building research capacity is not just about building the next cohort of professors and senior academics, it can also relate to the building of one's own personal capacity to engage with research and practice.

Source: Fowler, Z., Proctor, R. and Stevens, M. (2008) 'Mapping the ripples: an evaluation of TLRP's research capacity building strategy', *Teaching and Learning Research Briefing no. 62.* London: Teaching and Learning Research Programme. www.tlrp.org/pub/documents/fowlerRB62final.pdf

This passage constitutes one of many arguments in the report. The *claim* is in the final sentence: there is more to building research capacity than just making everyone a top expert; it is also about helping individuals to gauge their own potential and ambitions. The *warranting* is the quote in the first sentence, where a researcher reveals that the research experience resulted in a recognition of what sort of future work would be most comfortable for them. Quoting from a respondent is one kind of *evidence* that can be used in warranting. Since this study entailed online surveys with researchers and their project managers, quoting in this way is an appropriate form of evidence.

What makes an argument convincing?

In the example from Fowler and colleagues in the box, note how the claim is based on one quote from one respondent. Part of the job of the critical reader is to evaluate whether the warranting provided for a claim is adequate to make the claim convincing. The reader might feel that a single voice does not carry much weight and so look for other, supporting evidence, such as a statistic: 38% of the respondents felt that their experience as researchers had helped them decide what sort of future career they did and did not want. However, the reader might equally decide that the point of the claim is not that it is necessarily a majority view, but that it exists at all. In such a case, the reader might be satisfied that even if this view is restricted to one person, it is sufficient for warranting the claim. Such decisions cannot be taken in the abstract. They will take into account the nature and purpose of the study and also the reader's other knowledge and experience, and interests in reading the text.

To explore further the quality of an argument, let us return to our example from Chapter 1. Here is the (fictional) extract from Browning again:

> In the reading test, the five children who were taught to read using phonics performed better overall than the five children taught using the whole word method. This shows that the phonics method is a better choice for schools.

The conclusion is a single claim: 'the phonics method is a better choice for schools'. Browning offers research evidence as the warranting for his conclusion: 'the five children who were taught to read using phonics performed better overall than the five children taught using the whole word method'. But we saw that Browning's claim was vulnerable, at least as depicted in the extract. It was unclear how he could justify his claim that the phonics method was best for all schools on the basis of this small amount of evidence. What Browning's claim illustrates is the drawing of a conclusion with *inadequate* warranting. Here is the example reader's commentary from Chapter 1:

> Browning (2005) found that children taught to read using phonics did better in a reading test than children taught using the whole word method. However, the study was small, the test rather limited, and the subjects were not tightly matched either for age or gender. An examination of Browning's test scores reveals that, although the mean score of the phonics group was higher, two of the highest scorers in the test were whole word learners. Since this indicates that the whole word method is effective for some learners at least, Browning is perhaps too quick to propose that 'the phonics method is a better choice for schools' (p. 89).

The commentator is evaluating Browning's claim by critically assessing whether the warranting is strong enough to make the conclusion convincing. First, the limitations of the empirical investigation are noted: 'the study was small, the test rather limited, and the subjects were not tightly matched either for age or gender'. Second, a notable degree of overlap is highlighted between the range of findings for the two groups of subjects, something that was evidently reported by Browning but was ignored by him in warranting his conclusion: 'An examination of Browning's test scores reveals that, although the mean score of the phonics group was higher, two of the highest scorers in the test were whole word learners'.

Note that these two evaluatory comments comprise the *commentator's own warranting*. That warranting is used to *back the commentator's own conclusion:* 'Browning is perhaps too quick to propose that "the phonics method is a better choice for schools"'. The commentator is claiming that Browning's warranting is inadequate to make his sweeping conclusion convincing. As the reader of this commentary, you must decide whether you find the *commentator's* warranting adequate, or whether you think Browning did enough.

In all cases, a claim is as convincing as the adequacy of the warranting that justifies it. Whether you are writing about your own research or commenting on someone else's, you need to warrant your claims. So, when you are commenting on what others have claimed about their work, you must be careful that your counter-claims are warranted. It is rather easy to criticize the shortcomings of others' conclusions, and then to draw similarly flawed conclusions oneself!

Meanwhile, in the same way, you need not accept at face value the conclusions that a commentator draws about someone else's work. Has the commentator supplied sufficient warranting to justify the conclusion that Browning's claim should be rejected? In order to decide, you might need to go and read Browning's work for yourself and see whether you feel that the commentator has been fair.

Tracking down and reading the original work is of great importance for evaluating the arguments in a text that reports the work second-hand. Retelling a story tends to simplify it and second- or third-hand accounts can end up appearing much more definitive than the original. Thus, even though Browning offers too little warranting for his conclusion about phonics being the best choice for any school, this does not necessarily mean that phonics is the worst choice, or that the whole word method is the best choice. A range of possibilities opens up regarding alternative claims. One is that Browning is right, but just has not been able to provide satisfactory evidence from his own study. Another is that Browning has failed to see certain patterns, or to relate his findings to others that might have supported his conclusions. Our commentator has not chosen to provide the kind of information that you would need in order to see what options there are. So only by reading the original study for yourself, rather than relying on an intermediary, could you ensure that you were fully informed in making your own evaluation.

CONVINCING ARGUMENT =	CONCLUSION +	ADEQUATE WARRANTING
	(containing claims)	(based on sufficient appropriate evidence)

The claims in the *conclusion* need *adequate warranting* for an *argument* to be convincing. Warranting is adequate when you, as the reader, are satisfied both that there is *sufficient* evidence and that this evidence is of an *appropriate* kind. Note that people may differ in their views about what counts as adequate evidence. This is because the strength of the warranting depends only indirectly on the evidence itself. The relationship is mediated by our *interpretation*. The reason why critical readers in the social sciences might question the adequacy of the warranting of claims forming the conclusion of a research paper is usually because they differ from the author in their judgement about the amount and quality of evidence necessary for warranting the acceptance of that conclusion.

Identifying the conclusion and warranting of arguments

Academic discourse offers us several ways of relating ideas to each other, and there is more than one formulation that can connect a conclusion and its warranting. Key indicators are words or phrases, such as: *therefore, because, since, so, it follows that, it can be concluded that.* Note how the following formulations all say essentially the same thing:

- *Since* research shows that girls mature faster than boys, studies should take age and gender into account when exploring child development.
- Child development studies should take age and gender into account *because* research shows that girls mature faster than boys.
- Research shows that girls mature faster than boys. *Therefore,* studies of child development should take age and gender into account.

Other variations may weight the warranting, implying that it is reliable in its own terms but it may not be universally the case:

- *In so far as* girls are believed to mature faster than boys, studies of child development should take age and gender into account.
- *In conditions where* girls mature faster than boys, studies of child development should take age and gender into account.
- *Where it is relevant to the investigation that* girls mature faster than boys, studies should take age and gender into account.

Incomplete or flawed arguments

In your reading (and your own writing) look out for incomplete arguments. Table 4.1 shows some common flaws and the ways in which you can ask questions to identify where the problem lies.

As these illustrations suggest, when you adopt the role of critical reader you are, in a sense, interrogating the author, to answer the questions that your reading has raised in your mind.

Thinking your way into the mind of the author

How can you focus on *your* questions when the author's agenda may be different? Imagine that you have the opportunity to talk to the author face-to-face. What questions would you ask to pursue your own agenda? Use the author's text to try to work out how the author would answer your questions.

TABLE 4.1 Identifying flaws in arguments

Type of flaw in an argument	Example (at the level of a few sentences)	Critical questions as a reader, suggesting there may be a flaw	Example resolution
Conclusion without warranting	The best musicians make the worst teachers	Why do you think that? How do you know?	The eye for fine detail possessed by the best musicians tends to make them over-critical and discouraging with pupils (Goodman, 2009)
Potential warranting without a conclusion	Johnson's research shows that people often sign legal agreements without reading them. Legal documents can be difficult to read	So what? What do these different pieces of evidence, together, imply?	People may fail to read legal documents because they are too difficult
Warranting leading to an illogical conclusion	People in English-speaking countries tend not to know another language. This indicates that they are poor language learners	Does this reasoning add up? Aren't there other more plausible conclusions?	This may suggest that English speakers do not see the need to know other languages
Conclusion not explicitly linked to warranting	Statistics show that teenagers are drinking far too much to be good for their health. Alcoholic drinks should be increased in price	What causal relationship between the factors are you meaning to suggest?	Since teenagers have only limited money, raising the price of alcohol might result in their drinking less
Conclusion with inadequate warranting	Trainee managers learn more effectively when they are praised than when their efforts are criticized. In a survey of female trainee managers in a retail company, 77% said they liked to be praised	Is the evidence adequate to justify the extent of the claim? Is the evidence appropriately interpreted? What is the link between 'liking to be praised' and learning more effectively?	However, males and females may respond differently to praise

Five Critical Synopsis Questions

The five questions introduced below map onto the more detailed approach to critical reading to be explored in Part Two. As will become clearer then, the extent to which you apply the in-depth level of engagement will vary, depending on how central a given text is to what you are trying to achieve. In many cases, the five basic Critical Synopsis Questions are all you will need and, even where you undertake a more detailed analysis, they may well have been your starting point:

A. Why am I reading this?
B. What are the authors trying to achieve in writing this?
C. What are the authors claiming that is relevant to my work?
D. How convincing are these claims, and why?
E. In conclusion, what use can I make of this?

Critical Synopsis Question A: Why am I reading this?

In Chapter 2, we reviewed some of the most likely answers to this question. In the early stages of your study of a new area you may be reading something because you were advised to or because you want to gather some background information. However, the more you work in an area, the more you will be choosing what to read with attention to your own agenda in relation to your study task. This is where a review question, as discussed above, could valuably come in. It would offer you a focusing device that ensures you take charge of your critical reading and are not distracted into following the authors' agenda at the expense of your own.

Critical Synopsis Question B: What are the authors trying to achieve in writing this?

If you are to assess the value of authors' findings or ideas for your own interests and priorities, you need to have a clear understanding of what the authors were trying to do. It should be fairly clear what their purpose is, often from the abstract or introduction and, failing that, the conclusion. These are the places where authors tend to make most effort to convey to the reader why their piece of work should be taken seriously. Authors may be trying to do any of the following:

- Report the findings of their own research.
- Review others' work.
- Develop theory.

- Express particular values or opinions.
- Criticize what is currently done.
- Advise on what should be done in the future.

It is also useful to consider who their target readers might be. The primary readership for academic journal articles and research monographs is academics. Sometimes the student will feel rather like an onlooker as an academic debate rages. Edited books vary in their target readership, according to what they cover. Some offer an up-to-date overview of a field. Others are based on conference presentations and can be so eclectic as to be quite misleading to the student entering the field for the first time. Besides the level of knowledge, the target readership is also defined by the *scope* of knowledge. Students from a non-psychology background will find a book written for psychologists difficult to understand because it will assume a breadth of knowledge they do not have.

Critical Synopsis Question C: What are the authors claiming that is relevant to my work?

This simple question covers several aspects of any text that may be important to you:

- What the text is actually *about* – what it reports, how any empirical work was carried out, what was discovered and what the authors conclude about it.
- Where any overlap lies between the authors' concerns and your own interests – the authors are unlikely to have been asking exactly the same questions as you are.

Critical Synopsis Question D: How convincing are these claims, and why?

We have already touched on this crucial question for the critical reader. It invites you to evaluate the quality of the authors' data and arguments, particularly with regard to the strength and relevance of the warranting for claims that are made. Other things that you might keep an eye on are any underlying assumptions made by the authors that you do not share, and whether the claims are consistent with other things that you have read or that you know about from your own research or professional experience.

Critical Synopsis Question E: In conclusion, what use can I make of this?

For the purposes of fulfilling your study task, does this text count amongst the many that you will refer to quite briefly, or the few that you will want to discuss in depth? Are you minded to write about this work positively or negatively, and would you want to imply that, overall, you agree or disagree with the claims the authors make? If your reading is guided by a review question, how (if at all) does the text contribute to answering it?

Applying the Critical Synopsis Questions to an abstract

We saw in Chapter 3 that one can generate a lot of free-ranging questions from reading the abstract. How does that exercise relate to employing the five Critical Synopsis Questions? Asking questions of the abstract is a way to practise identifying what you need to know. Now, you can adopt a more focused approach to the questioning of an abstract by applying the five questions to it before tackling the article itself. The five questions will help you identify, from the abstract, what specific things you need to know when you read the article. As a result, when you go to the main text to answer the five Critical Synopsis Questions, you will have prepared lots of insightful ideas about exactly what you need to look for in that paper. The example in Table 4.2 is based on the abstract used in Chapter 3.

As column 1 in Table 4.2 shows, the abstract is least helpful in giving direct answers to Critical Synopsis Question D and, consequently, E. But column 2 shows how one can still identify from the abstract what to look for in the main text. Many students find that answering question D is by far the most difficult part of a Critical Synopsis, because the information is least likely to be given directly by the authors. Rather, it entails drawing together what the authors say with your own judgement about the significance of what they say, as well as your observations about what they did not say, could have said, and so on. Having questions inspired by the abstract gives you specific things to look for.

Of course, by the time you have generated questions from the abstract in this way, you may realize that the paper is not relevant. If so, you have saved yourself some time. Conversely, it may be that you can immediately see how very important this paper is to your research. As a result, you may recognize that a short Critical Synopsis will not be sufficient, and that the full Critical Analysis that we introduce in Part Two of this book is appropriate. For now, though, we will assume that you have established, by the techniques just laid out, that the paper is relevant and it can be written about fairly succinctly. So, you need to generate a short, informative evaluation of it for your literature review. Later in this chapter we show you how to use the answers to your questions to do that. But first, you need to find the answers to the Critical Synopsis Questions.

TABLE 4.2 Targeting your reading using the Critical Synopsis Questions and the abstract

My initial answers to the Critical Synopsis Questions, from the abstract	What I need to find out from the paper itself in order to answer the Critical Synopsis Questions adequately
A. Why am I reading this?	
My research is into the effectiveness of early years educational support	• Is this paper relevant? Do the authors, who don't appear to be educationalists, align with my understanding of what 'early years educational support' is? Do they define that term?
B. What are the authors trying to achieve in writing this?	
Reporting patterns in data from a large survey – it is secondary data and their main message is about how they analysed it	• Do they say what they are trying to achieve? • Are they primarily looking at this general data set, and happen to be looking at education in this paper? Or do they have something particular to say about early years support? • Do they have an implicit position on the desirability of ethnic minority representation in early intervention education? • As it's not their data, how have they ensured they understand what it does and doesn't represent, why it was collected, etc., so that it does enable them to achieve what they want to?
C. What are the authors claiming that is relevant to my work?	
The following characteristics are associated with high representation in EI/ECSE: male gender, low birth weight, congenital abnormalities, behavioural problems. The following characteristics are associated with low representation: low socioeconomic status, high language and numeracy, ethnic minority group. Of these, it's the last that remains after factoring out interfering variables	• Do they make any important claims that are not mentioned in the abstract? • Do their definitions of key terms, (e.g., 'ethnic minority group', 'early intervention', 'special education', 'other than English') align sufficiently with mine for their claims to inform my study? • What were the 'additional factors' they mention? • Are any reasons given for the disproportionate under-representation they find?

(Continued)

TABLE 4.2 *(Continued)*

My initial answers to the Critical Synopsis Questions, from the abstract	What I need to find out from the paper itself in order to answer the Critical Synopsis Questions adequately
D. How convincing are these claims, and why?	
	• Is this sample size big enough for the kind of questions they want to answer? Do they make clear how they know their sample was big enough to get reliable results? For example, how much variation might there be across different states and/or different minority groups? • Who says that the ECLS–B is nationally representative? Has anyone challenged that? • How have they done the calculation showing that ethnic minority grouping is the only real effect on representation level? • Do they make any claims about how their findings generalized beyond the United States, and if so, do they explain why they think this? • Do they take into account the difference between large minority communities (e.g., Spanish) versus being the only kid with that language in the neighbourhood?
E. In conclusion, what use can I make of this?	
	• Do the claims convince me? Am I convinced that a study done in the United States is relevant to the country I am researching? If so, then I can cite this study as evidence that before you can make early years support effective you have to make sure that all children have access to it • Would the statistical test they used work with a smaller study like mine? If so, I could replicate their method and cite the paper as part of the justification • Were they able in this study to separate out factors that I think are important, such as the social and educational aspirations of different ethnic minority groups? If not, then I may cite it as an example of research that has not been able to capture that important variable

A Critical Synopsis of a text

The sequence of five Critical Synopsis Questions provides a structure for ordering your thoughts in response to any text you read. It is important, especially to begin with, that you write down your answer to each Critical Synopsis Question rather than just thinking about it. Critical Synopsis Question A can be written down before you start reading, Critical Synopsis Questions B, C and D as you go along and E once you have finished reading. Taken together, your answers comprise your Critical Synopsis of the text, available for you to refer to when moving from preparatory reading to writing your account for assessment.

We strongly recommend that you download the Critical Synopsis Template from the SAGE website (https://study.sagepub.com/wallaceandwray3e). The template enables you to write as much as you like in answering each Critical Synopsis Question. We suggest that you fill in a copy for each text that you read. If you use the electronic template, you can file each completed Critical Synopsis form electronically, where appropriate with the same file name as the PDF version of the downloaded article to which it refers. You can also print out any completed form and attach it to the original text or a photocopy, so you can quickly remind yourself of the key points. The accumulated set of completed forms will provide you with a summary of what you have read and how it relates to your developing interests. The evaluative code at the end of the form is useful for sorting the forms later – a rapid means of generating a short-list of texts that you want to return to for a more in-depth consideration.

Trying out a Critical Synopsis of a text

We invite you now to familiarize yourself with this structured approach to developing a Critical Synopsis by completing one for yourself. The text for you to read is in Appendix 1. It is an abridged version of a paper by Wray and Staczek (2005), exploring possible reasons why a mismatch in two people's knowledge of a dialect expression led to an expensive court case. In order for you to focus your reading, and to complete Critical Synopsis Question A, let us imagine that you have been given the task of writing an essay entitled: 'Discuss the ways in which language can be the focus of a court dispute'. Following our earlier advice, you have turned the essay title into a review question to help you focus your reading: 'In what ways can language be the focus of a court dispute?' You have made the critical choice to read the paper by Wray and Staczek because it looks like a piece of research literature about a court dispute where language is the focus. Turn now to Appendix 1 and, as you read, answer the questions on the downloaded blank Critical Synopsis

Template. *First* answer them using only the abstract, generating your own questions, as explained in Chapter 3. Then read the paper as a whole, referring, as you need to, to the questions you generated, to help you answer the five Critical Synopsis Questions more fully.

When you have finished, reflect on how well you have got to know the paper as a result of having to answer the Critical Synopsis Questions. The more Critical Synopses of texts you complete, the more naturally you will ask these questions. As critical reading in this way becomes automatic, you will eventually find that you no longer need the prop of the Critical Synopsis questions. But since this is your first attempt, you may not yet feel sure how to answer each Critical Synopsis Question. So, for comparison, you may wish to look at the Critical Synopsis answers we generated for this paper. For convenience, we have included an indication of the questions that the abstract might generate.

Items in the template for a Critical Synopsis

Author, date, title, publication details, library code (or location of copy in my filing system):

A. Why am I reading this?
B. What are the authors trying to achieve in writing this?
C. What are the authors claiming that is relevant to my work?
D. How convincing are these claims, and why?
E. In conclusion, what use can I make of this?

Code:
(1) = Return to this for detailed analysis; (2) = An important general text; (3) = Of minor importance; (4) = Not relevant.

Example completed Critical Synopsis of a text

Author, date, title, publication details, library code (or location of copy in my filing system):

Wray, A. and Staczek, J. (2005) 'One word or two? Psycholinguistic and sociolinguistic interpretations of meaning in a civil court case', International Journal of Speech, Language and the Law 12(1): 1–18 [abridged as Appendix 1 in Wallace, M. and Wray, A. (2016) Critical Reading and Writing for Postgraduates (3rd edn). London: SAGE].

A. Why am I reading this?

Part of reading to answer the review question 'In what ways can language be the focus of a court dispute?'

B. What are the authors trying to achieve in writing this?

Abstract: *They're questioning the relative weight of psycholinguistic and sociolinguistic explanations. (But what are those two explanations and how convincing are they?) They seem to be defending the person who gave offence. (How do they justify that position?)*

Full reading: *They provide an explanation, from psycholinguistic theory (Wray's) for why two people had different understandings of the same word or phrase. They show that sociolinguistics and psycholinguistics play a role in how we understand language. But they don't propose that court cases should always take these things into account.*

C. What are the authors claiming that is relevant to my work?

Abstract: *If you encounter an unknown word/phrase, you break it down to understand it. But if you do know it, then you don't need to break it down to understand it. So you can miss seeing that it is offensive. (What sort of psycholinguistic theory is used to make that case?)*

Full reading: *An African-American woman sued her employer after she was sent a certificate calling her a 'Temporary Coon Ass'. 'Coonass' (usually one word) is a dialect word that does not relate historically to 'coon' or 'ass', and refers to white people from Louisiana. The case revolved around whether the sender should have realized that the woman would find 'coonass' offensive because it contains 'coon'. The authors' 'Needs Only Analysis' model shows how the sender could fail to notice 'coon' inside 'coonass', because he had never had to break the term down into its components. Meanwhile the recipient, not knowing the dialect word, would automatically break it down to reveal two offensive words.*

D. How convincing are these claims, and why?

Abstract: *The authors claim a 'psycholinguistic rationale'. (But how plausible is it that someone could fail to see an offensive word inside a longer word or phrase? What other explanations could there be, and are they considered? Is their claim generalizable to other court cases?)*

Full reading: *Their argument is convincing in itself, but draws only on one theory. They don't mention any other court cases, so it is not clear how common this sort of dispute is. There is no mention of other kinds of disputes in the courtroom either. There is good quality evidence about what happened and what the individuals believed 'coonass' to mean: original court transcripts, other court documentation. Other supporting evidence from dictionaries and a survey is offered.*

(Continued)

(Continued)

E. In conclusion, what use can I make of this?

Abstract: *It's about language, but so far I can't tell if it is convincing enough to use.*

Full reading:

(a) It will be useful for demonstrating that one way in which language can be the focus of dispute is when two people fundamentally disagree on what a word or phrase means – but is this case representative? I need to find other cases that are similar and also cases that illustrate different kinds of dispute.

(b) It could inform a discussion of what causes disputes, bringing in psycholinguistics and sociolinguistics – but I may need to look at alternative theories too.

Code: *(2) or (1)*

(1) = Return to this for detailed analysis; (2) = An important general text; (3) = Of minor importance; (4) = Not relevant.

Our reading was driven by the review question posed above. Bear in mind that our answers may differ from yours, since they reflect our perceptions and evaluatory judgements. But what we have written can help you to gauge which aspects of the Critical Synopsis process you are most confident about, and which aspects you may need to concentrate on when undertaking your own Critical Synopses.

From Critical Synopsis to Critical Summary

In Chapter 5, we will take this Critical Synopsis of Wray and Staczek's paper as a starting point for developing a Critical Summary of a text, thus moving seamlessly from critical reading into the art of self-critical writing. You may, understandably, be more concerned with writing than with reading, since it is what you write that will be assessed. But your capacity to develop a convincing argument in your account is heavily dependent on the quality of your preparatory critical reading. It is important that you feel confident about the ideas presented in this chapter before moving on, since they are the foundation of your self-critical writing.

5

Getting Started on Self-Critical Writing

Keywords

assessment; Critical Summary; readers; self-critical writing; sense of audience

Writing a good account of the literature requires care, otherwise you can waste a lot of words covering irrelevant issues (for hints on spotting irrelevant material, see the Linkage Tracker Test in Chapter 17). As with your critical reading, remember that you are in charge. You must decide, and map out, the story that *you* need to tell. This skill may not come easily. Initially, you may be tempted to write descriptively, just summarizing the work in the same order as the content was presented in the original. A straight summary like this, however, will draw you into the concerns of the author and away from your agenda. In order to keep your focus, look for where the text intersects with your review questions. Then you can extract solely the information that relates to these questions, and weave it together into answers. Your evaluatory views on the validity and relevance of the claims will determine what you tell your readers about the text. Your readers should be able to see why you have mentioned the work and what you think of it.

This chapter shows you how to make a text work for you by using a Critical Synopsis (Chapter 4) as the basis for a written account. We begin with an exploration of the role you adopt as commentator. We next examine some characteristics of the target readers for whom you are writing. Many students are so concerned with what they have to say that they forget that they are not writing for themselves. When your critical readers are also your assessors, it is vital to understand how to communicate a convincing argument. We conclude the chapter by showing how the answers to Critical Synopsis Questions can be incorporated into the writing of a Critical Summary of a text, whether as a short review or as part of a more extensive piece of work.

Developing your own argument

When you are instructed, for an essay or longer assignment, to give your own view on an issue, this does not mean simply presenting your instinct or opinion. Rather, it implies assessing evidence in published (and maybe also unpublished) material, to build up a coherent and convincing position. That is, you construct an *argument* using the available evidence as the *warranting* for your *conclusion*. In Chapter 4, we suggested that, as a critical reader, you should be convinced only when authors' conclusions are adequately backed by the warranting provided. Now, in becoming a more self-critical writer, you should apply the same standards to your own writing so that you can convince your target readers.

Compare the following extracts from two essays entitled 'Should phonics be adopted for teaching reading in schools?'

1. 'There are many different opinions about this question, but I think that phonics should be taught.'
2. 'Taking into account the various arguments in the literature that I have discussed, it seems reasonable to conclude that phonics is a sufficiently reliable method to be adopted in schools.'

In (1) the claim is not backed up by evidence. Even the mention of the 'many different opinions' is not being used as warranting (to do so it would have to be more directly linked to the conclusion, e.g., 'On the basis of the many different opinions ... I think'). As a result, the reader gains the impression that the author is probably just presenting the same opinion, maybe biased and uninformed, that she or he had before beginning to read. Of course, the author might in fact have developed this view on the basis of reading the literature. But unless that is made explicit in the account, a reader will not know.

In (2) the author makes clearer how the literature has been used: the various arguments have been discussed in the course of the essay. Additionally, the author has made the relationship between the warranting and the claim rather tentative ('it seems reasonable'). This tactic suggests that the author feels it inappropriate to take a strong view. Such an impression is supported by the proposal that 'phonics is a *sufficiently* reliable method', which is much less extreme than, say, 'phonics is entirely reliable' or 'phonics is methodologically very sound'. Indeed, it sets a tone implying that no one could hope to find a perfect method and a reasonable compromise is to select a method that stands a good chance of working satisfactorily.

Where the sweeping statement in (1) could disguise a greater insight than the reader can detect, the reverse is not true of (2). The statements in (2) would be difficult to construct convincingly unless one really had discussed the arguments and come to a balanced conclusion. It follows that a reader or assessor will tend to have confidence that a wording like (2) is an accurate reflection of what the author really knows and thinks.

Writing for your audience

As the discussion above indicates, successful academic writing involves anticipating what your target readers will need to know and delivering it in the most effective way. To write convincingly for your audience entails knowing something about who your readers are: what they know, what they believe, what they expect, what they are likely to find convincing. It also entails understanding what their purpose is in reading your work. In other words, if they were to complete the five Critical Synopsis Questions (Chapter 4) about your essay (or dissertation), how would they answer Critical Synopsis Question A: 'Why am I reading this?' During your postgraduate study, their answer is likely to be 'in order to assess it' or 'because it is my job to provide feedback on a draft'. But you are, of course, also writing for readers who want to learn from your work.

Self-critical writing in the wider context

Awareness of audience is a generic skill. It demands different emphases according to the purpose and destination of the material. However, in all cases, unless you provide adequate warranting for the claims in the conclusion of your argument, your readers will find it unconvincing. If they do, it will undermine the achievement of your purpose in writing the text.

How strong is your sense of the audience for your academic writing?

Look carefully at each statement in our profile of the academics who may assess a postgraduate's written work. Then consider the two questions at the end of the exercise.

(Continued)

(Continued)

Profile of the postgraduate student's target readers (assessors)

Age	**Old enough** to have read plenty of other postgraduate work, so they will have a measure by which to judge yours.
Lifestyle	**Busy**, so they will appreciate a logical structure, clear focus and fluent writing style that communicates efficiently.
Attitudes	**Fair and respectful**, concerned solely with the quality of your argument.
	Sceptical, so they will not accept your argument unless you provide adequate warranting for the claims in the conclusion.
	Open-minded, so they will be ready to be convinced by your argument if your conclusion is well warranted, even if their own views are different.
	Empathetic, having once been postgraduate students themselves, they will have a sense of how you are feeling and how difficult it can be to navigate a new topic.
Best subject	**The field of enquiry:** knowledgeable about the area in general but possibly not about detailed issues or your professional experience. Therefore, they will welcome a brief description of specific context and content, but only in so far as it is relevant to your argument.
Likes	**Logic**, as expressed in an account that is carefully constructed, well argued, balanced, meticulous on detail and reflective.
	Books and journals, so they know the literature well and will expect you to have read what you write about and to report it accurately (and they may wish to follow up some of your references to extend their own knowledge).
	Evidence that you have met the assessment criteria, since no work, however imaginative, can pass unless it fulfils the requirements that are laid down.
	Signposting, indicating what you are doing, what you have done and what you are doing next, and making clear how parts of the written account fit together in supporting your argument.
Pet hates	**Waffle:** ill-structured writing that is unfocused and leads nowhere.
	Avoidable errors that careful proofreading could have picked up, whether in spelling, punctuation, word choice or grammar.
	Over-generalization: sweeping conclusions that are unconvincing because they go far beyond the backing provided.
	Free-floating recommendations for practice: insufficiently justified proposals about what should happen.

Poor referencing: failure to acknowledge authors or inaccurate and incomplete reference lists.

Plagiarism: using chunks of someone else's text as your own work, passing off others' ideas as your own or failing to acknowledge your sources adequately.

Believe that **Conclusions must be warranted** by evidence from empirical research, literature or personal experience, if they are to convince.

Everything in a written account should be relevant to the focus and the conclusion.

Questions to ask yourself

A. To what extent are you already aware of the characteristics of your assessors and their concerns as they read your work?
B. Which of their concerns could you take more fully into account as you prepare written work for them to assess?

Let us focus on the target readership of someone completing assessed work at postgraduate level. We can profile the postgraduate assessor quite specifically, though surprisingly little needs to change for it to fit other kinds of academic reader that you might target. Academics may play a range of roles in regard to the reading of other people's writing, whether as consumers of published literature for their own research, reviewers for academic journals, or panel members for research funding bodies. They may be more indulgent of a student, as a learner, but will still be seeking evidence of the critical approach to reading and self-critical approach to writing that they expect generally from academics.

Structuring a Critical Summary of a single text

Here we focus on a short account of the kind that you will need in an essay-length work, or might use in a dissertation where the text you are reviewing is not the focus of detailed examination. (How to do an in-depth review will be discussed in Part Two.)

We have previously suggested that you should rarely, if ever, write a purely descriptive summary of a text. Even when you are writing about a single publication, it is possible to focus on your own agenda rather than that of the authors whose work you are critically summarizing. Wherever you choose to focus on a single text sufficiently to offer a Critical Summary of it, aim to introduce your readers to the text and then, in the role of commentator on this text, develop your own warranting for your evaluatory conclusion.

One approach is to structure your account according to the order of the five Critical Synopsis Questions. The projected length of our illustrative Critical Summary structure is up to 500 words. We have indicated the approximate number of words for each component, though this is flexible. (If you were writing a review of a different length, you could adjust the length of components proportionately.) Your answers to each Critical Synopsis Question relate to each component, so you can refer to them when writing your Critical Summary of the text and also refer back to the original text as necessary.

Structure for a critical summary of an article or chapter reporting research (500 words)

- *Title*
- *Introducing the text* (50–100 words), informed by your answers to Critical Synopsis Question:

  A. Why am I reading this?

- *Reporting the content* (100–200 words), informed by your answer to Critical Synopsis Questions:

  B. What are the authors trying to achieve in writing this?
  C. What are the authors claiming that is relevant to my work?

- *Evaluating the content* (100–200 words), informed by your answer to Critical Synopsis Question:

  D. How convincing are these claims, and why?

- *Drawing your conclusion* (100–150 words), informed by your answer to Critical Synopsis Question:

  E. In conclusion, what use can I make of this?

To learn how this structure works, we invite you to write a 500-word Critical Summary based on your completed Critical Synopsis of the Wray and Staczek article from Chapter 4. You will need to provide your own title. Try keeping close to the word length allocations in the outline above. Your answer to each Critical Synopsis Question will form the starting point for completing each component, and you can also revisit the original Wray and Staczek article in Appendix 1.

When you have written your Critical Summary, you can compare what you wrote with our effort below. (Do try writing your own Critical Summary first, to maximize your learning opportunity.)

Building up a Critical Summary: an illustration

Our Critical Summary reflects our purposes and the answers contained in our completed Critical Synopsis (Chapter 4), so it may differ from yours in places. We are imagining that our task is not just to write a Critical Summary of the Wray and Staczek article, but to incorporate it as one section in an essay on the ways in which language can be a focus of dispute in a court case. Here is how we proceed to introduce the text, develop our warranting and draw our conclusion.

Introducing the text

The first thing to do is indicate to the target readers why this text is worth mentioning (informed by the answer to Critical Synopsis Question A). The reason why we are writing a Critical Summary of the Wray and Staczek article is because it contributes towards answering our review question 'In what ways can language be the focus of a court dispute?' by offering evidence about one of these ways. Since our Critical Summary of this text is to be part of something larger, we also need to provide a link from what was under discussion previously. We assume here that our essay has begun with some broad observations about how and why language can be a matter of dispute generally. These observations are brought to a summary, as a way of leading into the main discussion of language disputes in the courtroom. (Alternatives to this particular introduction might include talking about the importance of language in the oral proceedings of a courtroom, or beginning with a concrete example of what can happen when language falls into dispute in the courtroom, as a means of setting the scene for a structured account of the phenomenon.)

> *... As this brief discussion has demonstrated, language can be the basis of dispute when there is an unintentional mismatch between the beliefs of speaker/writer and hearer/reader. This may occur when the hearer/reader mishears, misreads or misunderstands a word, or when the literal or implied content of a sentence is misconstrued. We have seen that such 'disputes' are usually resolvable through repetition/rereading or explanation. It follows that only particularly difficult cases will get as far as the law court. Wray and Staczek (2005) report such a case, in which there was a fundamental difference between what two people believed the same piece of language to mean.*

The link-in illustrated here enables readers to see why, given what has gone before, it makes sense to consider the Wray and Staczek paper now. This passage also makes a basic statement about the content of the paper, drawing out the essence of the story it tells. We have managed, already, to tell readers that what we think is most interesting about this text is the kind of dispute that it illustrates.

Reporting the content

More needs to be said about the text itself, but without getting distracted into merely retelling the account in the source text. The basis of what is to be written lies in our answers to Critical Synopsis Questions B and C. We require only that part of the answer to Critical Synopsis Question B that is relevant to our developing account. The other part of our original answer to that question, about how courts should respond, would be a distraction here (but it might be mentioned later in the essay, if and when the issue of policy arises). Next, the answer to Critical Synopsis Question C is needed, so that readers have a rough idea of what the paper is about. This is the passage that may be most like a straight description. It needs to be kept short, with a firm eye on why this text is being critically summarized at all. Here is our account, bringing out the features that relate to our interest in how language can lead to legal disputes.

> *Wray and Staczek aim to provide a theoretically informed commentary on a past court case, in order to explore the possible psycholinguistic and sociolinguistic causes of the dispute. The case was one of alleged racial harassment, after an African-American woman was sent a certificate calling her a 'Temporary Coon Ass'. The dispute hinged on the fact that the sender knew 'coonass' (usually spelled as one word) to be a dialect term referring to white people from Louisiana. In contrast, the recipient found the term offensive because it contains 'coon'. On the basis of their theoretical psycholinguistic model, 'Needs Only Analysis', Wray and Staczek claim that the sender could have failed to notice 'coon' inside 'coonass' because he had never needed to break the term down into its components. Meanwhile, the recipient, not knowing the dialect word, would automatically have broken it down to reveal two offensive words.*

Note how many details have not been mentioned because they are irrelevant to the purpose of the essay (e.g., how the sender came to send the certificate and why the woman received it, the detailed etymological history of 'coonass', how the different regional backgrounds of the expert witnesses for the prosecution and defence affected the positions they took).

Evaluating the content

The next component of the Critical Summary is informed by the answer to Critical Synopsis Question D. Readers need to know whether we accept the authors' claims that we have just summarized: are they adequately warranted? This is the place to give a balanced view, identifying any reservations that are relevant to our story. Here is our evaluation.

> *The 'coonass' dispute is a particularly interesting one, since both parties appear to have had a plausible position. Wray and Staczek convincingly argue that unless the two interpretations have actually been pointed out, one or the other is likely to be overlooked. This explanation well accounts for the details of the case, though the authors do not offer an alternative with which it could be contrasted. Being a single case study, there is little indication of whether disputes of this kind are common or rare. Although the authors are obliged to speculate about the internal linguistic knowledge of the individuals involved, the court transcripts do provide a reliable source of direct evidence for what both parties said about their understanding of the disputed term.*

(If our reservations had not been relevant to our interests, we would have just mentioned them in passing. For example, 'Although one shortcoming is ..., nevertheless this work seems to demonstrate that ...'.)

Drawing a conclusion

Critical Synopsis Question E concerns what use can be made of the text in pursuing the summarizer's purposes. In our case, it has helped with answering our review question. This is where we can demonstrate to our readers what we have found out from this text and how we view its worth and relevance. The set of claims in the conclusion is warranted by our earlier account of the content and our evaluation of it. It is often also possible to use the conclusion component to provide the impetus into the next section of the work. Here is how we did so, leading into the next part of our essay.

> *The focus of interest here is the kinds of disputes that can arise in the courtroom on account of language. Wray and Staczek's paper demonstrates how disagreements about what a word or phrase means may not be easy to resolve, even in the court. What remains unclear is the extent to which their model of how such disputes happen would apply to other cases, and other kinds of disputes.*
>
> *Central to Wray and Staczek's case was the attempt to apportion blame. In other cases, however, it is not the question of blame that is at issue. Rather, it is a question of how serious the offence is judged to be. For instance ...*

Having worked through the development of our Critical Summary, you may now wish to re-read the components one after another to see how the Critical Summary looks as a whole.

Structuring an account to develop a convincing argument

The basic structure for a Critical Summary is flexible, but there are limits. Your target readers need to know what the text is about before reading your critical assessment. They also need to know how the Critical Summary contributes to what you are trying to achieve in your account, and they must be able to see that your conclusion is well backed by adequate warranting. The combination of these components is necessary for rendering a Critical Summary convincing to critical readers. In the next chapter, we will show you how this approach can be extended to enable you to compare several texts on the same topic.

6

Creating a Comparative Critical Summary

Keywords

Comparative Critical Summary; Critical Synopsis; text comparisons

We have aimed to show that, in writing for assessment, it pays to focus your reading via a review question. You can then construct a convincing answer to that review question by using your critical evaluation of relevant texts as the warranting for a robust conclusion. In the previous chapter, we concentrated on dealing with a single text. However, it is not always appropriate for your review question that you write sequentially about one text after another. You may be required to review texts whose authors develop contrasting arguments related to your topic, and to evaluate which is most persuasive and why. The amount you write will almost certainly be governed by an imposed word limit. However, the good news is that comparative writing is much more economical with words than a sequential account.

Comparing and contrasting evidence from several texts in relation to your own agenda is more complex than focusing on one text at a time. You have to make all the texts work for you, yet the authors of each text are attempting to convince their target readers about their own argument and are pursuing different (and possibly incompatible) agendas. It is easy to be swayed one way by one argument, then a different way by the next. So how can you pick your way between these different accounts and develop your own argument, as commentator, about whichever aspects of the various works are relevant to your purpose?

You will need to interrogate the texts quite determinedly to work out how each one relates to the issues that interest you. You will also need to probe beneath the surface: should you believe this claim? If you do, what does it imply about this other author's quite different claim? Are they compatible? What would each author be likely to say about the other's work? By comparing the arguments of each, can you see a pattern, contrast or similarity that neither of them could see alone?

This chapter examines how a Comparative Critical Summary may be built up. First, we indicate how a comparative account can be structured. Then we talk you through a worked example of a Comparative Critical Summary.

Structuring a Comparative Critical Summary

This structure parallels the one we presented in Chapter 5 for a single text. Your comparative account should be based on a Critical Synopsis of each text that you are evaluating. These Critical Synopses will have been completed during your preparatory reading. Your argument will be developed by comparing the different answers that each text has provided for a given Critical Synopsis Question. Effective comparisons are possible only if you have prepared all your Critical Synopses with the same review question or questions in mind. This is why it is important to identify your review questions as early on as possible.

Placing your completed Critical Synopses side by side will enable you to scan across them to see how your answers to the same Critical Synopsis Question compare with each other. Doing this as you go along will help you to firm up your thinking while you work on developing your argument. If you have attached the Critical Synopses to the original texts, you will easily be able to refer back to them if necessary.

As with the Critical Summary of a single text, the most straightforward structuring option is to follow the order of the five Critical Synopsis Questions. This time you will be comparing two or more texts within each section of the account in developing your own argument as commentator.

Structure for a comparative critical summary of several texts

- *Title.*
- *Introducing the texts,* informed by your answers to Critical Synopsis Question A for all the texts.
- *Reporting the content,* informed by your answers to Critical Synopsis Questions B and C for all the texts.

- *Evaluating the content,* informed by your answers to Critical Synopsis Question D for all the texts.
- *Drawing a conclusion,* informed by your answers to Critical Synopsis Question E for all the texts.

This structure is only a guide. The extent to which a comparative account is fully integrated can and should vary. Use your own sense of what works best for answering *your* review questions. It might suit your purposes, on one occasion, to integrate and compare the findings of research (informed by your answers to Critical Synopsis Question C for all the texts together). However, you might then talk separately about the limitations (informed by your answer to Critical Synopsis Question D) for one text at a time. On another occasion, it might make most sense to start by contrasting the aims of each researcher (informed by your answers to Critical Synopsis Question B) for all the texts together. Next, discuss the findings of each study separately (informed by your answer to Critical Synopsis Question C for one text at a time). Then jointly evaluate what they tell you about your own concerns (informed by your answers to Critical Synopsis Question D for all the texts together). In short, our guidelines are not a formula, but pointers that can help you make informed decisions about what will serve your purpose best. You are in charge, not us.

Building up a Comparative Critical Summary: an illustration

Here we demonstrate how to integrate a discussion of three texts. Accordingly, our example combines information on three publications. One is the Wray and Staczek (2005) paper (for which we wrote a Critical Summary in Chapter 5). Our completed Critical Synopsis for that paper is in Chapter 4. The other two texts are papers by Butters (2004) and Langford (2000), for which we have provided our completed Critical Synopsis forms below. At the top of the respective forms is the full reference to the papers, so you can obtain them for yourself if you wish. However, we shall assume that you have access only to our Critical Synopses.

Form for a Critical Synopsis of a text

Author, date, title, publication details, library code (or location of copy in my filing system):

Butters, R.R. (2004) 'How not to strike it rich: semantics, pragmatics, and semiotics of a Massachusetts Lottery game card', Applied Linguistics 25(4): 466–90.

(Continued)

(Continued)

A. Why am I reading this?

Part of reading to answer the review question 'In what ways can language be the focus of a court dispute?'

B. What are the authors trying to achieve in writing this?

Butters analyses the basis of two different interpretations of the instructions on a Lottery scratchcard. He raises theoretical questions about how linguistic and non-linguistic (semiotic) features relate to each other: specifically, how does the position of words on a card affect how the words are understood?

C. What are the authors claiming that is relevant to my work?

Butters describes a court dispute hinging on language in its broader context. A State Lottery Commission was taken to court by two apparent winners of $1m. The instructions on the scratchcard said that if they revealed the $1m prize in any *location on the card, they had won. But the intention was* any *location* within the relevant game *(there were two games on the card). The author looks at both sides of the argument. The words were not in dispute, only whether the buyer should infer from the design features of the card that there were two games, not one. He shows (p. 483) how there is no ambiguity in the 'small print' rules and that the addition of the word 'in' in two places on the card would have been enough to prevent the ambiguity. He concludes: 'A linguist who attempts to analyse the interpretations of the game card will be severely and unnecessarily restricted if he or she limits the linguistic testimony to evidence that does not clearly make use of semiotics' (p. 487). He explains why the line is drawn differently for a Lottery card than for warning instructions.*

D. How convincing are these claims, and why?

Butters shows convincingly that language is not in a vacuum when used in real situations: language is interpreted in the context of its presentation, including design features, customary practice and general knowledge (e.g., that there are different rules for roulette and dice). Butters had a vested interest in the case, as expert witness, but balances both sides. He includes evidence from the court case. He does not attempt to draw a strong conclusion about what is right or wrong.

E. In conclusion, what use can I make of this?

It helps identify the boundaries between language and other things in legal disputes. Butters raises several general issues and provides a helpful literature review of other studies on language disputes in the courtroom. It will be useful as a contrast to other language-related court cases because there was no question of what the disputed language was, or what it meant, just how it should interact with non-linguistic information.

Code: *(2)*

(1) = Return to this for detailed analysis; (2) = An important general text; (3) = Of minor importance; (4) = Not relevant.

Form for a Critical Synopsis of a text

Author, date, title, publication details, library code (or location of copy in my filing system):

Langford, I. (2000) 'Forensic semantics: the meaning of "murder", "manslaughter" and "homicide"', Forensic Linguistics 7(1): 72–94.

A. Why am I reading this?

Part of reading to answer the review question 'In what ways can language be the focus of a court dispute?'

B. What are the authors trying to achieve in writing this?

Langford demonstrates a way of making clearer the meaning of three important legal terms: 'murder', 'manslaughter' and 'homicide', using a particular method of simple meaning expression.

C. What are the authors claiming that is relevant to my work?

Langford talks about words that are used in the court, but maybe are not properly explained. It is one way in which (unintentional) disputes might arise (e.g., in the jury discussions about whether the defendant technically did commit murder or not). He provides a solution: complex terms could be defined through a series of simple descriptions using only 59 keywords. This makes it possible to pin down exactly where the differences lie between words with similar meaning, and also where there are differences between the normal (e.g., juryperson's) understanding of a word and the official legal one. He claims that this approach lets you translate the definitions accurately between languages.

D. How convincing are these claims, and why?

He shows convincingly that there is a potential problem with current legal definitions but no evidence is cited that there ever has been a misunderstanding of these terms in practice. His proposed solution seems effective, though it may not be practical (people might feel patronized if they got explanations of the kind he proposes). No evidence is given that it has been tried.

(Continued)

(Continued)

E. In conclusion, what use can I make of this?

Language is the medium of the court case, not the focus of the dispute (as with Wray and Staczek (2005) and Butters (2004)). But it is still important because different interpretations of the language could affect the outcome of the case. It might be interesting to see how his solution would work on the language-dispute cases. This is a useful pivot resource that I could use as one focus in a discussion on dispute resolution.

Code: *(2), maybe (1)*

(1) = Return to this for detailed analysis; (2) = An important general text; (3) = Of minor importance; (4) = Not relevant.

Introducing the texts

To help the reader understand the purpose of this Comparative Critical Summary, it is necessary to indicate why the publications under discussion are being introduced now. In our example, we need to identify how, together, the three papers present useful material relating to our review question: 'In what ways can language be the focus of a court dispute?' (informed by our answers to Critical Synopsis Question A). In the example in Chapter 5, we also demonstrated how one can link the introduction with a previous section. This time, instead, we show how an essay or substantive section of a longer work might *begin* with the introduction of the texts, illustrating one technique for doing so.

> *Since human beings so often misunderstand each other, it seems inevitable that, from time to time, language will become the focus of legal dispute. In this essay, evidence will be reviewed to establish the ways in which that can happen. First, two cases of legal disputes about meaning (Wray and Staczek (2005) and Butters (2004)) are reviewed. Then, themes from these cases contextualize the discussion of a third paper, Langford (2000), which highlights a different kind of linguistic problem in the court and proposes a radical solution to it.*

The scene has been set with the general observation that human beings often misunderstand one another. This observation provides warranting for the claim that there is likely to be something interesting to say about linguistically based legal disputes. Note that no attempt is made to provide warranting for the observation about people often misunderstanding each other. As part of the opening statement, readers are being expected simply to accept it. There is a risk here. If readers were to immediately think 'who *says* that humans often misunderstand each other?', then there would be a credibility problem with everything that depends upon this opening assumption. Therefore, it is advisable to make unwarranted claims only when you are very sure that readers are not going to feel uncomfortable about them. If in doubt, you can hedge the unsubstantiated claim by limiting its scope. In our example, we could have begun: 'In so far as human beings ...'.

Next, we have told the reader about the scope of the essay: how the broad issue of misunderstandings will be narrowed down into something manageable. Finally, we introduce the reader to the three papers, indicating how each is relevant to our theme and how they relate to each other. We reveal that two of the papers will be compared head-to-head and a third one will be brought in afterwards. This is a response to the way that these particular papers help us answer the review question effectively, and it is just one of the options for presenting material within the basic structure for a Comparative Critical Summary.

Reporting the content

If readers are to follow the comparison, some basic content information must be offered. However, it is often unnecessary to describe first and compare later. Answers to Critical Synopsis Question B, 'What are the authors trying to do in writing this?', are arguably of more importance in a comparative account than in a single text analysis, because it could be that differences in content (e.g., data, method, conclusions) are explained by differences in what the respective authors were trying to achieve. In our present case, the aims of Wray and Staczek and of Butters are rather similar in this regard. But the aims lead them to different outcomes.

> *The accounts by Wray and Staczek (2005) and Butters (2004) are a useful starting point because both aim to locate specific linguistic disputes within a broader theoretical perspective. However, there are also differences between them. Although Wray and Staczek explicitly deny any intent to comment on how a court should judge a linguistic dispute, their model does offer a means of explaining why misunderstandings might arise unwittingly. In contrast, Butters concludes that there is no theoretical framework that can help the court easily to characterize and resolve the kind of dispute he is dealing with.*

By now, readers have been told that these two papers can be compared and contrasted in a number of ways but have yet to be told what they actually report, so this must come next (informed by our respective answers to Critical Synopsis Question C). The essential story of each text can be kept separate.

However, it is then useful to point readers specifically towards the issues that the authors jointly address, corresponding with the review question.

> *Wray and Staczek (2005) report a case of alleged racial harassment, after an African-American woman was sent a certificate calling her a 'Temporary Coon Ass'. The dispute hinged on the fact that the sender knew 'coonass' (normally spelled as one word) to be a dialect term referring to white people from Louisiana. In contrast, the recipient found the term offensive because it contains 'coon'. Wray and Staczek's theoretical psycholinguistic model, 'Needs Only Analysis' demonstrates how the sender could fail to notice 'coon' inside 'coonass' because he had never had to break the term down into its components, while the recipient, not knowing the dialect word, would automatically break it down to reveal two offensive words.*

> *The case reported by Butters (2004) was brought against a State Lottery Commission by two apparent winners of one million dollars. The instructions on the scratch card they bought said that if they revealed the $1m prize logo 'in* any *location', they had won. But the intention of the Commission was that the winning logo must be in any location* within the relevant game, *and there were two games on the card. Butters discusses whether the design features of a card can reasonably be said to contribute to the interpretation of an ambiguous wording and concludes that the relationship between semiotics and language is too little understood for a model to be offered.*

> *There are notable similarities between these cases. Both were brought by aggrieved parties who believed that their interpretation of a text was valid and reasonable. However, the focus of the two disputes is not the same. The defendants in the Lottery card case at no point denied the meaning of the word 'any'. Thus, unlike the Wray and Staczek case, no difference of opinion occurred in relation to the language. Rather, the Lottery card dispute related to how a non-linguistic factor, the design of the card, might contribute to understanding which physical space 'any' refers to.*

The paragraph comparing the two cases has homed straight in on the central issue of the review question: what sorts of disputes can occur? The narrative has shown a fundamental difference between the two texts. Now we bring in the third text, which is different again, so much so that it brings out the similarities between the first two. First, we create a link and then give Langford's article the same short summary description, before bringing all three papers together into a discussion that draws on features of each.

> *Despite these differences, both cases do feature a linguistically based dispute that comes to court. However, this is not the only way in which language can be disputed in the courtroom. Langford (2000) draws attention to the way in which language, as a courtroom tool, is open to different interpretations. Technical terms that are understood by the professional legal teams may not*

be understood – or worse, may be differently understood – by those less experienced in the courtroom, including the jury. He argues that different beliefs about what words mean might create problems in reaching a verdict. His proposed solution is the adoption of a method for defining terms such as 'murder', 'homicide' and 'manslaughter' that uses only 59 keywords. He argues that this method makes it possible to pin down exactly where the differences lie between words with similar meaning, and also where there are differences between a jury member's understanding of a word and the official legal meaning.

Taken together, the three accounts demonstrate the potential for misunderstandings about word meaning to have far-reaching effects on people's lives. Language can impact on the litigants and defendants in direct disputes, and on any defendant who is the subject of a jury's unwittingly variant readings of significant technical terms. The argument that Langford makes for simplified definitions of technical terms resonates also in the wider world, where greater explicitness in what we write and say might prevent others misinterpreting our intention.

Evaluating the content

The final paragraph above draws out some potential points of contact between the studies. But what we have not yet done is offer any opinion on which of the studies, if any, is really robust enough to withstand the critical eye. We draw for this on the answers to Critical Synopsis Question D.

However, it would be hasty to propose that Langford's system is the panacea for all misunderstandings. Although he provides a robust demonstration of how the simplified definitions reveal the source of the problem, the reader is left unsure about whether they would really work in practice. He offers no evidence that they would, and one might anticipate that these simplified definitions could appear patronizing to a jury. Furthermore, he supplies no warranting, even anecdotal, to support his initial claim that there really is a problem in the courtroom with how technical terms are understood. In a similar vein, Wray and Staczek's psycholinguistic insights are offered without any clear evidence that they would, in reality, clarify a complex picture in any reliable way, or that they could be generalized to other similar disputes. Indeed, although Langford's and Wray and Staczek's studies draw the stronger conclusions, it is Butters' solution to the dispute he describes that is most succinct. He reveals that the ambiguity did not extend to the 'small print' instructions and that the simple insertion of the word 'in' in two places would have prevented ambiguity on the scratch card (p. 483). In doing so, he only heightens interest in the question of why, then, it should have occurred. He wisely concludes that 'A linguist who attempts to analyse the interpretations of the game card will be severely and unnecessarily restricted if he or she limits the linguistic testimony to evidence that does not clearly make use of semiotics' (p. 487).

Here, the limitations of the accounts are presented in a way that continues to inform the question of what a dispute is. It is revealed that in Langford's case there might not, in reality, even be a dispute at all. Next it is pointed out that Wray and Staczek's model works for their case, but might not be applicable to others – an issue of how representative the 'coonass' dispute is. Butters fares better and this is in part because his claims are more moderate, so there is less to challenge. Our sympathy with Butters' stance, as commentators, is indicated by our use of the qualitative judgement term 'wisely'.

Drawing a conclusion

If you succeed in writing a critical review that focuses, at every stage, on your review question, you may wonder what there is new to say at this final stage. But we have reached a crucial point in our Comparative Critical Summary. Readers need to be given an answer to the 'so what?' question. In effect, all that has gone before is one big warranting effort. Now, the conclusion that flows from it needs presenting. Your answers to Critical Synopsis Question E should give you hints as to how you considered each text, as you read it, to play a role in answering your review question.

The first thing is to remind readers of what the review question was. Next, threads may be drawn out from what has gone before, to provide a succinct answer to that question. It need not be a final answer, of course, because there may be other texts to consider. It is important to avoid writing a straight repetition, even in summary, of what has already been said. Readers have only just finished reading it and hardly need reminding. What they do need is a different viewpoint.

> *In exploring the question of how language can be the focus of a legal dispute, we have examined three cases in which the basis of the dispute is meaning. These cases reveal that meaning-based disputes are complex. Firstly, it seems that disputes about meaning are often in the eye of the beholder. In neither the 'coonass' nor the Lottery case did the defendants believe that there was a dispute at all and in the 'coonass' case it was, perhaps, less of a genuine dispute about the meaning of 'coonass' than of whether responsible managers should realize that the term might be interpreted in more than one way (Wray and Staczek, 2005: 18). Meanwhile, Langford has supposed that there is a potential for unrecognized disagreement about the meanings of words, without actually providing evidence that this problem ever actually arises. Secondly, Langford's and Wray and Staczek's papers both show that a dispute does not need to be about one person being correct and the other incorrect. Rather, both interpretations can be genuine, yet different. Finally, Butters shows that language is not an island and that its interpretation is different according to how it is presented. This opens up the possibility*

that linguistic disputes will overlap with other kinds of dispute: how and where something was said, why something was written in one place or in one typeface rather than another, and whether it is part of our communicative competence to interpret a linguistic signal as part of a larger signal that also has non-linguistic parts.

We turn now to a different kind of linguistic dispute found in legal cases: differing claims about what was said ...

Our Comparative Critical Summary has concluded with three observations that address the question of how language can figure in legal disputes, focusing specifically on disputes about meaning. The conclusion is fully based on what has been previously said, yet makes new points, by coming at things from a different angle.

Having completed the exploration of disputed meaning, the account moves on to deal with disagreements about linguistic form. Here, if we were continuing, we would begin a new Comparative Critical Summary, based on reviews of other texts. After one or more such additional sections, we might aim to pull together the range of evidence that we had accumulated, to draw some general conclusions about the nature of linguistic disputes and why their intrinsic nature makes them difficult to resolve.

Making progress as a critical reader and self-critical writer

In Part One, we have introduced you to insights and techniques that can help you become a more critical reader and self-critical writer. These ideas can give you confidence that you are using your time productively. You can enhance your own learning by noticing good and bad practice in what you read and understanding how to model your own writing on what you find most effective in the writing of others. You can organize your approach to study by knowing how to choose what texts to read, identifying your purpose in reading them and making succinct, orderly notes that can be drawn upon for writing your critical account of the literature. You can easily compare across texts, knowing that your approach to reading has highlighted the key points that you need for an effective comparison. Your expectation of finding adequate warranting for every conclusion in what you read will transfer into your own writing, so that you expect of yourself, as a self-critical writer, a justification for any claim you make. As a result, you will be equipped to present your assessors with what they are looking for: robust arguments that reflect how your own interpretation of a range of evidence leads you to a well-warranted conclusion.

There is a lot more to be learned, however. In Part Two, we explore how to engage critically with one or more texts in greater depth.

Part Two

Developing an In-Depth Analysis

7

A Mental Map for Navigating the Literature

Keywords

assumptions; concepts; mental map; models; philosophical positions

In Part Two we develop the ideas from Part One, by demonstrating how to analyse texts critically in greater depth. As you embark on reading a range of literature using the Critical Synopsis Questions in Part One, you will probably identify a small number of texts as being particularly central for your topic. These are the texts with the greatest potential to inform your thinking and your subsequent writing. So it will be a good investment of time to scrutinize these texts more closely. Doing so successfully and efficiently requires a refined grasp of how academic enquiry works and a more extensive array of questions to guide your critical engagement.

To help you sharpen your in-depth critical analysis skills, we show you how to develop a *mental map* that can guide your thinking as you explore the social world. The map will enable you to find patterns in the ways that authors discuss their topics and in how they develop an argument that is capable of convincing their target audience. For many of our illustrations we draw on the abridged version of the journal article by Wallace (2001) in Appendix 2, referring to the way Wallace's text exemplifies ideas we are discussing.

The five components of the mental map are introduced in this chapter. Chapters 8, 9 and 10 look at them in more detail. Then, in Chapter 11, the mental map is put to work on a real example. We employ the mental map in demonstrating a structured approach to the Critical Analysis of Wallace's article, inviting you to try it out for yourself. In Chapter 12, we provide our own completed Critical Analysis of that article, as an illustration. Our Critical Analysis includes an accompanying commentary explaining our reasons for each step we have taken. Finally, in Chapter 13, we see how a Critical Analysis of this kind can be used as the platform for writing a Critical Review of a particular text, exemplified by our own Critical Review of Wallace's article. Thus, we mirror, with an in-depth analysis, the procedures we depicted in Part One for using the five Critical Synopsis Questions to create a less detailed Critical Summary. As in Part One, the approach that we first describe and illustrate for one text can be expanded to cover multiple texts. We end Chapter 13 with structured advice on how to conduct a Comparative Critical Review, making the transition from one text to several at the in-depth level.

We recommend that you turn now to Appendix 2 and read the abridged article by Wallace carefully, once through, before you tackle Part Two.

Developing your mental map

By 'mental map' we simply mean a structure for considering different aspects of a text – both a text you read critically and one that you write yourself. Since you typically read literature before you write for assessment or publication, we concentrate here on critical reading: how to identify the different aspects of a text that will help you explore and evaluate the argument(s) relevant to your own focus of interest. The five components of the mental map help you see not only what authors have done in their research and why, but also how they attempt to convince their target readers about what they claim to have found out.

Some components of this map will be familiar. Other components may be new in the way they direct your attention, but may still cover aspects of a text that you have met before in your studies. Let us briefly introduce the map, so you can quickly see which components relate to what you already know, and which may be less familiar. Figure 7.1 lays out the five components and how they are linked. Although we will examine them from left to right in the following chapters, it is useful here to start on the right, and move back to the left across the diagram. The reason is that claims to knowledge and the characteristics of the claims are the most tangible element – the aspects of a text that are most explicitly stated. We shall see how, in order to create those claims and establish their characteristics, authors feed in less explicit considerations – the reasons for studying the phenomenon and various tools and ways of thinking.

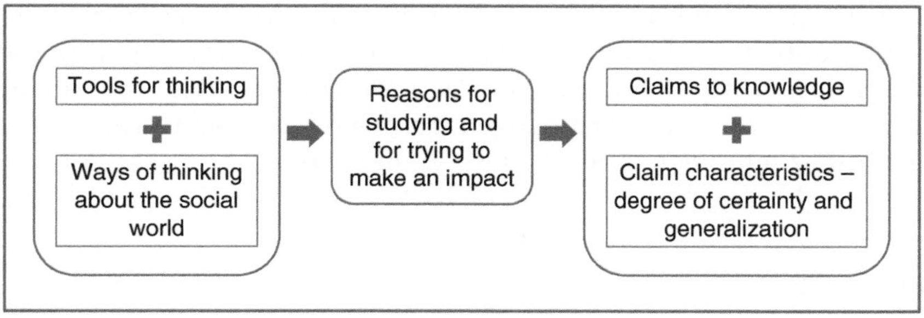

FIGURE 7.1 A mental map for navigating the literature

Claims to knowledge

In published work, authors typically make *claims* to know something new and significant. This knowledge may come from the findings of their empirical research, their theory for interpreting or explaining a phenomenon, or from their reflections on their experience as practitioners. For more exploration, see Chapter 10.

Claims to knowledge

Wallace (Appendix 2) makes several **claims** to have generated new knowledge from his studies of teamwork amongst senior staff in schools. One is that the maximum synergy (where all team members work collaboratively to achieve shared goals) may be achieved in situations where headteachers enable other members to make a relatively equal contribution, while the other members readily operate within limits that are acceptable to their headteachers. But the approach risks ineffective team operation if other members do not respect these limits (see page 261).

Claim characteristics

Claims to know something about the social world have two characteristics that the critical reader needs to note – certainty and generalization. These characteristics help you to assess whether the claims are sufficiently well warranted to be convincing. Authors make choices about how much certainty they express in relation to a claim – 'This indicates ...' or 'This probably indicates ...' or 'This may possibly indicate ...' signal to their readers different messages about the reliability of the finding. Authors also need to decide the extent to which they feel it is appropriate to generalize their claims beyond the precise cases or situation that they have examined – 'People do this ...' is much more generalized than 'People like these do this ...' or 'Some people do this in this context ...'. In Chapter 10 we will indicate how the author's decisions in relation to certainty and generalization alter the amount of warranting that you, as a critical reader, need in order to find the claims convincing. For more explanation, see Chapter 10.

Claim characteristics

Wallace's (Appendix 2) claim about maximizing synergy and the risk of ineffectiveness it carries (see above) is made with a particular degree of certainty and a particular degree of generalization. A low degree of **certainty** is indicated where Wallace states (page 266) that he 'seeks a tentative answer' to his questions about the benefits and risks for headteachers in sharing leadership through teamwork, and then concludes (page 273) by suggesting what prescriptions informed by his findings 'might be'.

A moderate degree of **generalization** is indicated where Wallace, having conducted his research in four British primary schools, states (page 274) that the principles could apply to 'British headteachers'. He is generalizing to all British primary and secondary schools, but not to schools elsewhere, consistent with his related claim (page 273) that prescriptions for school leadership should be 'informed by evidence, and so rest on principles that are context-sensitive'.

Reasons for conducting the research

Authors' claims to knowledge typically reflect the outcome of studying something. But why did they bother to do the study and write about it? There are many reasons why people do research. They may simply be curious about a phenomenon and want to generate new knowledge about it. Or their approach may be more evaluative, aiming to determine whether the phenomenon is good or bad. Or it may be practical, geared towards working out how to design an effective policy or to improve a particular practice.

Authors also want to tell others about what they have discovered, what their judgements are, what they recommend, or what they instruct practitioners to do as a strategy for improvement. Thus, usually, authors hope that their claims will convince others to change some aspect of their thinking or practice. The claims they make and how they make them will depend on what changes they hope to achieve, and whose thought or practice they are targeting. As a result, a critical reader needs to be alert to how authors' purposes and target readership affect what is claimed and how.

We can term the authors' motivations for the research their *intellectual project*. Identifying the authors' intellectual project is a quick way of alerting yourself to:

- the strengths and limitations of their approach;
- their likely target audience and what the authors need to do to convince this audience; and
- the form of impact they seek to make and how they use their text to help them achieve this.

In turn, intellectual projects can be presented in different types of frontline literature. The most common types (as we earlier highlighted in Chapter 2) are:

1. Research – reporting systematic empirical investigations into aspects of the social world.
2. Theoretical – presenting models and theories for interpreting and explaining patterns in practice.
3. Practice – presenting evaluations of others' practice, or practitioners' evaluations of their own practice and related advice to other practitioners.
4. Policy – advising policy-makers about advocated changes in practice, or policy-makers proposing changes that they desire.

Being aware of the type of literature you are reading can alert you to the kinds of evidence being used for warranting claims to knowledge, and so how authors hope to influence their target audience by persuading them to accept the authors' argument. For more explanation, see Chapter 9.

Reasons for conducting the research

The **intellectual project** pursued by Wallace (Appendix 2) entails informing improvement in a practical domain. He implies that his reason for studying team approaches to school leadership is to inform efforts to improve school leadership practice. His stated purpose (page 261) is to 'develop the normative argument that school leadership should ideally be shared but ... the extent of sharing that is justifiable in practice depends on empirical factors'. If you make yourself aware that this is his reason for studying school leadership, you are alerted to look out for evidence of the 'empirical factors' that, according to Wallace, affect how much sharing is justifiable in the circumstances he has investigated.

Wallace does not state whose thinking or practice he hopes to influence by publishing his article. But you can easily check from the journal's website who typically reads it. When Wallace's article was published, the journal was (and still is) published in association with a learned society whose 'members are a mixture of practitioners in schools, colleges and universities and working academics'. So you can guess that Wallace chose this journal because he wanted to reach an audience of school teachers and headteachers, plus academics who research in this area. He probably wanted to inform their thinking, so that practitioners who were convinced by his argument would follow the prescriptions for practice put forward in his conclusion (pages 273–4).

Ways of thinking about the social world

All research is infused with the knowledge, beliefs and assumptions of the investigator. They shape the focus and also the decisions made about what to find out and how. For example, we have beliefs about what is important to know or change, and about what is good and bad about a current situation. We make assumptions (whether we are aware of doing so or not) about what 'exists' in the social world to be measured or observed. As a critical reader, it is important to know how to recognize the authors' starting point and priorities in these regards and also to understand how your own knowledge, beliefs and assumptions will shape your interpretation of the authors' claims.

Assumptions may be made explicitly, or else left implicit. You can spot implicit assumptions from clues in the text, where you may also be able to gauge whether the authors are aware or unaware of the stances they are taking. As a critical reader, you need to decide whether you accept the authors' assumptions or reject them, and why. If you accept the assumptions, you are more likely to accept the argument that builds on them. If you reject the assumptions, you will probably reject the argument. For more explanation, see Chapter 8.

Ways of thinking about the social world

Wallace (Appendix 2) leaves implicit his **assumptions** about the nature of the social world and how we can know about it (we will examine them in the next chapter). But his assumption about what is right or wrong about this aspect of the social world (that is, how it should or should not be) – is explicit. Wallace (page 261) advances the argument that 'school leadership should ideally be extensively shared but … the extent of sharing which is justifiable in practice depends on empirical factors'. It is the word 'should' that indicates his assumption about how the world would ideally be.

Typically, authors' arguments reflect a bundle of linked assumptions, representing their *philosophical position* about the nature of the social world, how we can know about it and what is right or wrong about it. Authors sometimes indicate what their philosophical position is, but otherwise you can usually guess it from the individual assumptions you identify. Once you understand what authors' philosophical position is, you can see how their study approach and claims to knowledge reflect the set of assumptions that they subscribe to. You can then evaluate their argument by considering whether the assumptions on which it is based are acceptable to you, and so whether the claims that flow from these assumptions are convincing.

Tools for thinking about the social world

Authors necessarily use language as the basis for communicating their thoughts in the texts they create. Similarly, as a reader you use language to understand and evaluate their argument. Language tends to shape how we think about things, and we can conceive of it as a set of tools that draw our attention to some aspects of a phenomenon while pushing others into the background. For you as a writer, it is useful to have some awareness of how the tools you choose will frame the thoughts you express. As a critical reader, it is also important to be able to check how authors are using particular tools, and how their thoughts – and yours – are shaped and constrained by them, with an onward impact on how convincing their claims are.

The most fundamental tools for thinking are *concepts*: ideas derived by generalizing about or abstracting from experiences, or from other ideas, and expressed through language that frames the way people interpret both the physical and social worlds. Concepts are necessary for understanding the social world, because the social world is only 'real' in so far as we create a *conceptual reality* that gives meaning to our observations. We decide the significance of interactions between people or of the social structures that they create to facilitate or control that interaction. Thus, we work with concepts and we use language to convey them to others.

The concept of 'education', for example, is a social construct. 'Education' is an idea employed conventionally to refer to various experiences and activities, and even to the state of being experienced by an educated person. There is no one-to-one correspondence between whatever social world might exist 'out there' and people's interpretation of it in their minds. It is common to find that other people understand a social phenomenon differently from the way that we do. Our own educational experiences may frame how we conceptualize what education is or should be. One person may welcome opportunities for children to learn through play as 'valuable educational activities' while another sees the same events as a 'deplorable waste of time'.

Socially agreed terms for concepts are used to create a link between ideas in the minds of author and reader. So, when a reader sees the word *education* she gains some approximate entry into the mind of the author, by identifying, on her own terms, a concept that he wants her to focus on. To help narrow the gap between the concept in the reader's mind and the one in his own, the author can introduce other concepts to help classify, interpret, describe, explain and evaluate the phenomenon as he sees it. For example, his conceptualization of 'education' might be increasingly defined with reference to 'learning', 'skill formation', 'instruction', 'training', development', 'quality', 'standards', 'limitations', and so on. Since the social world is infinitely complex, authors use concepts to focus the attention of their readers on particular features, while others are backgrounded.

Often, several concepts need to be considered together, and they are bundled loosely under a single label: a collective concept that covers the group of concepts as a whole. A researcher interested in the management of change might include under the collective concept of 'organizational change' both the concept of 'innovation' (planned development of new products and processes) and the concept of 'adaptation' (response to emerging shifts in the organizational environment).

Combinations of concepts are also possible (as we will discuss more fully in Chapter 8). For example, where a bundle of concepts are in a clearly defined relationship with each other, we have the type of tool of thinking referred to as a *model*. Thus, an educational model might link individual 'learning' episodes to 'skill formation' over time, accelerated by 'instruction' techniques embodied in 'training' strategies, leading to overall 'development'.

Tools for thinking

Wallace's (Appendix 2) text features a range of individual **concepts** that are important for his argument. For example, he draws attention (page 262) to 'management', as expressed in the related concept 'management team'. He defines what he takes 'management' to mean here, stating that the term 'refers both to leadership (setting the direction for the organization) and to management activity (orchestrating its day-to-day running)'. Note how Wallace has to employ other related concepts (e.g., 'setting direction', 'orchestrating') in order to create his definition of management.

Tools for thinking are embedded in the language of the literature you read, and in the literature that you produce when writing for assessment or publication. Therefore, what we are introducing here is not new but a way of focusing your attention onto something that you have already encountered and used. By becoming more conscious of concepts and models that you have an implicit familiarity with, you will be able to ask questions that reveal hidden features of a text, including unspoken assumptions, logical flaws and unwarranted conclusions.

Tools are constructs too!

Be warned – these tools for thinking are themselves constructs that rely on the interpretation of language. As you will see, authors differ in what they mean when they talk about them: how they intend a term like 'concept' or 'model' to be defined, how they employ it, how they conceive of its relationship with other tools. No idea, even a tool for thinking, has a fixed and universally agreed definition. All the same, since academic communication fundamentally depends on common understandings of the discourse, there is an area of general agreement and shared meaning for most terms, which we have aimed to capture in our descriptions. Compare your existing understanding of each term against the way that we define it. Any differences may shed light on things that have puzzled you up to now (for instance, where your understanding of a term has been rather narrower, or rather broader, than is customary in academic usage).

Reordering the components: putting the mental map together

We have introduced the five components of this mental map, starting with the component that you are likely to be most aware of already and working through to components that might be less familiar, or that you may not have considered previously. But the map as a whole relates the components in a more logical order, to guide you in scrutinizing texts produced by other authors, as a critical reader, and creating them yourself as a writer subjecting your argument to the scrutiny of others.

Here is how the five components relate to each other, so you can get an impression of the map as a whole. As a critical reader, you are alerting yourself to the ways in which authors:

- use generic tools for thinking, and
- apply them in expressing their ways of thinking about the social world;
- are influenced in their approach by their reasons for conducting the research;
- make claims about what they have learned and why it matters, and
- express those claims with greater or lesser certainty and generalization.

As a writer for other critical readers, you become an author following the same logic, from using tools for thinking to making claims that have particular characteristics.

A visual representation of this map was given earlier in this chapter, as Figure 7.1, and in each of the next three chapters the relevant component of the map will be shaded to indicate which part of the map is under consideration. You should bear in mind that no mental map can be definitive, and a philosopher could offer something much more detailed and discriminatory than we use here. We offer an approach that is sufficiently defined to navigate by, while being streamlined enough to be usable. Let us turn now to a more detailed examination of the first map component.

8

Tools for Thinking and Ways of Thinking

Keywords

descriptive assumption; ideology; metaphor; perspective; stipulative definition; theory; value; value assumption

Here we add more detail about two components of the mental map for navigating the literature that were introduced in the last chapter. As noted there, we use language to share concepts with others. Several concepts may be combined in building towards an increasingly sophisticated interpretation of the social world.

Tools for thinking: concepts, metaphors, labels, perspectives, models, theories

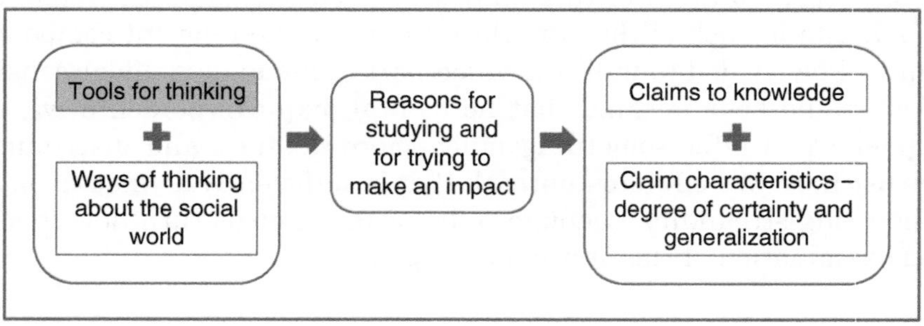

FIGURE 8.1 Focus on tools for thinking

More on concepts

Since experience is interpreted through language using concepts, there is room for interpretations to diverge. A concept may not mean the same thing to everyone who uses it in their writing or who comes across it in their reading. The extent to which concepts can be successfully shared by an author and a reader depends on the extent to which they both interpret the term in the same way. Suppose an author states an opinion about a concept (e.g., adult education is of little benefit to the economy) and the reader disagrees with it. This could be for one of at least three reasons:

1. The author and reader differently understand what the term refers to (e.g., author – adult education means evening classes in flower arranging; reader – it means mature student access to full-time university study).
2. They have different conceptualizations of the underlying dynamics of the phenomenon (e.g., author – adult education is largely about giving retired people access to pastimes; reader – it is an opportunity for people to make up for previously missed opportunities).
3. The reader does not share the author's opinion about the social significance of the concept (e.g., author – adult education is expensive and makes no difference to employability; reader – it is beneficial, because it stimulates the individual to make life-changing decisions).

Since no one has a monopoly on the definition of concepts, there is great potential for confusion. Readers may reject authors' claims because of poor communication about what is being referred to. If readers are to see things through the authors' eyes, the authors need to indicate what is meant by the terms they use. The best way is to offer a *stipulative definition* of the main concepts they are dealing with. A stipulative definition, literally, is what a person stipulates that something means for them. Others will be clear what this person's interpretation is, even if they do not agree with it. Stipulative definitions filter out all possible meanings of a concept except the one that authors intend. Readers can then see how close their own understanding of the concept is to that of the authors. If it is not identical, they can make a deliberate, if temporary, change to their own conceptualization, so as to follow the authors' argument.

Explicit and implicit definition of concepts

Wallace's (Appendix 2) definition of power (page 267) is explicit:

> Following Giddens (1984), a definition of power as 'transformative capacity' – use of resources to achieve interests – is employed.

(Continued)

(Continued)

Definitions can also be implicit, yet are easily detected if the first mention of the concept is followed by detail that contributes an account of what is meant by it. Wallace (Appendix 2) indicates what 'senior management teams' are by describing their role, typical membership and involvement in decision-making (page 262):

> ... senior management teams (SMTs) in British primary schools, whose role is to support the headteacher in leading and managing the institution. Typically, they consist of the headteacher, deputy head and other teachers with the most substantial management responsibility. Team members are variably involved in making policy and routine management decisions on behalf of other staff, whose views are represented in some measure.

Bear in mind that if you, as a reader, need authors to define their key concepts, then as a writer you risk confusing your readers unless you give them a stipulative definition of the key concepts that you employ.

Putting concepts together: metaphors

Concepts framing individual ideas can be combined in different ways. Where two concepts are linked on the basis of some indirect similarity, a *metaphor* is created. A *metaphor* is a way of describing one unfamiliar or complex phenomenon in terms of another, more familiar or simpler one. The characteristics of something familiar and easy to understand are used to explore, by analogy, the nature of the more difficult phenomenon. In the previous section, we likened stipulative definitions to a filter. A light filter selects certain wavelengths and excludes others. A particle filter holds back large particles while allowing small ones to pass through. Using these images, it becomes easier to think about a 'stipulative definition' as something that allows authors to define only those aspects of a phenomenon that are relevant for indicating what they take the concept to mean. Other possible aspects of the phenomenon are set aside.

A graphic metaphor: the 'garbage can' image of decision-making

March and Olsen (1976) used the metaphor of a 'garbage can' to characterize how ambiguity and unpredictability feature in organizational decision-making. The 'garbage can' metaphor captures the idea of various types of input in a meeting (such as individuals' presence and interest, issues that need deciding or local conditions) being 'thrown' into the decision-making process in a rather haphazard, unpredictable way. What gets 'tipped out' of the decision-making process – the decision itself – is a product of that mix.

(March, J. and Olsen, P. (1976) *Ambiguity and Choice in Organizations*. Bergen: Universitetsforlaget.)

In this way, a metaphor maps onto the concept that it describes, but not exactly. There are aspects of the concept that lie outside the bounds of the metaphor and also aspects of the metaphor that lie outside the bounds of the concept. In our 'garbage can' example, the metaphor draws attention away from the possibility that decision-making will sometimes be orderly and predictable. Conversely, a garbage can is periodically emptied out, whereas decision-making tends to be built on accumulated past decisions.

The boundaries marking where the metaphorical and base concepts no longer overlap are important. Pushing at them can be useful for exploring the phenomenon in new ways, but over-extending them will lead to 'shoehorning' things into unhelpful images. Consider what would happen if one explored an aspect of garbage can usage that March and Olsen could scarcely have included back in 1976: recycling. Would it help us understand more about decision-making in organizations if we thought metaphorically about how some items in a garbage can could be rescued and recycled? Or would that be an unhelpful step too far?

As a critical reader, you will often find yourself engaging with an account in which a metaphor has been adopted. It is important for you to reflect on which aspects of the social phenomenon being discussed are highlighted and which underplayed or ignored, and how the metaphor could be further exploited or is already being pushed beyond its usefulness.

Multiple concepts

Concepts are often grouped. Grouping concepts has the advantage of enabling us to attend to patterns in the phenomenon. But it will also obscure other patterns, which a different grouping would have drawn to our attention. This compromise is inevitable, since no one is capable of attending to everything at once. The key message for you is to be aware when a group of concepts is being used and to expect the author to provide sufficient information for you to know what is encompassed within the grouping. For our present purposes, we can identify two intersecting dimensions for grouping concepts (Figure 8.2):

- loosely, so as to draw attention towards diverse aspects of the same phenomenon, or more tightly to show how the aspects link together; and
- narrowly, to home in on specified aspects of a particular phenomenon, or more broadly to show how shared phenomena explain links between them – often causally.

The matrix in Figure 8.2 captures a loose or tight linkage between concepts (the left- and right-hand columns) and a narrow or broad focus (the upper and lower rows). Each cell depicts a combination of linkage and focus. The four combinations have each been given their own term: label, model, perspective, theory – though, of course, not all authors will use these terms in exactly the way that we do here. So we can illustrate further the notion of a 'stipulative definition' by outlining below what we mean by each of those four terms.

		Linkage between concepts	
		Loose	Tight
Breadth of focus	*Narrow*	LABEL	MODEL
	Broad	PERSPECTIVE	THEORY

FIGURE 8.2 Ways of grouping concepts together

What are labels?

Stipulatively, we are defining *labels* as the term for loose groups of concepts that have a narrow focus (Figure 8.2). For example, a researcher who is concerned with the impact on literacy of poverty, family instability and parental drug abuse might not only discuss these concepts individually but also bundle them under the collective label of 'social problems'. This tactic enables the author to refer in a loose way to the narrow set of concepts that is central to the argument being developed.

What are perspectives?

When several concepts are loosely grouped together but the focus is broader, they can be said to form a *perspective*. A broad focus does not mean no focus: some phenomena or aspects of them are still highlighted, while others are excluded. A cultural perspective, for example, brings together a range of concepts associated with a particular pattern of cultural behaviour (e.g., tradition, language, rituals, religious beliefs). Meanwhile, it pushes out of the way other factors, such as the psychological motivations of individuals within that culture, even though they, too, will determine how a person behaves.

The university degree ceremony provides an illustration. A behavioural perspective would draw to our attention the actions and words of the participants. A social relations perspective would examine the reasons why students elect to attend, perhaps in order to share one last special day with their friends and so that their parents can come and watch. A motivational perspective might reveal why individuals feel that it is 'worth' attending and how it affects their sense of identity and achievement to participate in the event and send some 'selfies' to their social network. A cultural perspective could examine how, through the 'rite of passage' ritual, academics symbolically acknowledge their students' achievements and the vice chancellor formally accepts them into the ranks of graduates of the institution.

Although it is quite difficult to manage multiple perspectives at the same time, it is possible to combine perspectives to a limited extent. A common approach is to examine a phenomenon first from one perspective, then from another. Difficulties can arise when the two perspectives embody concepts that are incompatible with each other. A cultural perspective on what happens in meetings may emphasize how people share beliefs and values to reach consensus, but a political perspective on the same meetings may emphasize how individuals use power to achieve their personal goals at others' expense. It might be difficult to decide which explanation to accept since they are all simultaneously valid. A researcher may need to combine the different perspectives, rather than deal with them independently. Doing so means confronting any conflicts in the stipulative definitions of the key concepts and resolving them. That is, the researcher makes a choice from within the range of possible definitions for a concept, so as to home in on one that is shared across the perspectives being used.

Combining perspectives

Wallace (Appendix 2) employs a combined cultural and political perspective on teamwork within the senior management teams that he researched. He justifies the combined approach as follows (page 267):

> The cultural and political perspective guiding the research integrates concepts about teacher professional cultures and micropolitics. It focuses on the reciprocal relationship between culture and power: cultural determinants of differential uses of power and uses of power to shape culture ...

In order to make the combined perspective work, Wallace has selected stipulative definitions of the core concepts 'culture' and 'power' that are compatible with each other. His stipulative definition of 'culture' is 'the way we do things around here', and allows for the possibility that different people may hold overlapping or contradictory beliefs and values about the culture. Equally, his stipulative definition of power as 'transformative capacity' is neutral and so allows for power to be used collaboratively or conflictually.

What are models?

When concepts are grouped together more tightly and with a narrow focus, they create a *model*. A process model of educational change, for example, might identify sequential 'stages', starting with 'initiation', followed by 'implementation', and culminating in 'institutionalization' (building into normal practice) or 'abandonment'. The tight grouping of a relatively narrow set of concepts means that, typically, a model refers to a specific aspect of a larger phenomenon. It is common, therefore, to see a specific phenomenon being modelled on the basis of the predictions or prescriptions of a more general *theory* (see below).

Modelling interaction: clarity versus comprehensiveness

Wallace (Appendix 2) develops a model of interaction between headteachers and other members of their senior management teams (pages 271–3). The core concepts are represented diagrammatically as a simple 'two-by-two' matrix of cells and arrows:

- The norm of people's belief in a management hierarchy is contrasted with the contradictory norm of people's belief in making an equal contribution to teamwork.
- The headteacher's potential to subscribe to each norm is contrasted with the potential for each norm to be subscribed to by all the other team members.

The four cells contain descriptions of the different outcomes of each combination, and they fall along a continuum from no synergy between the headteacher and other team members (when the headteacher subscribes to a belief in a management hierarchy and the other SMT members do not), to high synergy (when everyone adopts the norm of equality in the contribution to teamwork). Moderate and low synergy outcomes are also represented in the other two cells.

Note how Wallace has deliberately simplified even this quite specific aspect of teamwork by contrasting the headteacher's position with that of *all* the other members of the senior management team lumped together. The advantage of clarity that is gained through this simplification comes at a price. It ignores the possibility that amongst the other SMT members, individuals may differ regarding which norm they subscribe to at any given time. A more realistic model would have to consider multiple subgroups of team members, more linkages and more positions – but doing so would sacrifice clarity.

What are theories?

Theories are a tightly linked set of concepts with a broad focus, forming a coherent system. For instance, learning theories explain how individuals absorb, process and retain information. The concepts relating to parts of the system interrelate, and have implications for each other. Thus, a learning theory might focus on the interaction between prior experience, environmental influences and the cognitive processes through which individuals acquire information. How each part is defined (e.g., what range of factors are included under the label 'environmental influences') will affect the way this part is conceived to impact on other parts (e.g., how environmental influences shape cognitive processes). Theories may be used to interpret and explain what has happened and to predict what will happen. The breadth of focus may vary, from a particular range of social phenomena (as with learning theories), to more abstract explanations about society and history as a whole (such as structuration theory, which attempts to explain how social practices in general both produce and are reproduced by social structures). Some part of the tightly linked set of concepts embodied in broadly focused theory is often employed to construct a more narrowly focused *model*.

In some fields of enquiry, theories can be employed normatively, to prescribe what should be done to improve an aspect of the social world. Thus, a 'progressive theory of education' will make proposals about how education ought to be. It might be couched within a psychological perspective on individual development and employ the metaphor of 'nurturing growth'.

The theory behind the normative model?

Wallace's (Appendix 2) normative model of how school senior management teams ought to operate in a context where headteachers face strong demands for accountability is consistent with the much broader contingency theory of organizations. This theory attempts to explain how the most appropriate approach to organizing depends on the kind of task being undertaken and the environment in which the organization is set. While Wallace does not explicitly mention contingency theory, he does state in his abstract (page 261) that the model he puts forward is justified on the basis of a 'contingent approach to sharing school leadership'. If there is a link, Wallace leaves it implicit. So to check this hunch, it would be necessary to check Wallace's related publications in case the link is acknowledged elsewhere.

Ways of thinking: assumptions, philosophical positions, ideologies

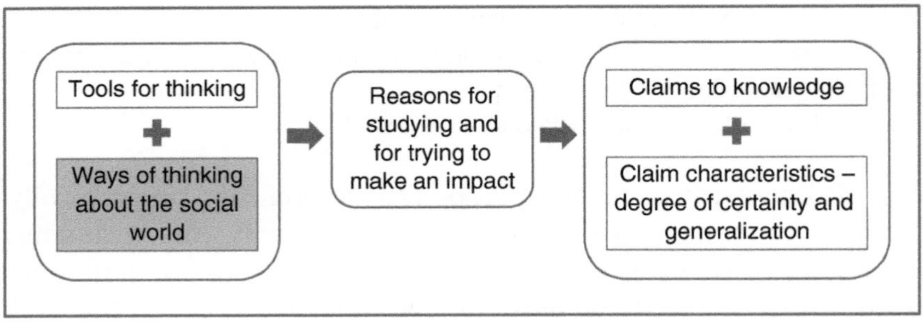

FIGURE 8.3 Focus on ways of thinking about the social world

Tools for thinking, as outlined above, are used to introduce key *ways of thinking* about the social world (Figure 8.3). We can identify three levels. The starting point for studying and making claims about the social world is to make certain assumptions. They are basic beliefs about what exists, how we can know about it and how it should or should not be. Irrespective of whether authors are aware of the assumptions they make, it is usually possible to work out what they are. Assumptions are then grouped into coherent *philosophical positions* or *ideologies*.

What are assumptions?

Any study of the social world is founded on two types of assumptions:

- *descriptive assumptions* – beliefs about how the world is, has been, or will be; and
- *value assumptions* – beliefs about what is right and wrong, so how things should be, or how they can be improved.

The term 'descriptive' implies a concern with social facts – though because we are dealing with assumptions, we will not take it for granted that those facts which are attended to encompass everything that might be taken into account. *Values*, on the other hand, imply a concern with what is desirable: especially what is right *in principle*, and how a principle might be reflected in what is the right thing to do ethically in a particular situation. The arguments developed by authors of any study will be underpinned, whether explicitly or implicitly, by both types of assumption. All claims to knowledge rest on beliefs about what reality is and how we can understand it, and values about what is worth paying attention to and how to do so.

Assumptions are a way of managing a complex world fraught with fundamental problems about existence, knowledge, and ethics. Table 8.1 shows how descriptive and value assumptions map onto three core philosophical approaches – ontology, epistemology and axiology:

- *Ontology* – the study of reality, being and existence.
- *Epistemology* – the study of the nature and scope of knowledge, and what counts as acceptable knowledge in a field of enquiry.
- *Axiology* – the study of judgements about values.

As Table 8.1 illustrates, these philosophical approaches progressively challenge the way we engage with research: what, how, why, and with what risk? The fundamental problems and the associated branches of philosophy are reflected in descriptive or value assumptions that are, in effect, the explicit or implicit answers to the questions in the final column. Researchers will have different answers, according to their specific assumptions. As a result, they will

TABLE 8.1 Fundamental problems reflected in assumptions that inform methodological concerns

Fundamental problem	Branch of philosophy	Type of assumption	Implications for study methodology
What exists?	Ontology	Descriptive	What can be studied?
How can we know what exists?	Epistemology	Descriptive	What methods can be used to generate evidence, and from which sources?
What is right or wrong about what exists?	Axiology	Value	What is worth studying to make an impact, and on whom?
What is right or wrong about ways of studying what exists?	Axiology (ethics)	Value	How should any people involved or affected by research be treated?

make different choices about the focus and methodology of their research. Working out authors' assumptions and seeing how they are reflected in their study methodology will help you identify why it is that you do, or do not, find their claims easy to accept. You may establish that the problem lies in one particular descriptive or value assumption that you do not share, and that, perhaps, you feel they are mistaken about. Or you may realize that they have not actually followed through on an assumption: there may be a break in the logic between what they assume to be the case and the way they have then proceeded, which contradicts with this assumption. It is easy to see that there are considerable opportunities for the critical reader to pin down the reason for a perceived problem with an author's claim. The reader can engage at a quite sophisticated, even philosophical, level with the nature of that problem, rather than only being able to say, rather superficially, that the claim somehow seems unsafe.

What are philosophical positions?

A word of warning: the following account is very simplified. Our modest purpose here is to alert you to some common philosophical positions in the social sciences as part of your map for navigating the literature. To enable yourself to make best use of the map you need also to study the philosophy of the social sciences in greater depth elsewhere, such as in a research methods textbook. Common philosophical positions in the social sciences include:

- *Positivism* – studying an observable social reality.
- *Realism* (and critical realism) – studying an underlying social reality that must be inferred from perceptions.

- *Interpretivism* – studying perceptions and actions taken in the light of these *perceptions.*
- *Post-structuralism* – studying how discourses frame perceptions and actions.
- *Pragmatism* – studying both an observable social reality and perceptions informing actions.

Table 8.2 summarizes these philosophical positions and shows how they relate to the three philosophical approaches – ontology, epistemology and axiology – that were introduced earlier. In particular, note how each position is linked to particular ontological assumptions about what exists and epistemological assumptions about how we can know. However, the axiological emphases differ widely between the positions. Some concern researchers' values about how to conduct a study; others concern researchers' values about the phenomena they study. The set of ontological, epistemological and axiological assumptions for each philosophical position informs the main methods that the researcher uses for generating evidence.

Checking for assumptions behind a philosophical position

In the previous chapter we noted how Wallace (Appendix 2) does not make explicit his assumptions about the nature of the social world and how we can know about it. Referring to Tables 8.1 and 8.2, however, it is possible to infer his assumptions, and consequently also his philosophical position, from his choice of data collection methods for his research (page 266–7). Wallace conducted 'focused, interpretive case studies' of senior management teams (SMTs) entailing interviews with SMT members and others involved, and observation of SMT meetings. Wallace's use of the term 'interpretive' suggests he is aware that his approach centres on what SMTs mean to people and on how these meanings are reflected in the actions of SMT members in team meetings. He may also be aware that the meanings that he comes to are derived from his interpretation of their perceptions and actions. His **philosophical position** appears to be 'interpretivism'. Two linked assumptions are implicit:

- the nature of the social world (ontology) – school SMTs exist insofar as people perceive a group of senior school staff as a team and act accordingly;
- how we can know about it (epistemology) – we can know about school SMTs by gathering the perceptions and observing the actions of people who are involved within particular contexts, and coming to our own interpretation of these phenomena.

We have previously seen how the third linked assumption concerning what is right and wrong about what exists (axiology) is made explicit. But even the modest clue provided by the choice of methods is enough to identify his likely position. Knowing this makes it possible to consider whether the assumptions underlying it are acceptable as starting points for his research, and so whether his claims to knowledge as an outcome of using these methods are likely to be convincing.

TABLE 8.2 Common philosophical positions, their underlying assumptions and methods

	Assumptions			
Philosophical position	**Ontology: What we know about what is**	**Epistemology: How we find out about what is**	**Axiology: What is right or wrong with what is, and how we find out about it**	**Methods**
Positivism	Social entities and their meanings exist objectively – there is a single reality external to and independent of social actors being studied and to the researcher, who has direct access to it	Data can be gathered about observable social facts that exist independently of the detached researcher, focusing on causality and law-like generalizations that explain observations, reducing phenomena to the simplest terms	Research is conducted in a value-free way. Research is objective, because it is independent of the data	Highly structured, large samples, measurement, quantitative, but may also use qualitative data
Realism (and critical realism)	Social entities exist objectively and meanings exist subjectively – social entities are external to, and shape social actors' meanings, but social entities are inferred from these meanings	Data can be gathered about observable social phenomena and their meanings, including meanings for the researcher, to determine underlying causal mechanisms which produce particular outcomes in specific contexts	Seeking underlying mechanisms implies criticism of common sense beliefs. Critical realists value emancipation from domination	Qualitative and quantitative

(Continued)

TABLE 8.2 *(Continued)*

	Assumptions			
Philosophical position	**Ontology: What we know about what is**	**Epistemology: How we find out about what is**	**Axiology: What is right or wrong with what is, and how we find out about it**	**Methods**
Interpretivism	Social entities and their meanings exist subjectively – there are multiple socially constructed realities based on 'common sense' meanings of actors, continually evolving	One can identify the range of actions (meaningful behaviour) and related perceptions of actors, including those of the researcher, to develop a contextualized understanding (as experienced and interpreted by the researcher)	The researcher's values inform the focus of study and its interpretation, and are made explicit through reflexivity about the impact of the researcher on the phenomenon being studied	Qualitative – naturalistic fieldwork (since phenomena occur in the social world) that observes a small sample of actors, narratives, case studies, etc.
Post-structuralism	Social entities and meanings exist subjectively, but are shaped by social discourses, and also shape them, so discourses are constitutive of social reality	One can identify the content and evolution of discourses shaping the meanings of actors, and how actors shape discourses	Researchers' values inform a focus on domination through discourses	Qualitative – analysing texts to show they may generate multiple meanings for different readers, rather than the author's intended meaning
Pragmatism	Social entities and their meanings exist both objectively and subjectively through intersubjectivity – there is a single reality and actors have different interpretations of it	Data can be gathered about social patterns that are independent of actors' meanings. Information can also be gathered on these actors' meanings and their associated actions. The transferability of knowledge derived from one context to others must be established empirically	The researcher's values on generating useful knowledge inform the focus, as does the researcher's reflexivity about his or her impact on the phenomenon being studied	Mixed qualitative and quantitative, theorizing observations, and assessing the application of a theory to a social setting

What are ideologies?

An *ideology* is a system of beliefs, attitudes and opinions about some aspect of the social world, based on particular assumptions. Political persuasions such as socialism, republicanism, and so on, are examples of ideologies. Ideologies are heavily influenced by values, and they guide action to achieve particular interests or goals. One person's ideology-driven action may prevent others from realizing their own interests, and may make it difficult to interpret aspects of the social world dispassionately.

For instance, many teachers and lecturers espouse an ideology built upon their beliefs, attitudes and opinions about education. One such ideology might be that 'education is about developing a lifelong love of learning'. This ideology is intrinsically value-laden because it cannot be based on facts alone. Rather, the ideology draws in addition upon views about the purposes, content and methods of education, and about the ideal balance of control between the different participants in educational activity over deciding what should and should not be done.

Ideology as a neutral or a critical term

The concept of an 'ideology' is often employed neutrally in discussion, referring to any system of beliefs, whether true or false. However, some use 'ideology' critically, to imply a false or distorted set of beliefs, representing a partisan interest that is not being made explicit. Take the superficially neutral educational ideology that 'the purpose of formal education is to provide the skilled workforce necessary for our nation's economic competitiveness in a global economy'. Marxists point out that this ideology is far from neutral. They argue that it protects the employers' position of advantage, by deflecting employees from a recognition that they could better their own economic position.

In your critical reading, it is important first to identify when authors' claims about the social world reflect their ideology, and then to question the assumptions and values that underlie the ideology itself.

Thinking about thinking

The first two map components can already enhance your critical thinking power. You will be alert to how tools for thinking shape the form of ideas, individually and in combination. You will be able recognize how ways of thinking shape the content of ideas, because they are founded on assumptions that frame the author's approach to research and claims about it. You can ask yourself whether an author has defined core concepts and adequately acknowledged assumptions. Equally, you can apply this discipline to making your own writing more convincing to your readers and assessors.

But the thinking that underpins the process of studying the social world is just the start. It has an onward influence on the reasons that authors adopt for undertaking their research. Time to consider the next map component.

9

Reasons for Conducting the Research

Keywords

action; critical evaluation; intellectual projects; knowledge; literature; policy; practice; research; theory; training; understanding; value stances

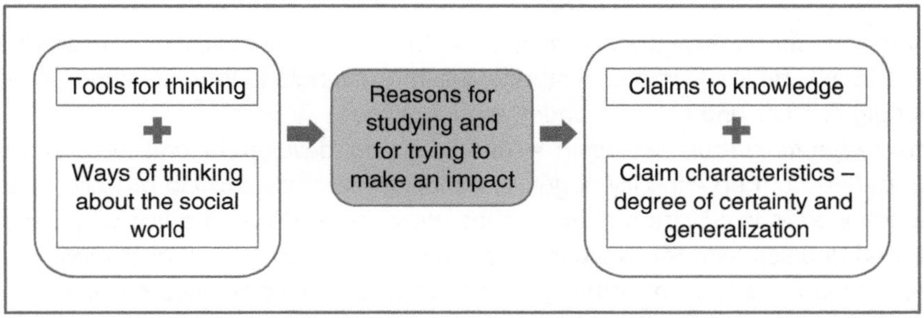

FIGURE 9.1 Focus on reasons for conducting the research

We now take a more detailed look at the 'intellectual projects' that lie behind studies of the social world. An author's intellectual project gives you insights about what they were trying to achieve through their study: why they were doing it, and whom they were seeking to influence through the claims they made. In turn, this information provides clues about how they will have gone about achieving their purpose and what the strengths and limitations of their approach may be.

Authors' intellectual projects are driven by what they find interesting, important, or right or wrong about the aspect of the social world they are investigating. What they argue, and how, will be determined by whose thinking or practice they want to influence. We shall see below that the type of literature that they have produced, the kind of knowledge claims they are making and the assumptions and values that lie behind their claims will all be linked to their intellectual project. So once you are clear about the authors' intellectual project, you will be in a strong position critically to assess how convincing their claims are.

To illustrate, consider the claim 'our findings show that it has been a bad year for criminal gangs'. We cannot interpret, and thus evaluate, this statement without knowing whose interests the authors are presenting – and that depends on their topic of interest and what they are trying to achieve. If the authors are researching the victim's perspective, then a 'bad' year is when there is a lot of criminal gang activity. But if they are researching the criminal's perspective, then a 'bad' year is when, say, the police crack down on the gangs.

Four sorts of intellectual project

It is possible to make a broad distinction between four main intellectual projects pursued in the social sciences, named for the outcome they seek to generate:

- *Knowledge-for-understanding* – attempting to develop theoretical and research knowledge from a relatively impartial standpoint. The rationale is to understand (rather than change) practice and policy or underlying ideologies.
- *Knowledge-for-critical evaluation* – attempting to develop theoretical and research knowledge from an explicitly negative standpoint towards existing practice and policy. The rationale is to criticize and expose the prevailing ideology, arguing why it should be rejected and sometimes advocating improvement according to an alternative ideology.
- *Knowledge-for-action* – attempting to develop practice-relevant theoretical and research knowledge, taking a positive standpoint towards practice and policy. The rationale is to inform efforts aimed at generating and implementing policies to improve practice, within the prevailing political ideology.
- *Training* – attempting, through guidance, training and consultancy, to impart practice knowledge and associated skills, taking a positive standpoint towards practice and policy. The rationale is directly to improve practice within the prevailing ideology.

As a student, you are similarly engaged in an intellectual project when developing your work for assessment or publication. Typically, academic studies emphasize *knowledge-for-understanding, knowledge-for-critical evaluation* and *knowledge-for-action*. In all three of these intellectual projects, critically reviewing the literature plays a central part in supporting or challenging the claims to knowledge.

We can work out what the dominant intellectual project is in a piece of research by looking at the following features, which will vary across the different types of project:

- *Reasons for undertaking the study* – this feature indicates how authors' explicit or implicit values about some aspect of the social world, their theorizing, research methodology and methods may affect their focus and the nature of the knowledge claims they make.
- *Typical mode of working* – indicates which kinds of knowledge authors are attempting to develop and how they make use of different types of literature.
- *Value stance towards the aspect of the social world* they are studying – indicates authors' attitudes towards policy and practice and towards attempts to improve them.
- *Value governing the significance of the study focus* – whether this aspect of the social world is intrinsically interesting, or is instrumentally important so relevant activity should be challenged, or improvement should be sought.
- *Values about what is right or wrong* about the behaviour of different groups involved in this aspect of the social world, and the consequences for them.
- *Typical question* or questions they ask about the social world – indicates which aspects authors are attending to or ignoring, and the focus of the answers they are offering.
- *Assumptions about the place of theoretical knowledge* in the study – indicates how authors employ any explicit definition of concepts, and the extent to which they are drawing ideas from the social sciences or from practical experience.
- *Types of literature produced* – indicates the kinds of knowledge authors are attempting to create, and where they publish.
- *Target audience to influence* – indicates the people whose thinking or actions authors wish to influence by convincing them to accept the authors' argument.

In Table 9.1, these different features are represented in the rows, and the four intellectual projects are in the columns. The cells therefore indicate how a given feature is manifested in the relevant intellectual project. The final row offers an illustrative, fictional example of a study of leadership framed by each sort of intellectual project.

Be mindful both that these categories are simplistic and that, in reality, intellectual projects are not always pursued separately. While one intellectual project is usually most central, you may expect to come across authors whose activity spans different intellectual projects. For instance, an account of social science-based research, designed mainly to generate knowledge-for-understanding, may include in the conclusion some recommendations for improving policy and practice (reflecting a knowledge-for-action agenda). Or a social science-informed normative theory of good practice in some policy domain, following a knowledge-for-action agenda, may also, as a spin-off, underpin the production of a diagnostic tool (contributing to a training agenda) for assessing the quality of existing practice.

TABLE 9.1 Four intellectual projects for studying aspects of the social world

	Intellectual project for studying an aspect of the social world			
	Knowledge-for-understanding	**Knowledge-for-critical evaluation**	**Knowledge-for-action**	**Training**
Reasons for undertaking the study	To understand policy and practice through theory and research	Critically to evaluate policy and practice through theory and research	To inform policy-makers' efforts to improve practice through research and evaluation	To improve practitioners' practice through training and consultancy
Typical mode of working	Social science-based basic research and theory	Social science-based basic research and theory	Applied research, evaluation and development activity	Designing and offering training and consultancy programmes
Value stance towards an aspect of the social world	Relatively impartial towards policy and practice	Negatively critical of policy and practice	Positive towards policy and the possibility of improving practice	Positive towards policy and the possibility of improving practice
Value governing the significance of the focus	Positive, because it is intrinsically interesting to understand how policy and practice operate	Positive, because it is instrumentally important to show how policy and practice benefit some groups at the expense of other groups	Positive, because it is instrumentally important to help those responsible for policy and practice to make them work as well as possible	Positive, because it is instrumentally important to find practical ways of making policy and practice work as well as possible
Values about what is right or wrong	Neutral towards any group advantages or disadvantages that result from the behaviour of the different groups involved	Negative towards advantages that the behaviour of some groups gives them over others Positive towards changing policy and practice to minimize advantages or disadvantages for any group	Positive towards (or not noticing) any advantages that the behaviour of some groups gives them over others Positive towards (or not noticing) the help that advantaged groups may get from the investigation to sustain or increase their advantage over others	Positive towards (or not noticing) any advantages that the behaviour of some groups gives them over others Positive towards (or not noticing) the help that advantaged groups may get from the practical intervention to sustain or increase their advantage over others

	Intellectual project for studying an aspect of the social world			
	Knowledge-for-understanding	**Knowledge-for-critical evaluation**	**Knowledge-for-action**	**Training**
Typical question about the social world	What happens, and why?	What is wrong with what happens, and why?	How effective is what happens, and how may it be improved?	How may my programme improve practice?
Place of theoretical knowledge in the study	Informed by and generates social science theory	Informed by and generates social science theory	Informed by and generates practical theory	Largely atheoretical, informed by a practical theory of training
Common types of published literature produced	Academics' social science-based theory and research (reference may be made in associated policy literature)	Academics' critical social science-based theory and research	Informed professionals' practice and academics' applied research (reference may be made in associated policy literature)	Trainers' and consultants' practice literature (reference may be made in associated policy literature)
Main target audience to influence through published literature	Policy-makers, academics, practitioners on advanced education programmes	Policy-makers, academics, practitioners on advanced education programmes	Policy-makers, academics, trainers, practitioners on advanced education programmes	Practitioners, other trainers, those practitioners on education and training programmes
Fictional example of a leadership study	A comparison of perceptions as leaders and followers in different groups	A study of the inhibitory impact of childrearing on women's career chances as business leaders	Measuring the impact of senior managers' leadership behaviour on organizational performance	Development of a diagnostic tool for identifying individuals' potential as business leaders, marketed to the human resources departments of companies

Where do *you* fit into this picture, as a person studying something in the social world? Your intellectual project may be tentative so far. Nevertheless, a few elements of one sort of intellectual project are likely to fit your reasons for studying and your associated values (even if the texts you are expecting to write are for assessment by your academic tutors rather than for publication). While your own intellectual project may still be emerging, the intellectual project of the authors whose texts you read is likely to be fully formed. So you can expect to gain useful insights by applying this component of the mental map to published frontline texts.

Having said that, authors rarely state what their intellectual project is, and some are not very explicit about the outcomes that they are trying to achieve. But you can often work out their main intellectual project from their writing. Promising places to check include:

- The title, chapter headings, or subtitles – authors usually indicate what their purpose is.
- The abstract if there is one – authors may say what the focus and outcomes of the study are.
- The introduction – where authors may set out their purpose and specify their research question(s), and where they may show how they will develop their argument in the remaining sections or chapters of the text (for example, highlighting their research methods).
- The conclusion – where most authors state in detail their main claims about what they have found out, as a result of the study they have undertaken.

A shortcut for identifying the intellectual project being pursued

Wallace's article (Appendix 2) offers indications that he is pursuing a *knowledge-for-action* intellectual project. Using Table 9.1 as a checklist, here is the evidence for this conclusion from clues contained in just the title and abstract of Wallace's paper:

1. What is the *reason for undertaking the study*? To conduct research whose findings have potential to inform training for senior school staff, in order to improve school leadership practice.
2. What is the *mode of working*? Evaluative research, where judgements are made about what happens and then used as a basis for model-building and, in turn, as a basis for identifying implications for training.
3. What is the *value stance towards the aspect of the social world being studied*? Positive towards sharing school leadership through teamwork.
4. *What value governs the significance of the study focus?* Implicitly, that it is of instrumental importance to inform training and thus help improve school leadership.
5. *What values are held about what is right or wrong?* It is both right for school leadership to be shared and right for headteachers to decide if they need to minimize the risk of things going wrong by restricting the scope of sharing.

6. What is the *question* being addressed? Implicitly, something like 'how effective are attempts to share school leadership through teamwork and how may they be improved?'
7. What is the *place of theoretical knowledge* in the work? The author generates practical theory from his research findings.
8. What *type of literature* is this? Primarily research literature because it hinges on data.
9. What is the *main target audience to influence*? Implicitly those who might be in a position to do something about addressing the training needs that are identified – senior school staff, trainers and policy-makers.

It does not matter whether you are a member of the authors' target audience for their text or not. Guided by this third component of the mental map, you can generally work out the main intellectual project being pursued by authors, from evidence of their reasons for studying and how they attempt to influence their target audience.

The next step now is to discuss the fourth and fifth components of the mental map in more depth, as your evaluation of any text will hinge on the claims to knowledge that are made, how well warranted they are and, consequently, whether they convince you, or not.

10

Knowledge Claims and Their Key Characteristics

Keywords

arguments; certainty; generalization; level of abstraction; practical knowledge; research knowledge; theoretical knowledge

At the heart of any text will be the authors' claims to knowledge. You will need to home in on them, so you have something to evaluate. In this chapter we explore in more depth the different kinds of knowledge that these claims relate to, and the types of literature in which you are likely to find them. Claims found in different types of literature are susceptible to certain typical limitations, and we will show you what to look for when critically evaluating those claims. The final section goes into greater detail regarding how authors characterize their degree of certainty and generalization about their claims. Recognizing these characteristics is a powerful preparatory step for evaluating whether the degrees of certainty and generalization are sufficiently well warranted to be convincing.

Kinds of knowledge claim and types of literature associated with them

We shall consider three kinds of knowledge claim and show which predominate in each of the four types of literature introduced in Chapter 2.

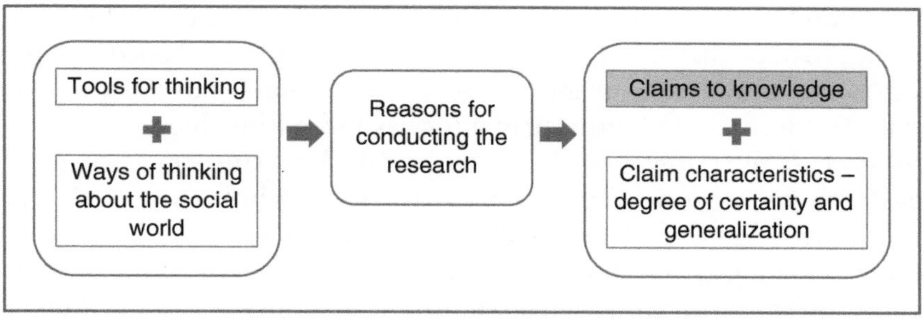

FIGURE 10.1 Focus on claims to knowledge

It is important to realize that you cannot always allocate a text to just one kind of literature, because it may contain examples of different kinds of knowledge, and aim to deploy the knowledge in more than one way. In this section we alert you to ways of working out what the main kind of knowledge and type of literature are in a given text. This information primes you on where to look when checking if the evidence is sufficient and appropriate to back the claims adequately, and so make them convincing. The three kinds of knowledge about the social world that we distinguish are theoretical, research and practice knowledge. Three of the types of literature map onto them – theoretical, research and practice. The fourth is policy literature.

Theoretical knowledge of the social world consists of theories (or more narrowly focused *models*, or looser *perspectives*) explaining how something works – whether a specific aspect of the social world, or society as a whole. It is developed through *systematic reflection*, and based on a set of closely inter-related concepts. Texts that predominantly offer theoretical knowledge can be termed *theoretical literature.*

To be credible, theoretical knowledge needs to be developed from some sort of evidence, otherwise it is just a hunch. Typical bases for theoretical claims are patterns noticed, either generally in society, through personal experience in a domain of practice, or as a result of specific investigations. When evaluating theoretical knowledge claims, here are some of the sources of evidence that you can check for their power to convince you:

- How the constituent concepts are defined, whether they are used coherently, and how logically they link together.
- Whether the claims build adequately and appropriately on others' theorizing, research or accounts of practice in the literature.
- What the quality of empirical evidence is; if either the authors' theorizing involves abstraction from research findings, or predictions from the theory are tested empirically.

Research knowledge describes what happens in the social world. The focus may be narrow or broad. It is developed through *systematic empirical investigation* to answer one or more research questions that data will be used to answer. Texts that predominantly offer research knowledge can be termed *research literature.* (However, keep in mind that this term is also used generically to refer to academic literature as a whole, since all types of academic knowledge entail 'research'. What we mean here by 'research' is narrower: experiments, observation, surveys, focus groups, and so on.)

The tools for thinking that we considered in Chapter 8 are used when conceptualizing research question(s) and interpreting the data produced. Even research that appears to be atheoretical is framed by concepts that have potential to be incorporated in theories, or are derived from theories. The empirical focus of research is typically a domain of practical experience, and findings entail surfacing patterns in them. Sources of evidence to check, as a critical reader, include:

- How convincingly the research topic and the findings are conceptualized.
- Whether the empirical investigation builds appropriately on others' research approaches and findings, or applies or tests a theory.
- How the authors' philosophical position is reflected in their methodological strategy and detailed methods for generating and analysing data, and what the implications are for the form, quality and quantity of the empirical evidence they produce.

Practice knowledge generates claims designed to *evaluate* how well something happens, usually regarding an everyday activity in some social domain. Investigating and challenging habitual activity is a feature of action research, which usually generates practice knowledge. Practice knowledge claims are developed through practitioners' actions in the social world, and based on their *personal reflections* on their experience, or a more *systematic evaluation* conducted by informed professionals. Texts that predominantly offer practice knowledge can be termed *practice literature.*

Practice knowledge entails judgements founded in the 'know-how' for the skilful performance of practical tasks. To generate practice literature, know-how needs to be raised to consciousness by reflecting on practice. Doing so entails employing concepts that bring certain aspects of this practice into the foreground. The concepts are likely to be influenced by theories. (For example, consider the impact that Marx's economic theory has had on political regimes across the world.) Practice knowledge claims may well be informed by research findings. Sources of evidence to check here include:

- How the practice is conceptualized, and especially what value assumptions are made about good practice.

- Whether the authors are informed by others' accounts of what happens and what works well, particularly from research that is independent of any stakeholder groups within the practice domain.
- The quality and quantity of experience, and how systematically it is drawn upon as the grounding for claims.

The bulk of frontline literature consists of claims to theoretical, research and practice knowledge, as indicated above. The fourth type of literature, *policy literature*, includes government policy statements and reports commissioned from informed professionals or academics. Focusing on significant, generic social or economic changes, it can be seen as an application of the three kinds of research knowledge, in different combinations, to achieve a particular purpose. Policy literature does not, therefore, tend to generate theoretical, research or practice in itself. Nor is it driven by an intellectual project for study. Rather, it is driven by a political ideology.

Authors of policy literature have a vision for improving something within a government's jurisdiction. To this extent policy literature is similar to practice literature. But policy literature is more ideologically and politically directed. It is written by, or on behalf of, people who have the authority to make policy, or else to represent the interests of other groups who stand to be affected by it.

Policy literature entails the authors' evaluation of the present situation. It will usually rely on other types of knowledge and literature to make the case. But the evaluation of them will be influenced by the values and assumptions underlying the authors' political ideology. Identifying a text as policy literature alerts you to check:

- What value assumptions underpin the authors' evaluation and vision, how acceptable these values are to you, and why.
- Whether the authors draw explicitly or implicitly on any theory in framing the policy problem they diagnose and their proposed solution for it, and how coherent their conceptualization is.
- Whether the authors provide any warranting from the practice knowledge of informed professionals or from research knowledge, and how robust this knowledge base is, to support their evaluation of what is wrong with the present situation, and predictions about what will work better.

To summarize, it is usually straightforward to work out what the main kind of knowledge is within a claim, provided you are aware that the other kinds of knowledge are also often involved, in a subordinate role. For example, claims to theoretical knowledge will usually be supported by research knowledge: the author's explanations are based on evidence. Theoretical knowledge claims are also often followed up with some claim about practice knowledge. Here the author answers the 'so what?' question: what difference can your theoretical knowledge claims make to something in people's practice? The type of literature you are dealing with reflects in large part the dominant kind of knowledge, but also the intentions of the author. Therefore, when considering literature produced by researchers it is useful to refer back also to the authors' 'intellectual project' for study, as described in Chapter 9.

A hierarchical mix of types of literature

Many texts give unequal emphasis to more than one kind of knowledge. Combinations include:

- *Theoretical literature* illustrated by examples drawn from *practice literature* (e.g., an account of systems theory using the authors' experience of higher education organizations to illustrate its application to practice).
- *Research literature* interpreted through *theoretical knowledge* (e.g., research using a political perspective as a theoretical framework).
- *Research literature* commissioned by policy-makers to inform *policy* designed, in turn, to change *practice* (e.g., systematic reviews of research commissioned by a central government agency).

Wallace's article (Appendix 2) is clearly concerned with research knowledge generated by his empirical investigation as a professional researcher. Early on he states (page 261): 'I wish to explore empirical factors connected with the contexts of schools and consequent risks – especially for headteachers – that may inhere in their endeavour to share leadership'.

But his research focus is also informed by his combined cultural and political perspective. This conceptualization channels his attention towards those empirical factors connected with uses of power as determined by different cultural allegiances. He both draws on theoretical knowledge and generates a model of his own to synthesize his findings. Further, his explicitly normative argument culminates in practical prescriptions, designed to influence the development of practice knowledge by school managers and trainers.

So this example of academic literature relates unequally to all three kinds of knowledge. At the top of the hierarchy are Wallace's claims to research knowledge. For this reason, we judge it to be research literature. But he also draws upon theoretical knowledge and claims to have developed his own (in the form of his perspective and model). And he makes normative claims about profitable directions for practitioners to develop more effective practice knowledge through changes in practice.

Communicating knowledge claims in different types of literature

It is worth identifying what type of literature a text conforms most closely to, because each is prone to certain limitations affecting the validity of the knowledge claims it contains (see Table 10.1). You can thus alert yourself to what you should look for, when deciding how convincing the claims are.

TABLE 10.1 Types of literature and indicative limitations of claims to knowledge expressed in them

Type of literature	Common features	Some potential limitations of claims to knowledge
Theoretical (emphasizes theoretical knowledge)	Academic theorists develop a system of related concepts and apply them, in order to understand an aspect of the social world. Sometimes they subsequently advocate improvement in practice or policy	• Key concepts may not be defined • Concepts may not be mutually compatible • Concepts may not be linked together logically • Assumptions about the social world may be false • Attention may be drawn away from important features of the social world • A supposedly impartial theory may be affected by implicit values reflecting a particular ideology • Explicit values underlying any advocated improvement may be unacceptable • Evidence from the social world may not support the theory
Research (emphasizes research knowledge)	Academic researchers or practitioners report on the outcomes of a systematic investigation into an aspect of the social world. Sometimes they subsequently make recommendations for improving practice or policy	• The focus of the research may be diffuse • The research may be atheoretical or employ theoretical ideas unsystematically • Any conceptual framework may not be rigorously applied to inform data collection and analysis • The design and methods may not be given in sufficient detail to check the rigour of the investigation • The design and methods may be flawed • Generalizations about the applicability of the findings to other contexts may lack sufficient supporting evidence • The findings may contradict those of other research investigations • Recommendations for improving practice and policy may not be adequately supported by the findings • Values connected with an ideology about the aspect of the social world under investigation may affect the choice of topic for investigation and the findings

(Continued)

TABLE 10.1 *(Continued)*

Type of literature	Common features	Some potential limitations of claims to knowledge
Practice (emphasizes practice knowledge)	Professionals, trainers or experienced practitioners offer an account of lessons for good practice in an aspect of the social world, based on personal experience or on the evaluation of others' practice	• Significant factors affecting the capacity to improve practice may be ignored • Criteria for judging the quality of practice may be implicit and unjustified • Generalizations about the applicability of any advocated practice and means of improvement to other contexts may lack sufficient supporting evidence • Values connected with an ideology about good practice and how most effectively to improve it may influence recommendations for improving practice • The evidence base may be flimsy, narrow and impressionistic
Policy (emphasizes practice knowledge)	Policy-makers and their agents articulate a vision for improved practice in an aspect of the social world and the means of achieving their vision	• Implicit or explicit assumptions about the need for improvement and the content of the vision may be based on values connected with a political ideology which is open to challenge • Any analysis of the current situation, the vision and means of achieving it may be under-informed by research and may contradict research findings

These potential limitations underline how open to challenge and alternative interpretation our knowledge of the social world can be. Becoming a critical reader entails developing the habit of questioning whether such limitations have a bearing on claims made in the literature you encounter. In turn, becoming a self-critical writer involves habitually checking whether your own claims might be subject to such limitations, then addressing those that you can resolve or work around, and acknowledging those that you cannot. (In the next chapter, we explain how you might react to these limitations when developing a Critical Analysis of a text.)

A shortcut for identifying the type of literature

There are often clues in the title of a text that help you to work out which type of literature you are dealing with (italicized in these fictional examples):

- Theoretical literature – 'An Ironic *Perspective* on Organizational Life'.
- Research literature – 'The Impact of Marketing on Consumer Decision-Making: A *Large-Scale Survey* of English Householders'.

- Practice literature – 'Effective Hospital Management: The Evidence from *Inspection*'.
- Policy literature – 'Generating Profitable Commercial Spin-Offs from Innovation: *The Way Forward*'.

Failing that, you may get clues from an abstract, the blurb on the cover of a book, or the introduction and conclusion of the text. Theoretical literature will have a strong emphasis on one or more tools for thinking. Research literature will include a report or discussion of empirical evidence. Practice literature will focus on experience in some practical domain. Policy literature will tend to assert that existing practice needs improving or that a new practice should be implemented.

Look at the abstract for Wallace's article (Appendix 2). Within it, certain keywords indicate what type of literature it is: *empirically backed* ... *findings* ... *research* ... *model*.

Wallace is developing an argument about how leadership should be shared. His conclusion about sharing is backed by warranting that consists of findings from empirical research, which he reports. In the light of the research, he develops a model that uses patterns in the findings as a means of supporting his argument about the value of a contingent approach to sharing school leadership. This piece of research literature is therefore providing evidence to support a model, which itself legitimizes a conclusion. By this means, Wallace aims to convince the target readers of the paper that his conclusion is valid.

Elements of research and theoretical literature are being combined here. But this is *research* literature because the empirical investigation underpinning the model is the central feature of the author's work. Whether the conclusion is convincing rests on the adequacy of the claims made possible by the investigation.

Knowledge claim characteristics: the degree of certainty and generalization

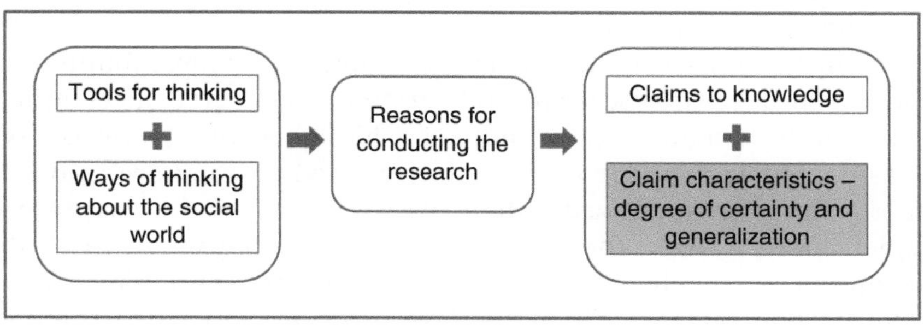

FIGURE 10.2 Focus on claim characteristics

As highlighted in Chapter 7, when a claim to knowledge is made – that something is, or normatively should be, the case – it has two key characteristics: the degree of certainty with which it is made; and the degree to which it is generalized to a wider range of instances of a phenomenon than just those the authors have studied. As a critical reader, how you evaluate the evidence for claims is intricately related to the degree of certainty and generalization associated with it. Furthermore, while the two characteristics can be considered separately, they also interact. Figure 10.3 shows that each characteristic operates along a continuum, from a low, through moderate, to high degree of certainty or from a low, through moderate, to high degree of generalization. Note that the degree of certainty is independent of the degree of generalization, so any combination is possible.

Figure 10.3 demonstrates how, if a claim is to be sufficiently warranted, it requires a certain level of evidence, which is different according to the degree of certainty and of generalization. In Chapter 4, we saw how warranting can be provided, and be appropriate, but still be inadequate – not sufficiently convincing for the critical reader. An inadequately warranted claim often fails to convince because:

- it is based on an insufficient amount of robust and appropriate evidence to support the degree of *certainty* with which this claim is made;
- the evidence does not justify the extent to which the claim is *generalized* beyond its immediate context;
- or both.

Certainty about a claim

The academic literature is not short of highly speculative claims to knowledge of the social world, made with enormous confidence that they are certain truths. Yet, as discussed earlier, no knowledge of the social world can ever be beyond all doubt. It is always appropriate for the critical reader to ask whether there is sufficient evidence to support the degree of certainty with which a claim has been made.

To home in on how sure authors are that they really have found out what they claim, you need to look for an indication of the degree of certainty with which this claim is made. An example of a highly certain claim is: 'Trainee managers demonstrably learn more effectively when they are praised than when their efforts are criticized.' Often the degree of certainty expressed in a claim is left implicit, as in the version of this claim that we saw in Table 4.1 (as an example of a conclusion with inadequate warranting): 'Trainee managers learn more effectively when they are praised than when their efforts are criticized.' Removing the word 'demonstrably' means there is no explicit

Degree of certainty: low ← moderate → high

Degree of generalization: low ↔ moderate ↔ high

Degree of generalization	*Tentative whether a claim is true* (low)	*Moderately confident that a claim is true* (moderate)	*Confident that a claim is true* (high)
low — ***Applies to a specific context at a low level of abstraction***	*Low vulnerability* to rejection since the claim is tentative and generalization to other contexts is minimal ***Warranting check:*** • **Is there sufficient evidence from the specific context to support this tentative claim?**	*Fairly low vulnerability* to rejection since the claim is moderately confident and generalization to other contexts is minimal ***Warranting check:*** • **Is there sufficient evidence from the specific context to support this moderately confident claim?**	*Moderate vulnerability* to rejection since the claim is confident but generalization to other contexts is minimal ***Warranting check:*** • **Is there sufficient evidence from the specific context to support this confident claim?**
moderate — ***Applies to some contexts at a moderate level of abstraction***	*Fairly low vulnerability* to rejection since the claim is tentative and generalization to other contexts is moderate ***Warranting check:*** • **Is there sufficient evidence from the specific context and other contexts to support this tentative claim which is moderately generalized?**	*Moderate vulnerability* to rejection since the claim is moderately confident and generalization to other contexts is moderate ***Warranting check:*** • **Is there sufficient evidence from the specific context and other contexts to support this moderately confident claim which is moderately generalized?**	*Fairly high vulnerability* to rejection since the claim is confident and generalization to other contexts is moderate ***Warranting check:*** • **Is there sufficient evidence from the specific context and other contexts to support this confident claim which is moderately generalized?**
high — ***Applies to all contexts at a high level of abstraction***	*Moderate vulnerability* to rejection since the claim is tentative but generalization to other contexts is extensive ***Warranting check:*** • **Is there sufficient evidence from the specific context and other contexts to support this tentative claim which is extensively generalized?**	*Fairly high vulnerability* to rejection since the claim is moderately confident and generalization to other contexts is extensive ***Warranting check:*** • **Is there sufficient evidence from the specific context and other contexts to support this moderately confident claim which is extensively generalized?**	*High vulnerability* to rejection since the claim is confident and generalization to other contexts is extensive ***Warranting check:*** • **Is there sufficient evidence from the specific context and other contexts to support this claim which is both confident and extensively generalized?**

FIGURE 10.3 Characteristics of knowledge claims and their vulnerability to rejection

indication of the high degree of certainty. But the certainty of the claim is still there: the authors simply state that praise *does* help trainee managers learn more than criticism – not that it may do so, or that it may sometimes do so in particular circumstances.

From time to time you will probably come across claims made with a level of certainty that you feel is unwarranted. Such claims are vulnerable to being rejected once you scrutinize the match between the evidence provided in the warranting for them and the certainty with which they are proposed. The more certain a claim, the stronger the evidence required adequately to warrant it. The more tentative the claim, the less the evidence required, because much less is actually being claimed. As a critical reader, you can scrutinize any argument by first checking that it actually has both a claim and a warranting, and then checking the match between the degree of certainty of the claim and the strength of the evidence offered to warrant it being accepted. Remember each time to ask yourself:

- Is there strong enough evidence to support the degree of certainty adopted (or implied) for this claim?

In our example above, the certainty of the claim *could* be justified if the researcher had studied a very large number of trainee managers and always got a clear result. Some kinds of claims are compatible with strong certainty. The claim that 'the earth is round' could be warranted by the evidence that whenever you fly westwards for long enough you end up in the east, and that satellite photographs of the earth reveal its curvature. Little knowledge about the social world is that certain, so you are unlikely to find experienced social science researchers stating that their evidence *proves* a claim. You are much more likely to come across authors who state that their evidence *suggests* or *is consistent with* a claim. They may fine-tune by saying *may suggest* or *strongly suggests*.

There are other ways in which authors may signal their own lack of certainty. One is by stating that their claims are tentative or cautious. A formal means of signalling tentativeness is through *hypotheses*. A hypothesis is a claim consisting of a proposition or statement that something is the case but which is as yet unproven. It will often be predictive (as we saw earlier in Figure 2.1), implying that a particular outcome will flow from a particular action. An enquiry into an aspect of the social world might begin with a hypothesis, the validity of which is then tested by checking whether evidence supports it or not. Alternatively, an enquiry may produce hypotheses as outcomes, amounting to predictions that could be tested in future. However, many hypotheses in the study of the social world are so general that they are not amenable to straightforward testing. For instance, how could we convincingly test the hypothesis that 'learning how to learn is a more effective preparation for adult life than learning lots of facts'? What would count as sufficient evidence warranting the conclusion that the hypothesis was supported or should be rejected?

Generalizing a claim

The issue here for you, as a critical reader, is checking the extent to which findings from within the context studied also apply to other contexts. Some level of generalization is normally expected in research: one examines a phenomenon in a limited way in order to find out something that is likely to be true in other similar circumstances. Generalization, in part, is about how one judges what counts as a similar circumstance. A claim about, say, the effectiveness of an approach to supporting teenage mothers might be made on the basis of studying five social service units that offer such support in the UK. A judgement must then be made about whether it holds true for all UK social service units providing such support, and whether it might be extended to all social service units and other support arrangements for teenage mothers anywhere in the world.

Gauging the level of generalization of others' work is very important when it comes to designing your own investigation. You will want to compare and contrast your findings with those of others, but that is only valid if they implicitly generalize to the kind of population you are drawing from. For instance, if they are careful to state that their claims about the levels of stress at work relate *only* to Buddhist nurses in Thailand, then there is little value in your claiming to have countered their evidence by referring to findings from research on non-religious nurses in Canada.

Frequently, when a claim is characterized by a high degree of generalization, the author is not explicit about the range of contexts to which the claim applies. Rather, the extent of the claim is implied, as in our example in Table 4.1 'Trainee managers learn more effectively when they are praised than when their efforts are criticized', which is not only presented with high certainty but is also implicitly highly generalized. By implication, the claim is asserted to have universal applicability – to all trainee managers everywhere, past, present or future. But generalizations are, in themselves, just claims that something is known, not proof that it is known. If you scrutinize the evidence offered for warranting this claim (as depicted in Table 4.1), you are likely to find it unconvincing. It comes from a survey of only female trainee managers in just one sector: retail. So, as a critical reader it is always appropriate for you to check the match between the degree of generalization of the claims made and amount of evidence used to back that generalization. Make a habit of asking yourself:

- Is there a sufficient amount of appropriate evidence to support the degree of generalization adopted (or implied) for this claim?

You can scrutinize any argument by first checking it actually has both a claim and a warranting, and then checking the match between the degree of certainty of the claim and the strength of the evidence offered as warranting for the degree of generalization.

The broader the range of contexts to which a claim is generalized, the more it may affect the *level of abstraction* from specific instances of the phenomenon. The broader the generalization, the more it must gloss over details of individual contexts, to capture some quite abstract feature that is supposedly common to them all. The generalization 'learning how to learn is a more effective preparation for adult life than learning lots of facts' glosses over the multiplicity of details that may vary between different contexts. They include learning environments (does it matter if you have a computer-equipped classroom or just an open space?), the characteristics of learners (is the claim equally true of adventurous and quietly reflective learners?) or purposes for promoting learning (can the learning be for its own sake or must it be aiming to contribute to society?). As a critical reader, you judge whether you agree with the authors that the detailed factors differentiating each context are not significant enough to affect the applicability of the claim across a wide range of contexts. To do that, you need to do more than just identify that there are differences. You have to present an argument for why they are important.

For example, the claim that 'trainee managers learn more effectively when they are praised than when their efforts are criticized' glosses over many differences between trainee managers. Some probably are not important (though we can never be sure), such as the month they were born in, the size of their feet, their favourite colour. It would be quite difficult to successfully argue, as a critical reader, that the authors had been remiss in generalizing across these aspects of variation – unless you had evidence to support your view. On the other hand, differences like the trainees' gender, age, work sector, past training experience or cultural background might indeed affect how far praise works better than criticism. Yet, how does one *know* that any or all of these factors is more relevant? Again, you need evidence: from your own research or that of others. In addition to variation in the trainees, what about variation in the praise? The claim implies that different kinds and amounts of praise and criticism, or the balance between them, have no major impact either.

The high degree of abstraction entailed in this highly generalized claim leaves it vulnerable to being rejected, unless the authors can show that the various possible differences between trainees and types of praise actually have no significance. Overall, the more generalized the claim, the more warranting it needs, to indicate how the claim applies across different contexts. Conversely, the more specific the claim, the less of such warranting is needed.

Scrutinizing the certainty and generalization of claims together

The situation of a claim made with *a high degree of certainty and a high degree of generalization* is depicted in the bottom right-hand corner of Figure 10.3. We have already seen how, for such a claim to convince a critical audience, it must be warranted by evidence that is adequate to justify the boldness of the claim. So, as a critical reader, be alert to high certainty, high generalization claims – whether explicit or implicit. Not every such claim will begin 'It is always the case that ...', and the certainty and generality associated with the claim may not be stated close to the main concluding statements. The signal might be a brief remark near the end of the text, or something said or not said in the abstract. Subtler cases might build certainty and generalization into a new claim, as in: 'The results of our study demonstrate that future training policy should focus on promoting the praise of trainee managers and minimizing criticism.' Here, the policy proposal is sweeping. It reflects the authors' assumption that the study's evidence adequately warrants a high degree of certainty and generalization. In your reading, watch out in particular for recommendations about ways of improving practice, whether directly, or through policy. They tend to make the strongest claims to knowledge, often combining a high degree of certainty with a high degree of implicitly or explicitly expressed generalization, at a high level of abstraction. Popular 'how to do it' management books typically make high certainty, high generalization claims along the lines of 'effective managers are visionaries who inspire others to go the extra mile to realize corporate objectives'.

High-risk writing: high certainty, high generalization

If as a critical reader you require extensive warranting when claims are made with high certainty and high generalization, the same is likely to be true of the critical readers who assess your written work. Beware of making such claims unless you are sure that you have adequate warranting, whether from your own research or the wider literature.

(Continued)

(Continued)

Otherwise your claims will be vulnerable to rejection as unconvincing. One way of reducing the vulnerability of high certainty claims is to make them conditional, as in 'If these results are reliable, this is definitely the case.' Similarly, high generalization claims can be made conditional, as in 'What I have discovered may also apply in other contexts, to the degree that this one is similar to them.' But critical readers might then question why you do not seem sure that your results are reliable or that other contexts are like yours. A more effective writing strategy is to judge for yourself just how reliable and generalizable you consider your findings to be, and then to adopt a clear and defensible position along each continuum.

The top left-hand corner of Figure 10.3 represents *low certainty and low generalization*, where a claim is tentative and is not held to apply to contexts other than the specific context studied. Such claims have low vulnerability to being rejected because of inadequate warranting. Since they are so tentative, only a modest amount of evidence is needed to warrant them. Further, as the claims are not generalized to other contexts, evidence can come solely from the context investigated.

A low certainty, low generalization claim is not very vulnerable to the criticism of being under-warranted precisely because there is not much of a claim in the first place – a modest claim needs only modest warranting. But a claim that is both tentative and confined to a specific context is not likely to be of much interest to most readers, because they are trying to establish the reliability of the claim in relation to the contexts that they work in themselves. A low certainty, low generalization claim will not be much use in establishing what is definitely known, let alone how far this tentative knowledge can be applied to diverse contexts.

So, as a critical reader, be alert to low certainty, low generalization claims. Tell-tale signs are qualifiers like 'it may possibly be the case that ...', 'it might be applicable only here', but authors may be more subtle. Sometimes only the absence of a more confident or generalized claim indicates how limited specific claims must be. Yet even when the claims are of low vulnerability, they still bear checking for adequacy of warranting. Unusually, you may judge that the authors have been more modest than they need be. Perhaps you know from your reading of the literature that evidence from other studies corroborates their findings. Collectively, that information may enable you, when you come to write, to express a greater level of certainty and generalization than they did.

Under-ambitious writing: low certainty, low generalization

As a self-critical writer developing your argument, beware of playing too safe. You risk your work being dismissed as under-ambitious and so failing to find out anything important. Critical readers will be most interested in claims with wide significance for the area of enquiry. If you are writing a paper for presentation at an academic conference or writing your dissertation, you may be expected to demonstrate robust claims about important new knowledge. So your claims need to be every bit as certain and generalized as you can adequately warrant using the evidence you can produce in support, both from your own investigation and from other literature.

How do you ensure your evidence is strong enough? By appropriately interpreting the claims in the research literature and by designing your own empirical studies to take into account from the beginning your eventual need to make claims with the highest warrantable degree of certainty and generalization (addressed in Part Three of this book). But bear in mind that when you write up your research, you can determine the level of vulnerability of your claims by careful choices in the way you word them, since the degree of vulnerability changes as one moves along the continuum in each dimension.

We have already noted how the two dimensions portrayed in Figure 10.3 vary independently. So a claim could conceivably be of low certainty and high generalization ('might be the case and applies universally ...'), or high certainty and low generalization ('is clearly the case in this context but its wider applicability has yet to be demonstrated'). Such claims are moderately vulnerable to rejection because they are ambitious along one dimension and play safe on the other. Equally, claims may reflect other positions, such as moderate generalization.

Whatever the position of a particular claim along the two continua, it will have some level of vulnerability to rejection. So, in sum, an incisive way to evaluate the major claims you come across as a critical reader is to:

- identify the degree of certainty and generalization of claims; and
- check how well this degree of certainty and generalization matches up with the amount of appropriate evidence employed in warranting them.

Meanwhile, as a self-critical writer, you will wish to make your writing robust to the demands and expectations of the critical readers of your work. Be cautious about asserting greater certainty over your claims to knowledge than you have evidence to support and about making broad generalizations – unless you can justify a high level of abstraction.

Hopefully, you have now got into your head a detailed mental map for navigating the literature, or at least some sense of:

- What *tools for thinking* are.
- How they are applied to *ways of thinking* about the social world.
- How they help to frame *reasons for conducting research* (an intellectual project).
- How studies result in *claims to one or more kinds of knowledge* expressed in particular types of literature.
- How these *claims embody two characteristics – a degree of certainty and a degree of generalization* – that need to be adequately warranted by evidence if they are to be accepted as convincing.

The best way to consolidate your acquisition of this mental map is to put it to work, referring back to the previous chapters as required. The more you use the map, the more familiar you will become with its components and how they can help you as both a critical reader and a self-critical writer. Soon it will be an integral and intuitive part of your critical thinking capability. It is time now to stop looking at the map and to do some practice in using it to navigate the literature.

11

Developing a Critical Analysis of a Text

Keywords

Critical Analysis exercise; Critical Analysis Questions

This chapter focuses on how you can use your mental map in developing an in-depth analysis of any text from the frontline literature. The framework we put forward and exemplify in use is an elaboration of the Critical Summary based on the five Critical Synopsis Questions that you met in Part One.

Completing a Critical Analysis of a text takes a lot of effort. But you will reap some very valuable rewards if you make that effort for the texts that are of most central significance for your work. First, you will get to know the texts extremely well and will have quite comprehensively evaluated them. Second, you will have assembled, in a structured format, the basis for writing an incisive Critical Review of each text individually, or a Comparative Critical Review of multiple texts (to be discussed in Chapter 13). Most importantly, the more Critical Analyses you do, the more familiar you will become with the components of your mental map, and with the Critical Analysis Questions that can be asked of a text. Eventually, using the map and asking the Critical Analysis Questions will become automatic. Then you will be in a position to use your mental map and Critical Analysis Questions selectively, without necessarily having to check whether you have forgotten to ask any questions, or needing to write your responses down.

We now introduce our structured approach for undertaking a Critical Analysis of a text. At the end of the chapter, once you have read through these ideas, we invite you to conduct your own full Critical Analysis of Wallace's article in Appendix 2, referring as you go along to the various sources of guidance we have provided. (In Chapter 12 we will offer our own Critical Analysis along with comments on our reasoning at each step, so that you can compare your responses with ours.)

From five Critical Synopsis Questions to ten Critical Analysis Questions

The five Critical Synopsis Questions introduced in Chapter 4 encouraged you to:

- Think why you are investing your time in reading a particular text.
- Get a sense of why the authors wrote it.
- Summarize what they have to say that is of relevance to you.
- Consider how convincing their account is.
- Draw a conclusion about how you might use the text for your purposes, in the light of its content and your evaluation of the authors' argument.

The ten Critical Analysis Questions do the same job (Table 11.1), but in more detail. The first expansion, in Critical Analysis Questions 2–4, helps you analyse what the authors are doing (and so alerts you to potential limitations of their work that might affect how convincing you find their claims). The second expansion, in Critical Analysis Questions 5–9, helps you evaluate the claims in a more sophisticated way.

TABLE 11.1 Linking Critical Synopsis Questions with Critical Analysis Questions

Critical Synopsis Question	Associated Critical Analysis Question(s)
EXPLORATION	
A Why am I reading this?	1 What review question am I asking of this text?
B What are the authors trying to achieve in writing this?	2 How and why are the authors making this contribution?
C What are the authors claiming that is relevant to my work?	3 What is being claimed that is relevant to answering my review question? 4 How certain and generalized are the authors' claims?

Critical Synopsis Question	Associated Critical Analysis Question(s)
	EVALUATION
D How convincing are these claims, and why?	5 How adequate is the backing for these claims? 6 How effectively does any theoretical orientation link with these claims? 7 To what extent does any value stance affect claims? 8 To what extent are claims supported or challenged by others' work? 9 To what extent are claims consistent with my experience?
E In conclusion, what use can I make of this?	10 What is my summary evaluation of the text in relation to my review question?

We will presently introduce a form that is completed as part of the process of conducting the structured Critical Analysis. The form contains ideas to guide your critical thinking at three levels:

1. The *Critical Analysis Questions* themselves, numbered 1–10.
2. For most of those questions, one or more *sub-questions*, lettered (a), (b) and so on, helping to highlight aspects of the question.
3. *Prompts*, enclosed in brackets and introduced by 'e.g.' to draw your attention to possible details you could look out for when working towards your answer to any Critical Analysis Question or sub-question.

We suggest you carry out your Critical Analysis at the same time as you read a text, rather than afterwards. The Critical Analysis Questions are grouped to form a sequence:

- Critical Analysis Question 1 encourages you to think about why you have selected the text and how your Critical Analysis of it may contribute to your enquiry.
- Critical Analysis Question 2 guides you in determining what the authors are attempting to do and alerts you to potentially fruitful lines of critical questioning.
- Critical Analysis Question 3 encourages you to summarize whatever content of the text is of significance to you.
- Critical Analysis Question 4 helps you identify two key characteristics of each claim: the degree of certainty and of generalization.
- Critical Analysis Questions 5, 6, 7, 8 and 9 are complementary. Together they help you to examine critically different aspects of this content to see to what extent you find it convincing.
- Critical Analysis Question 10 invites you to form a conclusion, in the light of your Critical Analysis, based on your informed judgement about the extent to which any claims relating to the focus of your enquiry are convincing, and why.

Below, we set out all the Critical Analysis Questions, sub-questions and prompts in the order that they appear on the blank Critical Analysis Template (which you can download from https://study.sagepub.com/wallaceandwray3e). Beneath each of the ten Critical Analysis Questions, we have offered our rationale (shaded) for why we consider it important to ask this question of the text.

We suggest you now read carefully through the explanations, checking that you understand the rationale for each Critical Analysis Question.

Advice on making effective use of Critical Analysis Questions

1 What review question am I asking of this text?

(e.g., What is my central question? Why select this text? Does the Critical Analysis of this text fit into my investigation with a wider focus? What is my constructive purpose in undertaking a Critical Analysis of this text?)

Rationale for Critical Analysis Question 1. It is crucial to begin by identifying a review question. In an essay, this question may map onto a central question, while in a longer piece of work it will probably reflect one aspect of the central question. The review question provides you with a rationale for selecting a particular text and a constructive purpose for reading it critically. Any text you select should potentially contribute to addressing your review question.

2 How and why are the authors making this contribution?

Rationale for Critical Analysis Question 2. You will be able to see *how* the authors make their contribution (e.g., developing theory to deepen understanding of a social phenomenon, reporting new empirical research findings) by identifying the type of literature (see Chapter 10) they have produced. Then establishing the authors' intellectual project will clue you in to *why* they are making their contribution by producing this type of literature. You will be aware of whom they are seeking to convince of their argument and associated claims to knowledge. Your awareness of how and why the authors have attempted to make their contribution will put you in a good position to evaluate what they have done. (See the section in Chapter 9 on different sorts of intellectual project, including Table 9.1.)

Sub-questions

a. What type of literature is this? (e.g., Theoretical, research, practice, policy? Are there links with other types of literature?)

b. How clear is it which intellectual project the authors are undertaking? (e.g., Knowledge-for-understanding, knowledge-for-critical evaluation, knowledge-for-action, training?)
c. How is the intellectual project reflected in the authors' mode of working? (e.g., A social science or a practical orientation? Choice of methodology and methods? An interest in understanding or in improving practice?)
d. What value stance is adopted towards the practice or policy investigated? (e.g., Relatively impartial, critical, positive, unclear? What assumptions are made about the possibility of improvement? Whose practice or policy is the focus of interest?)
e. How does the sort of intellectual project being undertaken affect the research questions addressed? (e.g., Investigation of what happens? What is wrong? How well a particular policy or intervention works in practice?)
f. How does the sort of intellectual project being undertaken affect the place of theory? (e.g., Is the investigation informed by theory? Generating theory? Atheoretical? Developing social science theory or a practical theory?)
g. How does the authors' target audience affect the reporting of research? (e.g., Do the authors assume academic knowledge of methods? Criticize policy? Offer recommendations for action?)

3 What is being claimed that is relevant to answering my review question?

Rationale for Critical Analysis Question 3. First, set aside arguments in the text that are not relevant to what you are trying to find out. Draw the remainder into a focused summary of the text. Try to avoid getting distracted by minor details. Concentrate on a small number of major ideas.

Sub-questions

a. What are the main kinds of knowledge claim that the authors are making? (e.g., Theoretical knowledge, research knowledge, practice knowledge?)
b. Excluding aspects that are obviously not relevant to the review question, what is the content of each of the main claims to knowledge and of the overall argument? (e.g., What, in a sentence, is being argued? What are the three to five most significant claims that encompass much of the relevant detail? Are the
improving policy or practice?)
c. How clear are the authors' claims and overall argument? (e.g
introduction or conclusion? Unclear?)
d. How consistent are the authors' claims with each other? (e.g., D
supporting an argument? Do any claims contradict each other?

4 How certain and generalized are the authors' claims?

Rationale for Critical Analysis Question 4. As preparation for a critical consideration of the authors' claims, it is helpful to work out the degree of certainty with which any knowledge claim is asserted and the degree to which the authors generalize beyond the context from which the claim to knowledge was derived. (See the last part of Chapter 10 for information on certainty and generalization.)

Sub-questions

a. With what degree of certainty do the authors make their claims? (e.g., Do they indicate tentativeness? Qualify their claims by acknowledging limitations of their evidence? Acknowledge others' counter-evidence? Acknowledge that the situation may have changed since data collection?)
b. How generalized are the authors' claims – to what range of phenomena are they claimed to apply? (e.g., The specific context from which the claims were derived? Other similar contexts? A national system? A culture? Universal? Is the degree of generalization implicit? Unspecified?)

5 How adequate is the backing for these claims?

Rationale for Critical Analysis Question 5. It is important to check whether the claims that are of interest to you are sufficiently well supported in the text to convince you of their validity. The authors may seek to back up their claims in various possible ways, including the presentation of their own empirical evidence, reference to others' work, logical reasoning, accounts of their own experience, and so on. (See Table 10.1 for the potential limitations of different types of claim to knowledge.)

Sub-questions

a. How transparent are any sources used to back the claims? (e.g., Is there any statement of the basis for assertions? Are sources adequately specified?)
b. What, if any, range of sources is used to back the claims? (e.g., First-hand experience? The authors' own practice knowledge or research? Literature about others' practice knowledge or research? Literature about reviews of practice knowledge or research? Literature about others' polemic? Is the range of sources adequate?)
c. If claims are at least partly based on the authors' own research, how robust is the evidence? (e.g., Are there methodological limitations or flaws in the methods employed? Do the meth-ods include the cross-checking or 'triangulation' of accounts? What is the sample size and [illegible] it large enough to support the claims being made? Is there an adequately detailed [illegible]t of data collection and analysis? Is there a summary of all data that is reported?)

d. Are sources of backing for claims consistent with the degree of certainty and the degree of generalization? (e.g., is there sufficient evidence to support claims made with a high degree of certainty? Is there sufficient evidence from other contexts to support claims entailing extensive generalization?)

6 How effectively does any theoretical orientation link with these claims?

Rationale for Critical Analysis Question 6. Any text must employ certain concepts to make sense of whatever aspect of the social world is being discussed. Many texts will feature an explicit theoretical orientation as a framework for understanding and possibly as a basis for the authors' recommendations for improvement. You will need to decide whether the claims being made are clear and coherent, and whether you accept the assumptions on which they rest. To assist your critical reflection, check which concepts and other tools for thinking have been used, what they are taken to mean and how they frame the claims being made. (See Chapter 8 on tools for thinking, Chapter 10 on kinds of knowledge and types of literature, including the potential limitations of claims to knowledge listed in Table 10.1, and Chapter 9 on different sorts of intellectual project.)

Sub-questions

a. How explicit are the authors about any theoretical orientation or conceptual framework? (e.g., Is there a conceptual framework guiding the data collection? Is a conceptual framework selected after the data collection to guide analysis? Is there a largely implicit theoretical orientation?)
b. What assumptions does any explicit or implicit theoretical orientation make that may affect the authors' claims? (e.g., Does a particular perspective focus attention on some aspects and under-emphasize others? If more than one perspective is used, how coherently do the different perspectives relate to each other?)
c. What are the key concepts underpinning any explicit or implicit theoretical orientation? (e.g., Are they listed? Are they stipulatively defined? Are concepts mutually compatible? Is the use of concepts consistent? Is the use of concepts congruent with others' use of the same concepts?)

7 To what extent does any value stance adopted affect claims?

Rationale for Critical Analysis Question 7. Since no investigation of the social world can be completely value-free, all claims to knowledge will reflect the value stance that has been adopted. So it is important to check what values have guided the authors of a text, how these values affect their claims and the extent to which the value stance makes the claims more or less convincing. (See Table 9.1 for guidance on values, and Table 10.1 for potential limitations in relation to value stance.)

Sub-questions

a. How explicit are the authors about any value stance connected with the phenomena? (e.g., A relatively impartial, critical or positive stance? Is this stance informed by a particular ideology? Is it adopted before or after data collection?)
b. How might any explicit or implicit value stance adopted by the authors be affecting their claims? (e.g., Have they pre-judged the phenomena discussed? Are they biased? Is it legitimate for the authors to adopt their particular value stance? Have they over-emphasized some aspects of the phenomenon while under-emphasizing others?)

8 To what extent are claims supported or challenged by others' work?

Rationale for Critical Analysis Question 8. It is unlikely that any study of an aspect of the social world will be wholly unrelated to others' work. One valuable check is therefore to examine whether authors make links with other studies. Another is to draw on your own knowledge of other literature, to determine how far the claims being made are supported by work that others have published (including work done since the authors' publication). Referring in this way to other texts that address phenomena related to the text you are analysing is an entry point to a Comparative Critical Analysis (see Chapter 13 and, for a more concise illustration, the Comparative Critical Summary in Chapter 6).

Sub-questions

a. Do the authors relate their claims to others' work? (e.g., Do the authors refer to others' published evidence, theoretical orientations or value stances to support their claims? Do they acknowledge others' counter-evidence?)
b. If the authors use evidence from others' work to support their claims, how robust is it? (e.g., As for 5(c).)
c. Is there any evidence from others' work (including work you know, but the authors do not mention) that challenges the authors' claims and, if so, how robust is it? (e.g., Is there relevant research or practice literature? Check any as for 5(c).)

9 To what extent are claims consistent with my experience?

Rationale for Critical Analysis Question 9. Your own experience of the social world will probably not be identical to that being studied in the text but it is still relevant. In considering how convincing the claims made in a text may be, it is worth checking whether these claims have significant similarities with your experience and evaluating whether they sound feasible or unrealistic, given what you know from this experience.

10 What is my summary evaluation of the text in relation to my review question?

Rationale for Critical Analysis Question 10. What you have learned from your answers to Critical Analysis Questions 2–9 provides the basis for your overall, well-informed and balanced judgement about how convincingly your review question (Critical Analysis Question 1) is answered by these authors' claims. All your answers will now be available for you to draw upon selectively as you write an account of the text when addressing the review question that has driven your critical reading activity.

Sub-questions

a. How convincing are the authors' claims and why?
b. How, if at all, could the authors have provided stronger backing for their claims?

As noted above, we recommend that you download the blank version of the Critical Analysis Template from the SAGE website: https://study.sagepub.com/wallaceandwray3e. By copying the downloaded template file, you can create a separate file for each Critical Analysis that you complete. When you enter your responses, the template will expand as required so that you can write as much as you like. If you save a completed Critical Analysis with the original text, you can quickly refer back to the text if necessary.

Your Critical Analysis of an article reporting research findings

It is now time for you to try out a Critical Analysis. Of course, you can pick your own text to analyse if you wish. However, we offer an opportunity in this book to get feedback on your attempt, and if that will be useful, you will need to conduct your first Critical Analysis on the text we give commentary on – Wallace's article in Appendix 2. To make the exercise work, we will specify the two review questions that you should ask of Wallace's text. (We have done this so that you can compare your responses with ours, which we will provide in the next chapter.) The review questions are:

1. What does this text suggest may be key factors promoting or inhibiting the effectiveness of a particular aspect of educational leadership and management practice?
2. To what extent are the factors identified applicable to the leadership and management of my organization or one known to me?

Remember that these review questions guide you into what you *do not* need to focus on, as well as what you do. You can refer, as necessary, to:

- the discussion in Chapters 7–10 relating to the components of your mental map;
- Table 10.1 for a list of potential limitations of each type of literature that you can look out for; and
- the advice in this chapter on making effective use of each Critical Analysis Question.

(We have indicated above that knowledge of other relevant literature is needed to complete Critical Analysis Question 8, sub-question (c). However, if our example paper is not within your subject area, you do not need to refer to other texts in this exercise.)

Students embarking on a detailed Critical Analysis like this for the first time often encounter difficulties in finding answers to one or more questions, but it is important not to give up too soon. Always think carefully about how the text might actually contain the information, perhaps implicitly, that you need. Expect to read the text with great attention in order to detect some of the indicators that you are looking for. Now complete your own Critical Analysis of Wallace's article in Appendix 2 (using the Critical Analysis Template you have downloaded from the SAGE website: https://study.sagepub.com/wallaceandwray3e). If you wish, you can begin by seeing how the abstract, on its own, points towards answers to the questions (see Chapters 3 and 4). Doing so will raise more issues than it answers, but it may help you identify what you are looking for.

Once you have completed your Critical Analysis, turn to the next chapter. You will be able to check your responses to each Critical Analysis Question or sub-question against ours, to see what our rationale was for each of our responses and to decide whether you agree or not.

12

A Worked Example of a Critical Analysis

Keyword

Critical Analysis example

This chapter takes you step by step through our completed Critical Analysis of Wallace's article (Appendix 2). Hopefully, you will already have completed your own Critical Analysis of this text to answer the two review questions that we set, as suggested at the end of the last chapter. If you compare your responses with ours as you read through the present chapter, it will enable you to consolidate your learning. (Additional examples of completed Critical Analyses can be found at https://study.sagepub.com/wallaceandwray3e).

After each of our responses to a question or sub-question, we have provided a comment explaining our reasons for making this response. We have sometimes given further information about the nature of Wallace's text and suggested what you might look out for in any text when conducting a critical analysis. In brackets, at the end of every comment where the title or abstract provided clues about what to look for as we read the main text, we have summarized this evidence. (To keep the example as simple and clear as possible, in our response to Critical Analysis Question 8, sub-question (c) we have not made direct reference to other literature. Normally, however, you would do so.)

When you examine your responses alongside ours, do not expect them to be identical. In particular, your answer to Critical Analysis Question 9 (and hence the second review question) will naturally be different because you will be referring to your knowledge of a different organization. Indeed, throughout, our Critical Analysis is as personal to us as yours is to you. Our answers are based on our perceptions and values, which we have supported through our explanatory commentary. Your answers may be different. You may even wish to challenge our analysis and the reasoning behind our answers. The article happens to relate to an applied field of enquiry and, since applied fields tend to be value-laden, people will differ in what they regard as significant, good or bad. The important point to note is that, like us, you should be able to justify why you respond as you do when conducting a Critical Analysis of a text. (Of course, you do not need to write a commentary on each response. We have provided the commentaries here to help you understand the process.)

You will find that some of our answers are already familiar to you, because we introduced the ideas in Chapters 7–10 when illustrating components of the mental map by referring to Wallace's article.

An illustrative Critical Analysis of a text

Wallace, M. (2001) 'Sharing leadership of schools through teamwork: a justifiable risk?', Educational Management and Administration 29(2): 153–67 [abridged as Appendix 2 of Wallace, M. and Wray, A. (2016) Critical Reading and Writing for Postgraduates (3rd edn). London: SAGE].

1. What review question am I asking of this text?

(e.g., What is my central question? Why select this text? Does the Critical Analysis of this text fit into my investigation with a wider focus? What is my constructive purpose in undertaking a Critical Analysis of this text?)

Review Question 1: What does this text suggest may be key factors promoting or inhibiting the effectiveness of team approaches to the leadership and management of educational organizations?

Review Question 2: To what extent are the factors identified applicable to leadership and management in universities in which we have worked?

Comment. We are imagining that our purpose in reading the text by Wallace is to prepare for writing a critical review of it, to answer two review questions. Review Question 1 reflects our interest in team approaches to educational management. Review Question 2 reflects the organizational situation in which we work – the university.

2 How and why are the authors making this contribution?

(a) What type of literature is this? (e.g., Theoretical, research, practice, policy? Are there links with other types of literature?)

This is primarily research literature based on Wallace's own investigation but Wallace is informed by theory, puts forward practical prescriptions and is critical of British central government policy.

> *Comment.* Our response is derived from the following observations. Wallace's argument rests for its backing on the evidence of his empirical research in four British primary schools. However, the focus of his investigation was guided by a cultural and political perspective; his argument and the model he develops are explicitly concerned with improving teamwork practice in schools; and he criticizes relevant British central government policies on the training of headteachers for failing to focus on sharing leadership through a team approach. (Help from the abstract: 'empirically-backed'; 'findings'; 'research'; 'model'.)

(b) How clear is it which project the authors are undertaking? (e.g., Knowledge-for-understanding, knowledge-for-critical evaluation, knowledge-for-action, training?)

This is clearly a knowledge-for-action intellectual project for study, but Wallace's argument is informed by research that appears to have had a strong knowledge-for-understanding emphasis.

> *Comment.* How do we know? Wallace states (page 261) that his purpose is to develop a normative argument about the extent to which he believes school leadership should be shared. This purpose implies that the rationale for his study of teamwork was to inform efforts to improve practice. In his conclusion, his criticism of central government training policy appears to be intended to convince policy-makers and trainers of the need to develop a stronger emphasis on teams. However, the research itself seems to have been driven partly by a wider concern to understand the phenomenon of team approaches. (Help from the abstract: 'empirically-backed'; 'normative'; 'model'; 'A contingent approach ... is justified'; 'implications for training'.)

(c) How is the intellectual project reflected in the authors' mode of working? (e.g., A social science or a practical orientation? Choice of methodology and methods? An interest in understanding or in improving practice?)

The knowledge-for-action project is reflected in the explicitly practical use of the research findings to support the development of a normative model and linked claims about what constitutes effective teamwork practice.

Comment. We made this judgement because even though the research approach may have had a strong social science orientation, it contained a major element of evaluation. Wallace made judgements about his findings on teamwork in terms of different degrees of synergy (pages 271–4). (Help from the abstract: 'implications for training'.)

(d) What value stance is adopted towards the practice or policy investigated? (e.g., Relatively impartial, positive, unclear? What assumptions are made about the possibility of improvement? Whose practice or policy is the focus of interest?)

A positive value stance is adopted towards teamwork as a way of sharing school leadership, especially where it is shared relatively equally. This stance is indicative of a knowledge-for-action project.

Comment. How did we reach this conclusion? Wallace evaluates a relatively equal sharing of leadership more positively than a relatively hierarchical sharing. But he does not claim that the latter approach is ineffective or wrong. Indeed, though he advocates relatively equal sharing (page 274), he also implies that a contingent return to relatively hierarchical sharing may carry less negative risk for headteachers in certain circumstances. While Wallace makes negative claims about central government training policy (page 274), he is not claiming that training is wrong, just that it could be improved. Therefore, this is not a knowledge-for-critical evaluation project. Wallace is positive towards the educational management practice he investigates. (Help from the abstract: 'normative argument'; 'ideally'; 'risks' – of what? for whom?; 'equal contribution'.)

(e) How does the sort of project being undertaken affect the research questions addressed? (e.g., Investigation of what happens? What is wrong? How well a particular policy or intervention works in practice?)

The research questions are not specified. However, Wallace does ask two questions (page 266) consistent with a knowledge-for-action project, namely, about the extent to which headteachers should be expected to share leadership and about the justifiability of them adopting a contingent approach to sharing. He sets out to answer these questions on the basis of his research findings.

Comment. Constraints on the length of journal articles often mean that research methodology and methods are not fully reported. The research appears to have addressed a knowledge-for-understanding research question – perhaps along the lines of 'how do SMTs operate, why and to what effect?' But Wallace uses the findings to address the two normative questions (page 266) and to support the context-sensitive principles that he formulates for justifying and prescribing practice (page 273). He clearly wishes to inform action. (Help from the abstract: 'Findings' – what are the research questions?)

(f) How does the sort of intellectual project being undertaken affect the place of theory? (e.g., Is the investigation informed by theory? Generating theory? Atheoretical? Developing social science theory or a practical theory?)

The research was informed by a social science-based cultural and political perspective. It led to the development of a model reflecting this perspective, consistent with a knowledge-for-understanding intellectual project. But the model forms the basis of Wallace's prescription of principles for practice, suggesting that his overall aim is to develop knowledge-for-action.

Comment. We have come to these conclusions because Wallace harnesses social science-based theoretical ideas to focus his research and underpin the development of a model. He employs this model as a practical theory to justify the principles that he prescribes for practice. If he adopts a knowledge-for-understanding element in his intellectual project, it seems to be there to serve his more fundamental intention of developing knowledge-for-action. (Help from the abstract: 'a model is put forward'; 'a contingent approach … is justified on the basis of this model'.)

(g) How does the authors' target audience affect the reporting of research? (e.g., Do the authors assume academic knowledge of methods? Criticize policy? Offer recommendations for action?)

The target audience is not specified, but the concluding section (pages 273–4) asserts implications for British headteachers, trainers and policy-makers. The inclusion of trainers, policy-makers and practitioners in the projected audience for a publication is typical of a knowledge-for-action project.

Comment. Specifying the audience for an academic journal article is rare. But there were enough clues in Wallace's abstract and conclusion to work out whom he is trying to

(Continued)

(Continued)

convince of his argument. We also note that he must have chosen to submit the article to this particular journal, whose international readership consists mainly of academics, trainers and practitioners (including senior school staff), some of whom are undertaking advanced courses of study. So he is likely to have been aware that he would reach an audience beyond the UK, including academics involved in the training of senior managers in diverse educational contexts. (Help from the title: 'a justifiable risk?' – for whom?; *Educational Management and Administration* – who reads this? Help from the abstract: 'implications for training' – training whom?)

3 What is being claimed that is relevant to answering my review question?

(a) What are the main kinds of knowledge claim that the authors are making? (e.g., Theoretical knowledge, research knowledge, practice knowledge?)

The main kind of claim is to research knowledge.

Comment. How could we tell? Wallace's claims to knowledge about how leadership is shared through different approaches to teamwork are derived from his investigation of practice in schools. His empirical evidence is based partly on observation. It also includes aspects of the practitioners' practice knowledge gathered through interviews. In addition, he draws on and develops theoretical knowledge to frame his research knowledge. (Help from the abstract: 'Findings … of research … in British primary schools' – what sorts of data did he gather?)

(b) Excluding aspects that are obviously not relevant to your review question, what is the content of each of the main claims to knowledge and of the overall argument? (e.g., What, in a sentence, is being argued? What are the three to five most significant claims that encompass much of the detail? Are there key prescriptions for improving policy or practice?)

The argument is that school leadership should be shared as widely as possible, contingent on the degree of risk for headteachers that sharing turns out to be ineffective. The most significant claims relevant to Review Question 1 are:

1. *Principles of staff entitlement and effective leadership outcomes are widely used to justify extensive sharing of school leadership, but theories reflecting these principles tend to rest on assumptions that may not be realistic for particular contexts (pages 262–6).*
2. *In UK state-funded schools, central government reforms have increased headteachers' dependence on their senior colleagues for support with implementation. However, they*

simultaneously increase the risk of being held uniquely accountable for sharing leadership if the outcome is judged ineffective (pages 265–6).

3. *Wallace's research in UK secondary and primary school SMTs implies that the culture of teamwork shared among headteachers and other SMT members includes contradictory beliefs. They believe in both (a) a management hierarchy where the headteacher is top manager and (b) the ability and entitlement of all members to make an equal contribution to the work of the team (pages 266, 268–73).*
4. *Wallace's UK primary school research suggests that maximum synergy (combining individual energies to achieve shared goals (pages 271–4) may be achieved if headteachers enable the other SMT members to make a relatively equal contribution to the work of the team, and the other members are willing to operate inside parameters with which headteachers are comfortable. Maximizing synergy holds most potential for maximum SMT effectiveness but also holds most risk of ineffectiveness (pages 265, 270).*
5. *In a context of high accountability, headteachers should aim to share SMT leadership as widely as they dare risk. However, they and other SMT members should accept that headteachers may 'pull rank' and operate hierarchically to ensure that the work of these teams remains inside parameters with which headteachers are comfortable (page 274).*

Comment. How have we singled out these key claims? Wallace gives explicit clues as to his overall argument but does not label his main claims as such. We are reading this article in the hope that its content may contribute to answering our two review questions. So we have used these review questions as criteria in deciding which claims are most relevant. We have concentrated mainly on the first question about factors promoting or inhibiting the effectiveness of team approaches. This is because the second question depends on our judgement when we are in a position to reflect on what we have learned about these factors. (Focusing on the two review questions may, of course, mean that other claims that Wallace makes are not included in the list. This is appropriate because the review must be driven by our own purpose in reading the text, not by its overall content, which might encompass issues that are irrelevant to our current interests.) (Help from the abstract: 'sharing ... depends on ... contexts ... and risks' – how? why?; model – achieving what?)

(c) How clear are the authors' claims and overall argument? (e.g., Stated in an abstract, introduction or conclusion? Unclear?)

The overall argument is clear – stated twice on page 261. Claims relating to the first review question are also quite clear, most being put forward and illustrated section by section.

Comment. Few authors explicitly label their overall argument at all, let alone as 'claims to knowledge'. But it is worth looking out for clues, as where Wallace states in his abstract and the introduction to the article what his overall argument is. Common locations for statements about main claims include the end of an introductory section, or a paragraph labelled as a summary.

(d) How consistent are the authors' claims with each other? (e.g., Do all claims fit together in supporting an argument? Do any claims contradict each other?)

The main claims do follow logically from each other and are consistent with the overall argument.

Comment. Wallace's argument is quite complex, so the article may require reading more than once to check whether the main claims and the overall argument fit together well. (It will probably be easiest for you to identify the arguments and claims that relate to your review questions first, and write them down, before you scrutinize them for logical consistency.) (Help from the abstract: there is a logic: 'normative' and 'ideally' indicate desirable outcome; achieving it 'depends on diverse contexts' which create 'risks'. Empirical work creates a 'model' used to suggest an 'approach'.)

4 How certain and generalized are the authors' claims?

(a) With what degree of certainty do the authors make their claims? (e.g., Do they indicate tentativeness? Qualify their claims by acknowledging limitations of their evidence? Acknowledge others' counter-evidence? Acknowledge that the situation may have changed since data collection?)

There is a low degree of certainty – on page 266 Wallace states that he is being tentative in using evidence from his research to back his argument about a contingency approach to sharing leadership.

Comment. Authors rarely state their degree of certainty as explicitly as Wallace did here. Remember to look for clues, for example whether authors suggest that something *may* be the case rather than something *is* the case. Wallace uses devices like the word 'arguably', as where he makes the claim that theories of leadership should be elaborated and refined to reduce their cultural relativity (page 274). (Help from the abstract: the phrase 'risks … *may* inhere in the endeavour to share leadership' implies tentativeness.)

(b) How generalized are the authors' claims – to what range of phenomena are they claimed to apply? (e.g., The specific context from which the claims were derived? Other similar contexts? A national system? A culture? Universal? Is the degree of generalization implicit? Unspecified?)

There is a moderate degree of generalization – Wallace makes clear that his source of empirical backing is research in British primary schools, drawing on an earlier study in secondary schools. In the conclusion he claims only that the principles he advocates for school leadership apply to the UK (pages 273–4). He has not specified whether his claims apply to private-sector as well as state-sector schools.

Comment. The proviso in our final sentence is important. Can we safely infer that the policy context that Wallace identifies as possibly having raised the risk for headteachers in sharing leadership is equally relevant to state-funded and private-sector schools? It is always worth checking whether authors have taken into account the full range of contexts to which they apparently assume that their claims apply. (Help from the abstract: 'model' and 'contingent approach' imply potentially generic usefulness – confirmed in the main text?)

5 How adequate is the backing for these claims?

(a) How transparent are any sources used to back the claims? (e.g., Is there any statement of the basis for assertions? Are sources unspecified?)

Sources of research evidence are transparent, specified in the section describing the research design (pages 266–7). Wallace also draws on a small range of relevant international academic literature to support his account of principles for sharing school leadership and his critique of influential leadership theories.

Comment. Wallace provides enough detail of his research design and theoretical orientation to give readers a reasonably clear idea of the scope of his investigation. He also refers to a book (page 266) that readers could, in principle, go to if they wanted more information. (Help from the abstract: it is stated that empirical research is reported – are data sources given in the main text?)

(b) What, if any, range of sources is used to back the claims? (e.g., First-hand experience? The authors' own practice knowledge or research? Literature about others' practice knowledge or research? Literature about reviews of practice knowledge or research? Literature about others' polemic? Is the range of sources adequate?)

Most claims are based on Wallace's own modest investigation – case studies of four primary school SMTs, involving observation of meetings, interviews and document survey. Research questions were informed by an initial postal survey and Wallace's previous research in UK secondary schools. Wallace also refers to a small amount of other research and theoretical literature. This range of sources seems adequate for the contextualized claims made.

> *Comment.* Authors reporting their research commonly summarize their design and the scope of data collection. But they may enhance the strength of their claims by referring to other sources, such as previous research with similar findings.

(c) If claims are at least partly based on the authors' own research, how robust is the evidence? (e.g., Are there methodological limitations or flaws in the methods employed? Do the methods include the cross-checking or 'triangulation' of accounts? What is the sample size and is it large enough to support the claims being made? Is there an adequately detailed account of data collection and analysis? Is there a summary of all data that is reported?)

The evidence appears to be moderately robust. Wallace observed primary school SMTs in action in their normal setting. He was in a position to triangulate accounts as he interviewed school staff both inside and outside the teams. A summary is given of findings related to Wallace's argument for each of the four SMTs. However, no outcome indicators of team effectiveness were reported that might have backed Wallace's claims about different degrees of synergy in the four teams. The sample of meetings and informants was small, limiting the extent to which Wallace can support generalization to other primary schools and to secondary schools across the UK.

> *Comment.* Our judgement of robustness of the evidence depended on the amount of information given about how the research was done and on the range of findings reported. We checked the findings section of the article to see if Wallace had reported relevant findings from all four of the SMTs he investigated. Limitations on the length of journal articles can lead authors to report findings from only part of their sample.

(d) Are sources of backing for claims consistent with the degree of certainty and the degree of generalization? (e.g., Is there sufficient evidence to support claims made with a high degree of certainty? Is there sufficient evidence from other contexts to support claims entailing extensive generalization?)

The sources of backing are consistent with Wallace's tentativeness about his claims. The sample is very small compared with the number of schools in the UK to which Wallace generalizes. However, in all schools that are affected by central government reforms, similar issues regarding the sharing of leadership are likely to ensue. The fact that he found such different approaches to sharing leadership in the four schools suggests that variation in practice across the country may be considerable. A larger sample and the use of outcome indicators for judging teamwork would have made his claims about variation in the degree of synergy and team effectiveness more convincing.

> *Comment.* Part of the knack of answering this sub-question is establishing the inevitable limitations of the study, which derive from the fact that one cannot include everything in a piece of research. All research involves compromise and Wallace's investigation was of only moderate scope. The design was also qualitative, giving the potential for depth of understanding but with potentially over-narrow coverage for convincing generalization from his sample to the wider population of SMTs in other schools. We judge that Wallace was not in a position to have made claims with greater certainty or to have generalized more widely than he does. (Help from the abstract: the claims here seem certain and generalized – are they are more nuanced in main text?).

6 How effectively does any theoretical orientation link with these claims?

(a) How explicit are the authors about any theoretical orientation or conceptual framework? (e.g., Is there a conceptual framework guiding the data collection? Is a conceptual framework selected after the data collection to guide analysis? Is there a largely implicit theoretical orientation?)

Wallace is explicit about the theoretical orientation guiding his data collection, defining the concepts he uses within his cultural and political perspective in the research design section (page 267). He makes extensive use of these concepts in reporting findings and he develops a model to explain the variation in practice that he found.

> *Comment.* Since Wallace claims to have adopted an explicit theoretical orientation, we checked the research design section for his account of it, to see if he defined the key concepts he used. We also examined the report of his findings and his model to determine whether he actually employed these ideas in framing his analysis. (Help from the abstract: 'model' – but what is it?)

(b) What assumptions does any explicit or implicit theoretical orientation make that may affect the authors' claims? (e.g., Does a particular perspective focus attention on some aspects and under-emphasize others? If more than one perspective is used, how coherently do the different perspectives relate to each other?)

The cultural and political perspective focuses on beliefs and values and the extent to which they are shared, in relation to different uses of power. However, it does not deal with other factors that may be relevant to understanding the effectiveness of team approaches to sharing leadership, such as individuals' psychological needs or responses to stress. So Wallace's claims are restricted to (a) those social factors connected with the cultural factors affecting uses of power in SMTs, and (b) ways in which power is used to try to shape the culture of teamwork.

> *Comment.* We have identified some limitations inherent in Wallace's focus. It is impossible to focus at the same time on all aspects of complex phenomena like team approaches. Due to our own experience of teams, we are aware that Wallace's cultural and political factors are not the only considerations relevant to our review questions. Therefore, even if we became convinced of his claims, we judge that there will probably be other important factors too. (Help from the abstract: 'contexts' affect sharing – how? What else might affect sharing?)

(c) What are the key concepts underpinning any explicit or implicit theoretical orientation? (e.g., Are they listed? Are they stipulatively defined? Are concepts mutually compatible? Is the use of concepts consistent? Is the use of concepts congruent with others' use of the same concepts?)

Key concepts are listed (page 267) and stipulative definitions offered. We are aware that some other academics define culture and power differently, but Wallace is consistent in his use of the concepts as he defines them.

> *Comment.* The statement in the introduction (page 262) that a combined cultural and political perspective was used alerted us to look in the research design section for stipulative definitions of key concepts, to check whether they were used to interpret the findings and, if so, how.

7 To what extent does any value stance adopted affect claims?

(a) How explicit are the authors about any value stance connected with the phenomena? (e.g., A relatively impartial, critical or positive stance? Is this stance informed by a particular ideology? Is it adopted before or after data collection?)

Wallace explicitly develops a normative argument about the degree to which school leadership should be shared in particular circumstances, and so is generally positive about team approaches as a way of doing so. He may have been relatively impartial prior to data collection. But, if so, he clearly made judgements about his data, because he uses his model of degrees of synergy to assert principles for effective team approaches in the UK political context.

> *Comment.* Wallace states in the introductory section that his purpose is to develop a normative argument (page 261). So we checked that he actually does this, especially in his conclusion (pages 273–4). (Help from the abstract: 'normative'; 'ideally'.)

(b) How might any explicit or implicit value stance adopted by the authors be affecting their claims? (e.g., Have they pre-judged the phenomena discussed? Are they biased? Is it legitimate for the authors to adopt their particular value stance? Have they over-emphasized some aspects of the phenomenon while under-emphasizing others?)

Given the central importance for Wallace of developing knowledge-for-action, it is legitimate for him to take a positive stance towards team approaches to sharing school leadership in general. However, his narrow focus on teamwork in practice means that he has taken for granted the policy context that so deeply affected this practice. It would have been legitimate for him also to question the managerial and educational values underlying central government educational reform policies – especially in the light of the consequence that he identifies, namely that the sharing of leadership is simultaneously necessary and risky for headteachers.

> *Comment.* Identifying Wallace's main intellectual project for study alerted us to consider what investigators following different intellectual projects might have attended to, which Wallace did not. We noted how he was critical of UK central government training policy (page 274) for failing to offer support with developing team approaches in the UK policy context. But he scarcely challenged the reform thrust and the acceptability of its consequences. (Help from the abstract: 'ideally', 'justifiable' imply that the author adopts a value-stance towards sharing school leadership – elaborated in the main text?)

8 To what extent are claims supported or challenged by others' work?

(a) Do the authors relate their claims to others' work? (e.g., Do the authors refer to others' published evidence, theoretical orientations or value stances to support their claims? Do they acknowledge others' counter-evidence?)

No reference is made to other research or theories that might support Wallace's claims about effective team approaches in the UK political context. Nor is any counter-evidence discussed. His claims would be more convincing if he had related them to others' work. It is notable that he questions the orthodox view that extensive sharing of leadership is always effective. If most of the existing research supported the orthodoxy that he sets out to challenge, when Wallace wrote his article there may have been little published evidence from elsewhere to support his view.

Comment. We looked out for references to other research, but we found only that Wallace criticizes leadership theories and associated prescriptions implying that school leadership should always be shared relatively equally. To the extent that such literature is based on research evidence, Wallace is implicitly rejecting the applicability of that evidence to the contexts he investigated. If we were conducting a literature review, we would expect to search for other literature supporting or countering Wallace's claims relating to our review questions.

(b) If the authors use evidence from others' work to support their claims, how robust is it? (e.g., As for 5(c).)

Wallace refers to no other evidence to support his claims.

Comment. If Wallace had referred to other research to support his claims, we would have tried to find out how strong that evidence was by looking for information about the research design, sample size and methods of data collection and analysis. If we were conducting a literature review, we might have checked by following up the references and reading the original accounts of this work.

(c) Is there any evidence from others' work (including work you know, but the authors do not mention) that challenges the authors' claims and, if so, how robust is it? (e.g., Is there relevant research or practice literature? Check any as for 5(c).)

The research that has led to the orthodox normative theories of educational leadership may be extensive. It seems likely that its findings would challenge Wallace's claims, just as he challenges the orthodox view.

Comment. If we were conducting a literature review, we might follow up Wallace's references, for example to transformational leadership (page 263), and assess how strong the counter-evidence was. If we knew of relevant papers published since this one, we might consider how they impact on it.

9 To what extent are claims consistent with my experience?

Wallace's account of the policy context is consistent with our recent experience of UK universities. Government-driven reforms have similarly included strong accountability measures, and additional measures have been developed within the universities themselves. The combined effect of these measures is to require more sharing of leadership. Fixed senior management teams are becoming the central mechanism in leadership and management within academic departments and across our university. So Wallace's claims are applicable to our context at a moderate level of abstraction. The loss of individual autonomy that academics used to be given imposes a greater need for maximizing synergy in managing their everyday work across departments or across the entire university. Maximizing synergy for effective teamwork is most important for individual teaching programmes and research project teams. Here the claim does potentially apply about sharing as equally as possible, while simultaneously allowing for the academic who is accountable to operate hierarchically where necessary to keep activity within parameters that are comfortable for him or her.

> *Comment.* Critical Analysis Question 9 is directly relevant to answering *our* second review question in the light of the earlier analysis. Our reflection focused on considering the extent to which the primary school context that Wallace investigates is similar to the university context in which we work, and which of the factors that Wallace identifies as affecting teamwork effectiveness in his school context also apply to that situation. (Help from the abstract: the summary claims remind me of our own experiences).

10 What is my summary evaluation of the text in relation to my review question?

(a) How convincing are the authors' claims and why?

Review Question 1: Wallace's conclusions are that school leadership should be shared as widely as possible, contingent on the degree of risk for headteachers, and that relatively equal sharing, subject to a contingent reversal to hierarchical operation, promotes effective teamwork. These conclusions are fairly convincing for the context of state-funded primary schools in the UK. He backs his claims with a coherent piece of research that is, however, modest in scope. We share his overall positive stance towards team approaches. Wallace himself restricts the asserted applicability of his claims to UK schools. His research was published more than a decade ago. We are uncertain how far these claims might apply now within UK schools, or beyond this context. But our university experience does suggest that they increasingly apply at only a moderate level of abstraction because of contextual convergence between UK schools, when Wallace's article was published, and UK universities now.

Review Question 2: Equal sharing with a contingent reversal to hierarchical operation does appear to be applicable to teaching programmes and research project teams in our recent experience. Important features of the primary school context from which his evidence was derived are increasingly applicable to the university where we currently work, where there is increasing reliance on fixed SMTs as a way of managing departments or the institution as a whole.

> *Comment.* Completing all the earlier Critical Analysis Questions with our two review questions in mind meant that we had already evaluated Wallace's claims in detail. Here we were soon able to compose a summative view by looking back at what we had already written in response to Critical Analysis Questions 5–9.

(b) How, if at all, could the authors have provided stronger backing for their claims? (e.g., If the authors were in the room, how would they respond to the criticisms you have raised?)

Wallace could in principle have provided stronger backing for his claims if he had drawn on a wider range of research literature on team approaches to leadership in schools and elsewhere, had investigated a wider range of organizational and national contexts, and included outcome measures in assessing the degree of synergy achieved in the four SMTs. However, given the modest scope of his research, he appropriately states that his claims are tentative. He avoids gross overgeneralization by indicating that he is making claims about UK schools only.

> *Comment.* By not expressing great certainty or generalizing beyond the UK schools context, Wallace has actually avoided claiming very much. Rather, he has put forward a strong, coherent argument with limited but sound empirical backing, offering a potent stimulus for readers' reflection rather than implying that his argument is fully proven or that his claims will necessarily apply to the readers' situation. (We think that Wallace would accept that he could have done more, and that was the reason why he made only tentative claims with a moderate degree of generalization.)

Taking charge of your Critical Analysis of texts

The Critical Analysis form is designed to apply to most types of frontline literature that you are likely to meet in the course of your studies, including material that you may download from the Internet. It is less useful for textbooks or other support literature. (As discussed in Chapter 2, textbooks are an excellent resource for identifying the frontline literature that you need to read and analyse, rather than key sources in their own right.)

Remember that it is up to you to decide which Critical Analysis Questions are most important for any individual text and what your answers to them must include. Conducting a Critical Analysis prepares you for writing about texts in depth. In the next chapter, we will offer ideas about how to develop a Critical Review of one text or a Comparative Critical Review of several texts, structured according to the answers given to each of the Critical Analysis Questions.

13

Developing Your Argument in Writing a Critical Review of a Text

Keywords

Comparative Critical Literature Review; Critical Literature Review; self-critical writing

By now, especially if you tried doing your own Critical Analysis, you will probably feel quite familiar with our structured approach to critical reading. We hope you are beginning to sense how all this structuring gives you scope to:

- drive the Critical Analysis according to your review question (or questions), restricting your concern with the content to searching for relevant material;
- alert yourself to how the authors attempt to convince their target audience;
- evaluate the authors' claims to knowledge thoroughly in assessing how far they are convincing to you; and
- draw a strong conclusion where you summarize how far the relevant content of the text contributes to answering your review question.

So far, so good. If your critical reading is in preparation for writing for assessment, you will now have to develop a convincing argument of your own, as commentator, about what you have read. In a Critical Review of a frontline text, your conclusion will consist of claims about what the authors reported, and you must yourself now provide adequate warranting. The basis for it is the evidence you have gathered, through your Critical Analysis, about what the authors were doing, their claims that are relevant to your review question and your evaluation of those claims.

In this chapter we show how you can use a completed Critical Analysis of a text as the platform for a Critical Review. We will invite you to write your own Critical Review of the article by Wallace in Appendix 2, drawing on your completed Critical Analysis (which we invited you to undertake at the end of Chapter 11). We will then offer our illustrative Critical Review of Wallace's article, based on our own completed Critical Analysis from Chapter 12. Finally, we will suggest how you can use the completed Critical Analyses of two or more frontline texts as the basis for constructing a Comparative Critical Review.

A Critical Review may be something you are required to produce for a coursework assessment, or for a component of an essay or a dissertation. But they also exist in the published literature. If you browse academic journals in your field, you will probably find reviews of single books, and comparative reviews of two or more books or articles on the same topic. In due course, you might wish to consider writing such a review, based on our approach, and submitting it for publication in an academic journal.

Structuring a Critical Review of a text

You have already seen in Part One the mechanisms for structuring a Critical Summary of a text. A Critical Review operates on the same principle but goes into more depth. A review can be structured in various ways, depending on its scope and purpose and on the nature of the text under scrutiny. But in all cases the author will have to develop an argument that is designed to convince the target audience. The review should therefore introduce readers to the topic, develop the warranting and provide a conclusion that this warranting adequately supports. You will probably notice, as you read a wider range of literature, that these three components (introduction, development of the warranting, conclusion) underpin the structure of most texts. Frequently, the development of the warranting is divided into a sequence of sections. The basic structure is flexible, enabling you to design your own text so that each component builds on the previous one, as best suits the material you want to cover. Every part of the text, from the title at the beginning to the reference list at the end, has its place in helping you to build up a convincing argument.

We offer here an adaptation of this basic structure that is appropriate for a Critical Review of an article or book chapter reporting research. The component on developing the warranting to make the conclusion convincing will be divided into a sequence of three linked sections, covering:

- what the authors were doing;
- the main claims about findings relevant to the review questions; and
- your evaluation of their claims.

You will see that your answers to particular Critical Analysis Questions on your completed form relate to particular sections within the structure. You can therefore draw on your responses when writing and also refer back to the text that you are reviewing. If you mention any additional literature, follow the normal conventions, referring to the publication by the author's surname and date in the text, with a full reference list at the end.

Note that the projected length of this illustrative Critical Review is 1,000 words (plus references). We have indicated the approximate number of words that each section might contain.

Structure for a Critical Review of an article or chapter reporting research (1,000 words)

Title

- Your choice of title should include the keywords that will indicate to the reader what you are doing (a Critical Review of a selected piece of literature) and the aspect of the social world that forms your focus.

Introducing the Critical Review (50–150 words)

- A statement of your purpose – critically to review the selected text (give the names of the authors, the title of the chapter or article and the date of publication) as a contribution to answering your review question or questions (Critical Analysis Question 1). You should list the review questions to give the reader an indication of the focus for your review. For this exercise, we will use the same review questions as those for the Critical Analysis of Wallace's article that you were invited to try out earlier:
    - What does the text suggest may be key factors promoting or inhibiting the effectiveness of a particular aspect of educational leadership and management practice?
    - To what extent are the factors identified applicable to the leadership and management of my organization or one known to me?

Introducing the text being critically reviewed – what the authors were trying to find out and what they did (150–250 words, beginning to build the warranting for your argument)

- A summary of the authors' purposes for the text and the kind of enquiry they engaged in, including an indication of the type of literature they produced and their intellectual project (use your answer to Critical Analysis Question 2).

- A brief indication of why this text is relevant to the review questions guiding your Critical Review (Critical Analysis Question 1).
- A brief summary of how they went about their investigation (e.g., the research design, methodology, sample, methods of data collection and analysis).

The authors' main claims relating to the review questions (150–250 words, continuing to build the warranting for your argument)

- A summary of the main claims made by the authors of the text, as relevant to answering your review questions (use your answer to Critical Analysis Question 3) – a synthesis of, say, up to five main points.
- An indication of the authors' degree of certainty about these claims, and the degree of generalization: the range of other contexts to which the authors claim, explicitly or implicitly, their findings may apply (e.g., they imply that their claims apply to all contexts or do not specify any limits on the extent to which they may be universally applicable). (Use your answer to Critical Analysis Question 4.)

Evaluating the authors' main claims relating to the review questions (200–400 words, continuing to build the warranting for your argument)

- Your evaluation of these findings and any broader claims, critically assessing the extent to which they are convincing for the context from which these claims were derived. (Use your answers to Critical Analysis Questions 5–8, possibly referring to additional literature to support your judgement in relation to Critical Analysis Question 8.) In your critique, you may wish to refer back to your earlier account of the authors' purpose, intellectual project, how they went about their enquiry (e.g., you may wish to assert that the value stance of particular authors led to bias that affected their findings), and how certain they were of their findings.
- Your critical assessment of how far the claims made by the authors of the text may be applicable *to other contexts, including those in your own experience* (Critical Analysis Questions 5–9, possibly referring to additional literature to support your judgement in relation to Critical Analysis Question 8). In your critique, you may wish to refer back to your earlier account of how the authors went about their enquiry and the extent to which they generalized their claims (e.g., you may wish to assert that the findings from a particular intellectual project were derived from a context that is so different from yours that you consider the prescriptions for practice emerging from this work are unlikely to apply directly to your context).

Conclusion (150–250 words)

- Your brief overall evaluation of the text, to assess its contribution to answering your review questions (use your answer to Critical Analysis Question 10).
- For this exercise, your summary answer to the first review question. This will include a statement of your judgement, with reasons, about how far the findings and any broader claims are convincing for the context from which they were derived.

- For this exercise, your summary answer to the second review question. This will include a statement of your judgement, with reasons, about how far the findings and any broader claims are applicable (e.g., at how high a level of abstraction?) to your professional context or one known to you.

References

- Give the full reference for the text you have reviewed.
- If you refer to any additional literature, list the texts to which you have referred, following the normal conventions for compiling a reference list.

Your Critical Review of an article reporting research

The suggested word lengths in the structure above can only be a guide. When deciding the length of each section in a Critical Review, it is important to ensure there is enough space to develop your argument effectively. Whatever the word length that you must, or wish, to comply with, you need to decide what proportion of the overall account should be given to each section. You will want to avoid the common error of giving too much space to describing the authors' claims and leaving too little space for the evaluation of them and the conclusion – offering only half of the warranting and a minimal conclusion will not make for a convincing argument.

Now write a Critical Review of Wallace's article in Appendix 2, of up to 1,000 words (plus references). Try to keep to the word length suggestions in the outline for the structure above, and draw on the completed Critical Analysis you were encouraged to write in Chapter 11. You will need to provide your own title and devise your own section headings. When you have written your Critical Review, you will be able to compare what you wrote with our effort below. (We strongly recommend that you write your own Critical Review before looking at ours, to maximize your learning.)

Our Critical Review of Wallace's article

Here is our illustrative Critical Review of Wallace's article, based on the structure we have outlined in this chapter and on our completed Critical Analysis from Chapter 12. As with the Critical Analysis material itself, our review will reflect our responses to the article, our organizational experience and our choice of headings. So it will differ from your review in some details. But we hope that you will find it easy to see both how we have drawn on our Critical Analysis and how we have developed our argument in attempting to convince our critical readers (including you).

Review of an empirical study of leadership in UK school senior management teams

Introduction

The purpose of this review is to critically analyse the article 'Sharing leadership of schools through teamwork: a justifiable risk?' by Mike Wallace (abridged from a paper originally published in *Educational Management and Administration* in 2001). Two review questions are addressed:

1. What does the text suggest may be key factors in promoting or inhibiting the effectiveness of team approaches to the leadership and management of educational organizations?
2. To what extent are the factors identified applicable to leadership and management in our universities?

Purpose and design

Wallace researched the extent to which headteachers of senior management teams (SMTs) in UK primary schools shared leadership with SMT colleagues. SMTs consisted of the headteacher, deputy head and other senior teachers. Their role was to support the headteacher in leading and managing the school.

Wallace sets out to inform the training and practice of senior school staff within the UK policy context. Central government education reforms had rendered the sharing of leadership simultaneously necessary for headteachers and risky. The obligation to implement reforms meant that headteachers depended on SMT colleagues' contributions. But, as team leaders, they alone were accountable for the SMT's effectiveness in managing the school.

This research relates clearly to the review questions because it highlights factors affecting team effectiveness that could have implications for practice elsewhere. Wallace was informed by research and theoretical literature on school leadership, including his study of secondary school SMTs. His case studies of four SMTs in large primary schools involved interviews and observation and were guided by a cultural and political perspective.

Findings relating to team effectiveness

Wallace claims, first, that principles based on staff entitlement and effective leadership outcomes are widely offered to justify extensive sharing of school leadership. But theories reflecting these principles are unrealistic for the UK context. Second, headteachers in UK schools increasingly depend on SMT colleagues to support the implementation of central government reforms, yet risk getting blamed for sharing leadership if it results in poor decisions. Third, Wallace's SMT research implies that headteachers' and other SMT

(Continued)

(Continued)

members' culture of teamwork includes contradictory beliefs: in a management hierarchy led by the headteacher, and in all members contributing equally to teamwork. Fourth, the primary school research suggests that maximum synergy is achieved where headteachers enable SMT colleagues to contribute as equals in teamwork, while other SMT members implicitly operate inside parameters set by the headteacher. This approach is most effective but also carries most risk of ineffectiveness. Fifth, in a context of high accountability, UK headteachers should share SMT leadership as widely as they dare, while all members should accept that headteachers must sometimes operate hierarchically to keep the SMT's work inside parameters they set.

Wallace suggests that these findings apply to all UK schools because of the system-wide impact of central government reforms. The findings imply that the generic leadership theories he criticizes should embrace contextual factors to extend their generalizability.

Evaluation of claims about team effectiveness

Wallace's findings appear quite robust. He is appropriately tentative, given the limitations of his research. His claims are backed by observation of SMTs at work and triangulation of individual informants' accounts. His generalization that headteachers of all UK schools face a dilemma over sharing SMT leadership is backed by reference to the UK policy context: central government educational reforms were designed to impact on all schools. But he reports no evidence of teamwork outcomes, so his claims about varying SMT synergy within the four case study teams are only moderately convincing. The sample of informants and SMT meetings is small, so the generalizability of the findings to other schools within the UK remains uncertain. Wallace's research does not address the possibility that diverse local contextual factors may contribute to team effectiveness elsewhere.

Use of the cultural and political perspective to guide data collection is convincing. Wallace defines key concepts and employs the perspective extensively in reporting findings, leading to the generation of a model explaining the variations in SMT practice that he found. However, this perspective does not embrace other factors that might significantly affect team effectiveness, including members' psychological motivations.

Wallace explicitly develops a normative argument and clearly values teamwork. Yet he does not question the existence of a management hierarchy entailing unequal sharing of leadership. Equally, he does not challenge the central government reforms despite claiming that they caused the headteachers' dilemma over sharing leadership.

Wallace does not relate his findings to other researchers' work. Therefore, they remain untested against other research or theories that might support or challenge them.

Wallace's claims apply to our higher education context at a moderate level of abstraction because academics no longer enjoy greater individual autonomy than school staff. In our recent experience, teamwork is significant both within teaching or research groups, and amongst central university leaders.

Conclusion

Wallace identifies a key factor promoting or inhibiting the effectiveness of team approaches to school leadership and management, at least in the UK. His conclusions, fairly convincing for this context, are that school leadership should be shared as widely as possible, contingent on the degree of risk for headteachers, and that relatively equal sharing coupled with a contingent reversal to hierarchical operation promotes effective teamwork. His claims are backed by coherent research, though of modest scope. It remains uncertain how far these claims might apply beyond the UK.

Equal sharing with a contingent reversal to hierarchical operation is potentially applicable to teaching-programme and research-project teams and to departmental and the university SMTs in our university context. Other important features of the primary school context from which Wallace's evidence was derived increasingly apply to our higher education institution, where SMTs are a way of managing departments and the university as a whole.

This study bears testing against a wider range of research and theoretical literature. Further research is needed on team approaches to leadership in schools and other organizations in different contexts, and should include leadership outcome measures.

Reference

Wallace, M. (2001) 'Sharing leadership through teamwork: a justifiable risk?', *Educational Management and Administration*, 29(2): 153–67 [abridged as Appendix 2 of Wallace, M. and Wray, A. (2016) *Critical Reading and Writing for Postgraduates* (3rd edn). London: SAGE].

Did we write the perfect review?

No – we hope we have convinced you by now that there is no single best outcome in critical reading or self-critical writing. Much depends on the authors' insights, values and capacity to argue convincingly, and on the readers' assessment criteria and values. But there are good and not-so-good practices. We have attempted to follow what we believe to be good practice: taking charge by asking review questions and developing our own argument about how the literature contributes to answering them.

If you were to count up the number of words in each section, you would find that it lies within our recommended range and so contributes proportionately to the review. The entire review (excluding the reference) comes close to our target of 1,000 words.

You may have noticed how we have sometimes taken material direct from our Critical Analysis of the article in Chapter 12, then edited it to fulfil our slightly different purpose in writing that part of our Critical Review. An electronically stored Critical Analysis of a text will enable you to 'cut and paste' material into any Critical Review that you write. However, avoid the mistake of just moving chunks of material around – a Critical Analysis of a text is not identical to a Critical Review of it. Editing will be required. Ensure that everything you write in your Critical Review is doing its job in contributing to the answering of your review questions.

Structuring a Comparative Critical Review of several texts

The structure for reviewing a single text can be adapted for reviewing several texts in depth. Rather than writing a sequential review of one text after another, a comparative approach requires you to review the texts together by grouping and synthesizing your answers to the same Critical Analysis Question across some or all of the texts at the same time. (Recall that we exemplified doing this at a less in-depth level in Chapter 6.) As with the single text structure, the Comparative Review structure may be modified to suit the nature of the literature.

Our suggested structure below has been adapted for reviewing several (up to maybe five) frontline texts reporting research – typically, published journal articles, book chapters or books. The projected length of the review is around 4,000 words, excluding references. We have used the same two illustrative review question types as in the single-text review, while leaving the field of enquiry unspecified. Obviously, you can modify it for the types of literature you are reviewing and identify your own review questions to address (they need to be the same questions for all the texts). To write a Comparative Critical Review, your first step will be to complete a Critical Analysis for each of the texts. Putting them side-by-side, your Comparative Critical Review will be relatively simple to construct, because parallel information about each text will be located in the corresponding place on each form.

Although we have not expanded this structure into a full 4,000-word review, you will find that our example Critical Review for one text above, along with the less detailed one- and three-text Critical Summaries that we exemplified in Part One, provide you with indications of how the structure below can be fleshed out.

Structure for a Comparative Critical Review of several texts reporting research (4,000 words)

Title

- Your choice of title should include the keywords that will indicate to the reader what you are doing (a Comparative Critical Review) and the aspect of practice that forms your focus.

Introducing the Comparative Critical Review (250–750 words)

- A statement of your purpose – to critically review the selected texts in depth as a contribution to answering your review question or questions (Critical Analysis Question 1).
- Your justification for selecting this focus (e.g., its significance for improving the aspect of practice), perhaps referring to other literature to support your argument.
- Your acknowledgement of the scope of your review (e.g., an indication of the texts you will analyse in depth, giving the names of the authors, title and date of publication for each, and the reasons why you selected them for in-depth review).
- Your acknowledgement of the limitations of your review (e.g., that your focus is confined to these few texts and there may be others relating to this focus which you will not be examining in depth).
- An indication of the topics to be covered in each of the remaining sections of your review, so that the reader can see how you will develop your argument.

Introducing the texts being critically reviewed (250–750 words)

- A cross-comparative summary of the authors' purposes and of the kind or kinds of enquiry they engaged in, including an indication of the type or types of literature they produced and their intellectual projects (use your answers to Critical Analysis Question 2).
- A brief indication of why these texts are relevant to the review questions guiding your Comparative Critical Review (Critical Analysis Question 1).
- A brief summary of how the authors went about their enquiry, for example:
  - for a research report, the research design, sample, methods of data collection and analysis;
  - for a research synthesis, the sequence of topics addressed and range of sources employed;
  - for a theoretical work, the main theoretical ideas, the sequence of topics and any use of evidence;
  - for a practical handbook, the sequence of topics addressed and any use of evidence.

(You may either present this summary in cross-comparative form, or outline each text separately, according to the nature of the texts and your judgement about which approach will be clearer for the reader.)

The authors' main claims relating to the review questions (500–1,000 words)

- A comparative summary of the main claims made by the authors of each text, as they are relevant to your review questions (use your answers to Critical Analysis Question 3) – a synthesis of, say, up to five main points for each text reviewed, indicating the extent to which there is overlap between texts (e.g., a particular claim was common to all the texts, or to three out of the four, etc.).

- An indication of the degree of certainty of the claims and the range of contexts to which the authors claim explicitly or implicitly that their findings may apply, paying attention to how two authors might ascribe different scopes of application to similar claims. (Use your answer to Critical Analysis Question 4.)

Evaluating the authors' main claims relating to the review questions (1,500–2,000 words)

- Your comparative evaluation of these claims, critically assessing the extent to which claims made by the authors of each text are convincing. (Use your answers to Critical Analysis Questions 5–9, possibly referring to additional literature to support your judgement in relation to Critical Analysis Question 8.) In your critique, you may wish to refer back to your earlier account of the authors' purpose, intellectual project and how they went about their enquiry.

Conclusion (250–750 words)

- Your brief overall evaluation of each of the texts reviewed, to assess their combined contribution to answering your review questions (use your answers to Critical Analysis Question 10).
- The summary answer to each review question, in turn, offered by all the texts reviewed. Each summary answer should include a statement of your judgement, with reasons, about the extent to which the claims across all the texts provide adequate warranting for the relevant conclusions drawn by the authors.
- If appropriate, any reasons why you think, in the light of your Comparative Critical Review, that there may be difficulties in finding definitive answers to your review questions.

References

- The list of texts to which you have referred, including those you have analysed in depth, following the normal conventions for compiling a reference list.

Gearing up for writing Critical Reviews of texts

The structures we have presented offer you a template that you can modify, whether by adding or subdividing sections or by changing their content, for in-depth reviews that are freestanding or part of something bigger. The length of each section can be adjusted according to the amount you need, or want, to write in total.

In Part Two, we have outlined a mental map for exploring the literature and indicated how you can apply it as part of a structured approach for the Critical Analysis of texts. We have shown that, in turn, Critical Analyses offer a platform for structuring a Critical Review of one text or a Comparative

Critical Review of several texts. The more you practise by using the mental map, completing Critical Analysis forms and writing Critical Reviews of texts, the more the ideas underlying these structures will become integral to your critical reading and self-critical writing. You will be able to employ the ideas flexibly and discard any props that you no longer need.

So far we have concentrated on helping you learn how to engage critically with a few texts: in summary in Part One and in depth in Part Two. In Part Three, we expand the focus to consider how to engage critically with a potentially unlimited number of texts in developing a Critical Literature Review.

Part Three

Putting Your Critical Reviews to Work

14

Focusing and Building Up Your Critical Literature Review

Keywords

Critical Literature Review; methodological review questions; substantive review questions; theoretical review questions

Part Three brings together the ideas from Parts One and Two. We will show how you can extend the scope of your critical reading and self-critical writing by using Critical Analyses and Critical Synopses together in constructing a larger-scale Critical Literature Review.

A Critical Literature Review addresses whatever texts are relevant to your review purpose. Unless you have been set the task of writing about one or more specified texts, your exploration of a topic is sure to engage with a range of material. Our techniques will help you decide what is most important. Applying the techniques will enable you to see whether to foreground or background the different texts that you want to mention. In other words, a good Critical Literature Review combines in-depth Critical Analyses of single and multiple texts, with more passing reference to Critical Synopses of other texts. These different levels of engagement must flow naturally as you build up your argument. It takes some skill to create a seamless account that brings in the appropriate amount of detail to achieve your objectives.

Literature reviews form the basis of some postgraduate assignments and are expected as part of a dissertation. A common assessment criterion at doctorate level is that your investigation must generate new knowledge in the field of enquiry. So you may wish to demonstrate through Critical Literature Reviews that your research and theorizing step significantly beyond the boundaries of existing academic knowledge. In due course, you may wish to try getting a Critical Literature Review published as a paper in an academic journal, especially if you are set on an academic career.

You will find that a *Critical* Literature Review is more manageable to write than a review that is merely descriptive. It will also enable you to develop a strong argument that maximizes your chances of convincing the critical readers who are your assessors (whether in the role of tutor, supervisor, examiner or academic journal referee). By taking charge, you can regard the literature as being available to serve your purposes. You make your own critical choice about what literature to seek and suit yourself in how you use it. Conversely, if you let yourself become a servant of the literature, you will rapidly become overwhelmed by trying to read and describe everything written in the field.

In this chapter, we define what we mean by a Critical Literature Review and propose some criteria that might mark one out as being of high quality, to give you something to aim for. We offer a structured approach to creating a self-contained Critical Literature Review that integrates the Critical Synopsis, Critical Summary, Critical Analysis and Critical Review structures from Parts One and Two. We then suggest how it is possible to start moving away from such heavy reliance on the direct translation of material from your Critical Synopses and Critical Analyses into your Critical Literature Review. You could make more flexible use of them, adapting the basic review structure to suit the development of your argument, and bringing in additional literature as appropriate.

Chapters 15 and 16 will consider how Critical Literature Reviews contribute to the research for your dissertation. Conducting Critical Literature Reviews before and during your empirical investigation will valuably inform what you choose to investigate and how you conduct the enquiry. After completing your investigation, you can refer back to your reviews and additional literature to help you interpret your findings and reflect self-critically on the strengths and limitations of your research. We show how, in writing up your account of your investigation, Critical Literature Reviews are often distributed across the dissertation. In Chapter 17 you will find tools that help you structure your dissertation in a manner consistent with using your Critical Literature Reviews to create a logical, warranted argument. Finally, Chapter 18 shows how the same logic applies to two other outputs: structuring a research report such as a journal article, and an oral presentation.

What makes a literature review critical?

Critical Literature Reviews are personal. They reflect the intellect of the reviewer, who has decided the focus, selected texts for review, engaged critically with and interpreted the evidence they offer, ordered and synthesized what was found, and written the final account. We define a Critical Literature Review as:

> a reviewer's constructively critical account, developing an argument designed to convince a particular audience about what the published – and possibly also unpublished – literature (theory, research, practice or policy) indicates is and is not known about one or more questions that the reviewer has framed.

Note that this definition excludes reviews that just describe texts, because the reviewer has not been critical. Such a 'review' simply restates what is in the texts rather than building any argument, targeting any identifiable audience or focusing on any specific question. (Our definition also excludes any review which is destructively critical. A constructively critical account will not indulge in gratuitously negative evaluation for the sake of demonstrating the authors' foolishness and the reviewer's intellectual superiority.)

Whether written for assessment or for publication, Critical Literature Reviews are integral to the knowledge-for-understanding, knowledge-for-critical evaluation and knowledge-for-action intellectual projects. They have several features. First, their purpose dictates their focus. Reviews relate to one or more explicit or implicit review questions that may be:

- *substantive* (about some aspect of the social world);
- *theoretical* (about concepts, perspectives, theories or models that relate to some aspect of the social world);
- *methodological* (about the approach to conducting an empirical or theoretical enquiry).

The attempt to address review questions drives the critical reading and self-critical writing process by providing:

- a criterion for selecting some texts for inclusion, rejecting others and homing in on a few of the most relevant selected texts for in-depth Critical Analysis;
- a rationale for reading selectively within any text, saving the time that reading the whole text in detail would take;
- a starting point for a Critical Synopsis (Critical Synopsis Question A) or for a Critical Analysis (Critical Analysis Question 1) of what has been read;
- a focus for synthesizing findings into a logically structured account that puts forward a convincing argument.

Second, in order to answer each substantive, theoretical or methodological review question, Critical Literature Reviews synthesize claims to knowledge from a range of relevant texts. Reviewers attempt to demonstrate to the target audience the basis of their informed judgement about what is known, how strong the evidence is and what is not known from others' work. Third, they enable reviewers to demonstrate the scientific or social significance of their review question and why an answer is worth seeking. The significance of a substantive review question may be as a contribution towards the development of research or practice knowledge in the field of enquiry. The significance of a theoretical review question may be to extend theory, and that of a methodological review question may be the justification of the research methods chosen for empirical work. Finally, Critical Literature Reviews enable reviewers to locate their own work within the wider body of knowledge in the area to which the substantive, theoretical or methodological review questions are applied.

Producing a high-quality Critical Literature Review is a challenging but rewarding task. As with a Critical Summary or a Critical Review of a text, you can help yourself to focus with precision by clarifying your review question at the outset, even if you need to refine it as you go along. Then sustain that focus as you develop the warranting of your argument through to the conclusion. Another tip is to be consciously constructive when evaluating the literature, ensuring that your judgements are clearly backed by what you have found. Suppose you discover that existing knowledge relevant to your review question is not particularly robust or conceptually coherent. Make this claim, but also show how the evidence, as you interpret it, warrants it. Then be prepared to suggest how, as appropriate, the knowledge base could be enhanced, practice improved or theory developed.

Aiming high

You will probably have sensed from your critical reading of the literature that there is a big difference between the best and the worst literature reviews that you have encountered. It is worth modelling your own Critical Literature Review writing on the best, high-quality reviews you encounter. In our view, a high-quality Critical Literature Review is likely to be:

- *focused* on an explicit substantive, theoretical or methodological review question;
- *structured* so as to address each review question in a logical sequence (see Chapter 15);
- *discerning,* so that some texts are given a more in-depth consideration than others, according to the reviewer's judgement of their centrality to the review questions and interpretation of the evidence they offer;
- *constructively critical,* evaluating the extent to which knowledge claims and the arguments they support are convincing, or whether a theoretical orientation is coherent;
- *accurately referenced,* so that each source can be followed up by readers of the review;
- *clearly expressed and reader-friendly,* with interim conclusions and signposting, to help readers get the reviewer's message easily and follow the development of the argument;
- *informative,* providing synthesis through a strong conclusion that summarizes the reviewer's judgement about how the cited literature answers the review question,

indicating the strengths and weaknesses of the evidence, and arbitrating between any opposing positions reviewed;
- *convincingly argued*, expressing the reviewer's 'voice' authoritatively because the conclusion is adequately warranted by evidence, as interpreted by the reviewer, drawn from the literature or the reviewer's experience;
- *balanced*, indicating that the various viewpoints expressed in the literature have been carefully weighed and that the reviewer's judgements are demonstrably based on a careful assessment of the relevant strengths and limitations of the evidence presented in that literature.

Structuring a Critical Literature Review from completed analyses

Here we suggest a straightforward way of constructing a self-contained Critical Literature Review. It enables you to build an account based directly on completed Critical Synopses and Critical Analyses. Essentially, it combines the structure we offered for a Comparative Critical Summary of several texts from Part One with the structure for a Comparative Critical Review of several texts from Part Two.

In preparation for writing a Critical Literature Review using this structure, you will need to have identified your review question, accessed relevant texts, completed a Critical Synopsis for each one and completed a Critical Analysis for those that are most central to your focus. If you have attached or saved a copy of each Critical Synopsis or Critical Analysis with the text it evaluates, you can organize your material into sets of Synopses (for brief mention) and sets of Analyses (for more comprehensive reporting).

You can now compare and contrast your Critical Synopsis and Critical Analysis forms, in order to determine what range of answers you have amassed to each of the Critical Synopsis Questions and, for the most central texts, the corresponding Critical Analysis Questions. Identify what the pattern of answers is: the most common, the range, the most unexpected, and so on. This information will provide you with a basis for your account of what is known, and the limits of what is known, regarding the answer to your review question. You can easily select from the Critical Summaries and Critical Analyses anything that you wish to highlight, and you can go back to the original texts if you want more detail.

We will indicate, below, what each section in our basic Critical Literature Review structure covers. In writing your own review using this structure, you would, of course, need to create your own heading for each section (as we did in the previous chapter with our Critical Review of Wallace's article).

Basic structure for a Critical Literature Review using Critical Synopses and Critical Analyses

Title

Use keywords indicating the focus for the study.

Introduction

- A statement of purpose – your focus, designed to answer one or more named review questions (Critical Analysis Question 1, Critical Synopsis Question A).
- Justification of the significance of your focus (e.g., its importance for improving practice).
- The scope of the review – the range of literature reviewed (e.g., concentrating on research reports, focused on business organizations) and why this range was selected for review.
- Limitations of the review (e.g., mainly concerned with a small number of key texts, restricted to sources from only one part of the world, confined to books and academic journal articles, based on what you could access from the Internet).
- Signposting – indicating how each of the remaining sections of the review will contribute to answering your review question.

Sections building up the warranting for the claims in the conclusion of your argument	**Based on answers to Critical Analysis Questions for central texts**	**Based on answers to Critical Synopsis Questions for more peripheral texts**
• An introduction to the texts being reviewed	2	B
• The authors' main claims relevant to your review question	3, 4	C
• Evaluation of the authors' claims, including any counter-evidence	5–9	D
Final section setting out the conclusion of your argument		
• Summary of your evaluation of literature reviewed to assess the texts' combined contribution to answering your review question	10	E

You may wish to extend the conclusion by:

- offering your self-critical reflection, in retrospect, on the strengths and limitations of your review (e.g., why it may have been difficult to fully answer your review question);
- highlighting possibilities for further work (e.g., research and theory-building) that you judge to be needed and, if appropriate, implications for policy and practice.

References

- A list (in author alphabetical order) of the texts to which you have referred, following the normal conventions for compiling a reference list.

What might such a Critical Literature Review look like?

Your entire Critical Literature Review constitutes one or more arguments: a conclusion for each of your review questions, backed up by your interpretation of the evidence warranting it. Using the structure we have just described, the warranting of your argument can be built up by writing paragraphs that synthesize your answers to particular Critical Analysis and Critical Synopsis Questions. Here is a fictional example, comprising part or all of each section. (We have indicated in square brackets and italic script how this account embodies elements of the structure outlined above. The texts by Jones, Nussbaum and Barthes et al. have been given full Critical Analyses. Other texts cited – Tauber, Jennings, Vrey and Lambert – have been given only a Critical Synopsis).

Learning the noun genders in a foreign language: a Critical Literature Review

Introduction

This review aims to shed light on why noun genders are so difficult for adult learners of the German language to master, and to consider how noun gender teaching might be improved [*statement of purpose*]. There are three genders in German, masculine, feminine and neuter, and although some nouns have features that indicate their gender, most do not and simply have to be learned [*justifying the significance of the focus*]. In order to understand more about this feature of German, the review explores the published literature in relation to two questions: (a) why are noun genders difficult to learn? and (b) how are they most effectively taught [*review questions*]. Since it is not just German that has noun gender, research on other languages has been included [*scope of the review*], even though it is possible that not all of the problems and solutions are transferable across languages (Tauber, 1991) [*limitation of the review*]. For clarity, the main texts under scrutiny are first introduced and the basic claims about noun gender learning are compared. Next comes a discussion of the strengths and weaknesses of the main claims, including a brief account of other published works that appear not to align with them. Finally, conclusions are drawn about the extent to which the reviewed texts shed light on the two review questions [*signposting*].

(Continued)

(Continued)

Research into noun gender learning [*introducing the texts*]

Despite the immediacy of the challenge of noun gender from day one in many languages, surprisingly few studies have been conducted on why gender is difficult to learn and how it might be better taught. Exceptions are the longitudinal study of Welsh noun gender learning by Jones (2004), the comparative study of classroom and naturalistic learners of German by Nussbaum (1998) and the classic study of French gender carried out by Barthes and his team in the 1970s (e.g., Barthes et al., 1979). Although old, this study is still widely identified as a landmark in language learning research. Several other works also bear on the questions addressed here. Tauber (1991) explains some of the similarities and differences between the noun gender systems of different languages. Jennings (2003) identifies noun gender as one of several hurdles that have to be crossed in first language acquisition. Meanwhile, Vrey and Lambert's (2005) normative approach to their 'revolution in language teaching' sets aside noun gender entirely, as 'an unwelcome and unnecessary distraction from the real fabric of the language' (p. 81).

Jones (2004) collected data from …

Like Jones, Nussbaum (1998) was interested in the first year of language learning, though her focus was German, making this comparative study particularly relevant to the present review questions …

In contrast, Barthes and colleagues (1979) focused on … and they investigated how …

Why are noun genders difficult to learn? [*main claims relevant to the first review question*]

All three studies just described propose that the age of learning plays a part, though Jennings' (2003) identification of gender as difficult for young children somewhat contradicts this. According to Nussbaum (1998), it is also *how* learners are first exposed to noun genders that determines how much effort they have to put into learning them (p. 36) …

How are noun genders most effectively taught? [*main claims relevant to the second review question*]

We turn now to the effective teaching of noun gender. Jones (2004) claims that teachers should attempt to distract learners from the noun genders until later classes. This proposal, however, does not sit comfortably with Barthes et al.'s (1979) data on what learners naturally pay attention to. For their part, Barthes and colleagues lay out a detailed set of guidelines for teachers, including four pages on gender. This level of attention contrasts starkly with Vrey and Lambert's (2005) total exclusion of it in their programme … Meanwhile, Nussbaum's (1998) contribution to answering this question is to note that 'more research is needed on what kind of exposure is most effective for learning' (p. 43).

Strength and limitations of the evidence [*evaluation of claims and any counter-evidence*]

At first glance, there seems to be consensus that noun gender learning is difficult – whether this implies that it should be carefully taught (Barthes et al., 1979), postponed (Jones, 2004) or ignored (Vrey and Lambert, 2005). However, there are important differences between the accounts, particularly in relation to the sort of intellectual project in which the authors are engaged. Only Nussbaum's study is fully centred in knowledge-for-understanding, while Jones (2004) and Barthes et al. (1979) share with Vrey and Lambert (2005) a strong interest in influencing practice and policy. As a result, all of these studies, it might be argued, demonstrate a vested interest in a particular methodology. It is perhaps not unrelated to this agenda that these are the studies in which the conclusions are made with most confidence, while Nussbaum (1998) remains tentative about what her findings mean …

… As noted earlier, care must be taken before assuming that the problems that a learner of, say, French has with noun gender are the same as those for a learner of German. As Tauber (1991) points out, 'our nomenclature for the phenomenon of word class tends to falsely impress upon us similarities between languages, for instance, that all have "genders" of "masculine" and "feminine"' (p. 911). Despite the evident dangers of a too simplistic equation of languages, Jones (2004) repeatedly draws backing for his claims about Welsh from research literature into other European languages, somewhat weakening his arguments …

Conclusion [*combined contribution to answering review questions*]

Inspired by the problems of learning German, this review has focused on establishing why noun gender is difficult for adults to master and how it is best taught. It has been revealed that, in fact, answers derived from languages other than German may not necessarily be wholly generalizable to it. This proviso notwithstanding, there does seem to be general consensus that something about the learning experience of the adult creates particular problems, even though children also struggle with noun gender (Jennings, 2003). It may relate to how adults pay attention to information, or to the absence of the opportunity in the classroom to focus on using language for communication.

The question of how noun gender is best taught remains unanswered, though there is no shortage of practice-focused and policy-focused commentators willing to propose teaching solutions, sometimes (as shown earlier) without much convincing evidence to support their claims …

There is evidently still much scope for research into these questions *[reflections]*. Carefully controlled comparative longitudinal studies, though difficult to conduct, would be of particular benefit. More work is needed, also, into how similar languages are in regard to how their noun genders are learned. An additional variable, apparently little considered in the literature, is the effect on learning one set of noun genders (say, German) of already knowing another set in one's first language (say, French). Finally, robust studies of the efficacy of different teaching methodologies are also urgently required. To sum up, there seems to be no magic bullet for the learning of noun gender and, until one is found, the learner may have to take the advice of Barthes et al. (1979), and 'study, study, study' (p. 561).

References

[*List of all texts mentioned, alphabetically by author, according to standard conventions*]

(NB: The texts and ideas in this example are fictional.)

Extending the structure for a review constructed from your completed analyses

The basic structure laid out above enables you to draw together what you have found out in the texts you analysed, whether in summary or in depth, by synthesizing the answers you gave to a particular Critical Synopsis and its corresponding Critical Analysis questions. It can be elaborated for more complex Critical Literature Reviews. We will describe two variations: one in which you have multiple review questions, and another in which you adopt a multi-thematic approach to evaluating the literature.

Structure for a review designed to answer multiple review questions

The basic structure may be elaborated by dedicating a separate section to developing an argument for each review question in turn. These arguments together comprise the warranting for the overall conclusion of the entire Critical Literature Review. Each section can itself be divided into an identical sequence of subsections, though obviously the content of each section will be different. The structure might then be:

Title

Keywords indicating the focus for the study.

Introduction

- Statement of purpose – say, three review questions that all relate to the overall focus (Critical Analysis Question 1, Critical Synopsis Question A).
- Justification of the focus, scope and limitations.
- Signposting to the remaining sections which indicates how each section will contribute part of the warranting for the claims in your conclusion to the Critical Literature Review as a whole.

Section addressing themes

Subsections building up the warranting for the claims in the conclusion of your argument for this section	Based on answers to Critical Analysis Questions for central texts	Based on answers to the Critical Synopsis Questions for more peripheral texts
• An introduction to the texts being reviewed	2	B
• The authors' main claims relevant to your review question	3, 4	C

Subsections building up the warranting for the claims in the conclusion of your argument for this section	Based on answers to Critical Analysis Questions for central texts	Based on answers to the Critical Synopsis Questions for more peripheral texts
• Evaluation of the authors' claims, including any counter-evidence	5–9	D
Final subsection setting out the conclusion of your argument answering this review question		
• Summarizing your evaluation of the reviewed texts' combined contribution to answering your **first** review question.	10	E

Section addressing the second review question

Subsections in the same sequence as above, leading to the conclusion of your argument answering the *second* review question	Based on answers to Critical Analysis Questions for central texts	Based on answers to Critical Synopsis Questions for more peripheral texts

Section addressing the third review question

Subsections in the same sequence as above, leading to the conclusion of your argument answering the *third* review question	Based on answers to Critical Analysis Questions for central texts	Based on answers to Critical Synopsis Questions for more peripheral texts

Conclusion for the whole Critical Literature Review

- Your summary account of how the conclusions of your arguments answering the three review questions relate together to provide the warranting for your conclusion to the review as a whole.
- Your self-critical retrospective reflections on the strengths and limitations of your review.
- Possibly, implications arising from your review for future research, theorizing or policy-making.

References

- A list (in author alphabetical order) of the texts to which you have referred, following the normal conventions for compiling a reference list.

If you foresaw the relevance of a text to more than one review question, you will have been able to expand your Critical Analysis or Critical Synopsis of the text to cover all the questions. However, sometimes, a new review question will arise only after you have completed the Critical Analysis or Critical Synopsis. In such instances, you may need to complete a new template (or add to the old one) to ensure you have material relevant to this new review question.

Structure for a review designed to develop several themes

Another variation on the basic literature review structure can be used where you wish to group thematically what you have found out in seeking to answer your review question. Here you create a section where you both summarize and evaluate the authors' main claims for each theme in turn. We illustrate a structure where there are two themes, but you could of course add more as required.

Title

Keywords indicating the focus for the study.

Introduction

- A statement of purpose – your focus, designed to answer a review question (Critical Analysis Question 1, Critical Synopsis Question A).
- Justification of the scope, focus and limitations.
- The scope of the review – the range of literature reviewed and why this range was selected for review.

Sections building up the warranting for the claims in the conclusion of your argument	**Based on answers to Critical Analysis Questions for central texts**	**Based on answers to Critical Synopsis Questions for more peripheral texts**
• An introduction to the texts being reviewed	2	B
• The authors' main claims and your evaluation of them, for Theme 1	3, 4, 5–9	C, D
• The authors' main claims and your evaluation of them, for Theme 2	3, 4, 5–9	C, D
Final section setting out the conclusion of your argument		
• Summary of your thematic evaluation of the literature reviewed to assess the texts' combined contribution to answering your review question	10	E

- Limitations of the review (e.g., mainly concerned with a small number of key texts, restricted to sources from only one part of the world, confined to books and academic journal articles, based on what you could access from the Internet).
- Signposting – indicating how you will synthesize the authors' main claims and your evaluation of them according to specified themes in order to answer your review question.

References

- A list (in author alphabetical order) of the texts to which you have referred, following the normal conventions for compiling a reference list.

Structuring a Review informed by Critical Analyses and Critical Synopses

The structures we have described above are useful but rather inflexible. In a more flexible approach, you might still draw on material from your Critical Analyses and Critical Synopses, but not all of it and not in any fixed sequence. Here, your Critical Analyses and Critical Synopses *inform* the content of your review but no longer dominate its structure. Parameters bounding your creativity in designing Critical Literature Review structures are set by the ingredients essential for developing a convincing argument. We suggest that any structure must include:

- An introduction setting out and justifying your review questions.
- Warranting that comprises a critical account of whatever evidence you have found in the literature relating to these review questions.
- A strong conclusion whose claims are backed by your warranting.
- Your reference list (so that readers can follow up your sources).

Illustrative structure of a Review informed by Critical Analyses and Critical Synopses

There is scope for a variety of structures within these parameters. Here is one illustration, developed for an 8,000-word assignment for a professional doctorate programme. In this example, the review questions, and therefore the structure required in order to address them, have flowed from a substantive concern: to improve how school leadership encourages teachers' commitment to their job within a developing country. While there is a large literature from organizational contexts in industrialized countries, it has become clear that little exists for such contexts in developing countries. As with the second structure we offered above, this one is designed to seek answers to three related review questions. But it looks quite different.

Title

Keywords indicating the focus for the study.

- 'The Impact of Leadership on Teachers' Motivation and Job Satisfaction: Implications for Schools in a Developing Country'

Introduction

- Statement of purpose – to examine what is known and the limits of what is known about the possible impact of leadership on teachers' motivation and job satisfaction, in order to assess what practical implications there may be for improving leadership practice in schools within a developing country. The review therefore seeks to answer three review questions (Critical Analysis Question 1, Critical Synopsis Question A):
  - What is meant by concepts of leadership, motivation and job satisfaction, and how are they assumed to relate to each other?
  - How strong is the evidence from educational organizations and elsewhere that leadership can positively influence the motivation and job satisfaction of those for whose work leaders are responsible?
  - To what extent does the evidence for leaders having a positive influence on the motivation and job satisfaction of those for whose work they are responsible apply to schools in a developing country?
- Justification of the focus, scope and limitations.
- Signposting to the remaining sections, indicating how each section will contribute part of the warranting for the conclusion of the Critical Literature Review as a whole.

Section on defining leadership, motivation, job satisfaction and their interrelationship

- Signposting – how this section will be divided into two subsections to address the first review question.

Material warranting the claims in a conclusion that answers the first review question, drawing on answers from Critical Analyses and Critical Synopses	Drawing on answers to Critical Analysis Question for central texts	Drawing on answers to Critical Synopsis Questions for more peripheral texts
• Subsection A: the main ways in which the concepts of leadership, motivation and job satisfaction are defined, and common assumptions about their interrelationship, especially how directly leadership impacts on either motivation or job satisfaction	3, 6	C, D
• Subsection B: conclusion about the degree to which leadership is commonly and convincingly conceived as impacting directly on motivation and job satisfaction	10	E

Section on evidence for the impact of leadership on motivation and job satisfaction

- Signposting – how this section will be divided into three subsections to address the second review question.

Subsections presenting material for warranting the claims in conclusions that combine to answer the second review question, drawing on answers from Critical Analyses and Critical Synopses	Based on answers to Critical Analysis Questions for central texts	Based on answers to Critical Synopsis Questions for more peripheral texts
• Subsection A: authors' main claims about the impact of leadership on motivation and job satisfaction	3, 4	C
• Subsection B: evaluation of these claims, including any counter-evidence	5–8	D
• Subsection C: conclusion summarizing how strong the evidence is from educational organizations and elsewhere that leadership can positively influence motivation and job satisfaction	10	E

Applicability of the evidence to schools in a developing country

Material warranting the claims in a conclusion that answers the third review question, drawing on answers from Critical Analyses and Critical Synopses	Based on answers to Critical Analysis Questions for central texts	Based on answers to Critical Synopsis Questions for more peripheral texts
• Subsection A: evaluation of the extent to which evidence from developed countries for leaders having a positive influence on motivation and job satisfaction applies to schools in a developing country	9	D
• Subsection B: conclusion about the extent to which school leaders in developing countries may positively influence teachers' motivation and job satisfaction	10	E

Conclusion for the whole Critical Literature Review

- A summary account of how the conclusions of the arguments answering the three review questions relate together to provide the warranting for the conclusion to the review as a whole:

  - The way leadership is conceived to impact directly on motivation and job satisfaction.
  - The strength of the evidence for this impact.
  - The degree to which contextual differences between developed and developing countries may affect the applicability of claims about this impact to schools in a developing country.
- Reflections, in retrospect, on the strengths and limitations of the review.
- Recommendations for training and other support for school leaders in a developing country.
- An indication of what further research may be needed to explore the relative importance of particular contextual factors potentially affecting the impact of leadership on teachers' motivation and job satisfaction in developed and developing countries.

References

- A list (in author alphabetical order) of the texts to which reference is made, following the normal conventions for compiling a reference list.

Developing independence as a critical reviewer of literature

The structures we have introduced allow for your growing competence in conducting Critical Literature Reviews. All these structures will help you keep the range of literature within manageable bounds by focusing on one or more review questions. The first three structures offer maximum security for the first-time reviewer because they most closely follow the logic of the Critical Analysis form. They enable you to:

- lay out side-by-side your completed Critical Analyses and Critical Synopses of individual texts;
- scan and synthesize your responses to specific Critical Analysis and Critical Synopsis Questions, using the sequence presented in the relevant forms;
- translate a synthesis of your responses to each of these Critical Analysis Questions and Critical Synopsis Questions directly into your review, either separating your account of authors' main claims from your evaluation of them, or combining the account and evaluation for texts relating to one theme at a time;
- build up logically the warranting for the conclusion of your argument as you write down the synthesis to each Critical Analysis Question and Critical Synopsis Question in sequence, culminating in a conclusion where you indicate what answer the literature gives to your review question.

However, security comes at the price of rigidity. As you gain experience, you can become more independent: work out how to develop the warranting and conclusion of the argument you wish to make by designing your own structure for addressing your review questions in whatever sequence works best (within the parameters we outlined earlier).

Your skills as an increasingly sophisticated critical reader and self-critical writer will stand you in good stead for the most complex of reviewing tasks facing most postgraduate students: incorporating literature reviews into a report of your own research, as with a dissertation. We now turn to this task.

15

Integrating Critical Literature Reviews into Your Dissertation

Keywords

core dissertation structure; Critical Literature Mini-review; dissertation; narrative creation; self-critical writing; writing convincingly

This chapter begins our exploration of the contribution that Critical Literature Reviews make to designing and writing up your larger-scale investigation. Here, we concentrate on what we will term the 'core' dissertation structure, which is common in the social sciences, and in some areas of the humanities. (Some alternative structures will be considered in the next chapter.)

We highlight the importance of Critical Literature Reviews in one or more locations in a high-quality dissertation narrative. We discuss how your account should follow a logical sequence, developing a convincing *overall argument*. Your Critical Literature Reviews, and the critical reading on which they depend, are vital for making the logic of your account compelling to your examiners.

Why the literature is important in empirical studies

Until now we have focused on conducting a Critical Literature Review. But dissertations usually involve not only literature reviews but also the generation and analysis of your own empirical evidence. So how may Critical Literature Reviews contribute to an empirical research project?

The published research literature offers an immensely rich (though not unlimited) source of evidence, ranging over theory, empirical research and engagement with practice. It extends way beyond the direct experience that any single individual could have. The literature therefore solves a problem for researchers – many things that you need to know in order to answer the questions driving your project can be found out without having to collect your own data. Instead, you can look at what others have done. You engage critically with their accounts because you need to be as confident of their claims as you would be if you had done the work yourself. This way of seeing the literature review is very important, placing it firmly at the centre of your *research itself*, rather than keeping it separate, as some kind of annoying preliminary to your empirical study.

As a reader of others' research, you will have noticed the inherent continuum between their own research and other research that they review. They are both part of the same thing for a reader. And as a writer, you need to sustain that sense of integration too. As a reader you value it when authors refer to other literature so as to demonstrate the level of consistency between their own claims and those of others. You are helped in your own study when authors reveal, through a critical evaluation of existing literature, some flaw or limitation in previous studies that their work is designed to address. In short, a skilled use of the literature by authors as a form of evidence is part of the reason why you find their claims about their own research findings convincing.

As a self-critical writer (whether of reviews, essays, a dissertation or some other written product) you will consciously search the literature for whatever useful evidence you can find there. You will employ it as part of your warranting to make the claims in the conclusion of your own argument as convincing as possible for your target audience. You may already have experience of relating a limited amount of literature to a piece of primary data that you had been given or had collected yourself. However, it is only with an extended piece of work such as a dissertation or thesis that the challenge is fully confronted.

Literature matters: what's new, and how can you show it's new?

If you are doing your dissertation research and writing it up for a masters or doctorate degree programme, you will be working towards submitting your completed account for assessment by academic examiners. You must convince these critical readers to accept your claims about what you have found out. They are required to evaluate your account against the programme criteria for assessing dissertations. So you must ensure that your account meets these assessment criteria as extensively as you can.

(Continued)

(Continued)

For both masters and doctoral dissertations involving empirical research, the criteria typically include twin expectations. First, you will use the literature beforehand to inform your own empirical work; second, you will consider afterwards what the implications of your findings are for the claims made in that literature. But an additional criterion is generally included for *doctoral* dissertations: what you have found out must make a *significant contribution to new knowledge* in the topic area. How can you demonstrate to your examiners that you have achieved this?

Ways of demonstrating that you have found out something new and important share a reliance on more than merely your own empirical findings. For although your findings are new for *you*, how can you show that you have not merely 'reinvented the wheel' – by repeating, unintentionally, what other researchers have already done, and finding out what they have already discovered? You need complementary sources of evidence from the relevant literature to show, first, that no one has previously studied exactly the same phenomenon in exactly the same way as you. (What 'exactly the same' means is relevant to our previous discussions of generalization – see Chapters 4 and 10). Second, you need to show that what you have found out is *important* because it has implications for other interested groups, maybe by adding to academic understanding or by informing efforts to improve practice.

The literature is your friend. Do not ignore it or just describe it – use it to as evidence to support your claim that you are generating significant new knowledge. There are many ways you can do this. Here are two examples to stimulate your thinking. One is to critically review the relevant literature, as discussed in the previous chapter, to inform the focus and design of your empirical investigation. Your review can demonstrate just how much is already known, what the limits of this knowledge are, and so what significant knowledge gap is left that your empirical investigation will contribute to filling.

Another is to investigate a phenomenon that has been studied before, but you study it in a significantly different context than other researchers have done. Your empirical research can assess the extent to which other researchers' generalized findings, derived from other empirical contexts, fully apply to your context. Will additional factors apply here, indicating that other researchers' generalization should be rejected or refined to take these factors into account? Your critical literature review could inform your choice of empirical context to investigate, and could establish which contextual factors the existing research does take into account. Then you could identify other relevant factors in your envisaged context, and so point to the possibility of generating new knowledge by checking the applicability of the generalization to this context.

The reality of the study process versus the written account

Students often remark that their finished dissertation was not quite what they had originally imagined. This is hardly surprising, given the amount of knowledge and research skill acquired along the way. The expectation placed on some students to propose an empirical project *before* they have read much literature may give them a particularly difficult challenge, since a worthwhile investigation should be inspired by, and build on, existing research. It makes sense to allow for the likelihood that your ideas will change during the study process. But equally, it is worth trying to minimize the chances of having radically to re-think your investigation and written account. You can do this by clearly establishing your research focus early on.

Irrespective of the journey, your final account of what you have done and what you have learned must be focused and logical. You will save unnecessary work if all the written work amassed as you go along fits easily into your assembled final draft of your dissertation. The secret is to make the process of investigating as close as you can to the written account you expect to end up with. You cannot know before you start exactly what you will find – what your conclusion will be – but you can frame your questions in such a way that you know what *sort* of conclusion you will have. For instance, by asking 'is learning by heart an effective method for increasing vocabulary knowledge in a foreign language?' you can know from the beginning that your conclusion will be some version of a 'yes', 'no' or (more likely) 'it depends on X'. With a planned focus on clear questions, you can ensure that your critical reading and empirical research are playing their part in generating the combination of literature-based data and the empirical data you need for your written account.

Therefore, it is important that, once you have done any initial background reading, your focused critical reading is always directed towards writing a draft of some part of your written account. We recommend that you begin drafting this account from the outset of your study, amending and adding to it as your understanding of what you are doing and knowledge of the field increase.

Maximizing your chances of convincing your examiners

In producing your dissertation, it is worth keeping in mind what your examiners will be looking for. They will normally expect a dissertation to include critical reviews of literature bearing on three aspects of your enquiry:

1. The *substantive* focus – the particular topic (or issue) that constitutes the substance of the investigation.
2. The *theoretical* issues – how particular concepts, perspectives, theories or models guide and inform the study, and what their strengths and limitations are.
3. *Methodological* approaches to conducting an empirical investigation – in one field, a particular methodology might be accepted as standard practice; in another, there may be more methodological debate amongst academics. Either way, you will need to establish which approach is most appropriate for your purpose.

(We briefly referred to these distinctions in Chapter 14 when discussing the need to focus a Critical Literature Review on specified review questions.) For the core dissertation structure, each aspect merits its own Critical Literature Review. You should expect to engage critically with literature in justifying your investigation of the substantive topic, your choice of theoretical orientation to frame your research and the interpretation of your findings, and the methodological approach and detailed methods through which you gather your data.

Reference to this literature may be made at various points during your investigation, and within your written account – wherever it helps to develop your warranting for the eventual claims in the conclusion of your overall argument. Thus, while you may have much of your critical evaluation of the literature in one or more chapters constituting a 'Literature Review', you will also mention relevant literature wherever necessary to contribute to building your argument. One way to do this is to incorporate what we will call *Critical Literature Mini-reviews* – short and narrowly focused reviews of a few texts – wherever you need to refer to relevant literature in addition to the main Critical Literature Reviews.

We have compiled a 'top ten' list of the features of a high-quality dissertation, indicating in *italic* script how Critical Literature Reviews or Mini-reviews and reference back to them are distributed across the written account.

A high-quality dissertation: 'top ten' features

A dissertation based on the core structure is likely to develop a convincing overall argument if it features:

1. A logical argument, developed from the title to the end of the account, which provides strong warranting for the claims to knowledge made in the conclusion. It should be possible to capture this argument in a sentence, which will form the core of the abstract if one is required.
2. A clearly-focused substantive topic about an aspect of the social world, justified as a significant focus of investigation through a *Critical Literature Mini-review.*
3. Explicitly stated aims for the investigation, whose achievement will contribute towards answering a well-defined broad central question.
4. Located in appropriate places, *Critical Literature Reviews relating to the substantive area, the theoretical orientation, and the methodology plus methods of data collection and analysis. Each Critical Literature Review is driven by review questions* linked to the broad central question, with clear connections drawn between existing knowledge and the present investigation. Answers to the review questions lead to the specification of detailed research questions or hypotheses.

5. A well-structured and explicit design for the empirical study, an appropriate methodological approach, detailed methods and carefully designed research instruments for answering the research questions or testing the hypotheses.
6. A set of data that is analysed thoroughly to indicate what answers have been found to the research questions or hypotheses. Clearly set out procedures for data preparation, summary and analysis.
7. Discussion of the findings and analysis, explicitly relating back to the research questions or hypotheses, and to the *Critical Literature Review on the substantive area*, and where appropriate, highlighting *implications for other literature domains through a Critical Literature Mini-review.*
8. A reflective conclusion, making *brief reference to the Critical Literature Reviews or Mini-reviews on the substantive, theoretical and methodological areas.* It summarizes the study's contribution to answering the broad central question, the study's strengths and limitations, any problematic issues that arose, implications for future research and (if appropriate) recommendations for policy or practice.
9. Accurate referencing, both in the text and in the reference list, so that, in principle, any *reference to the literature* may be easily traced and followed up.
10. Clear expression with attention to writing style, punctuation, spelling and grammar, so that the account can be easily understood.

Bear these features in mind when planning the structure and presentation of your dissertation. As we noted earlier, you will also find it useful to refer repeatedly to the dissertation assessment criteria, typically included in the students' handbook for the degree programme. Maximize your chances of your examiners awarding you a high mark by ensuring that your written account meets each of the criteria stated there.

You can make the most of your critical reading if each text you read and each area you review has potential for contributing to the development of your overall argument. Clearly, you cannot know in detail what your argument will contain before you have done any reading or data collection, so you cannot initially be sure how relevant a particular text is to this argument. But you can establish early on which areas of literature you need to review initially and – by formulating focused review questions – how the results of your Critical Literature Reviews will enable your overall argument to develop effectively. You need to maintain a sense of the logical sequence of steps required to build the warranting for your claims in the conclusion of your final written account. That way, you can plan how to keep the research process and the written account closely aligned.

Figure 15.1 depicts in summary form the progression of the logic within the core dissertation structure. The chapters that are often used to provide the

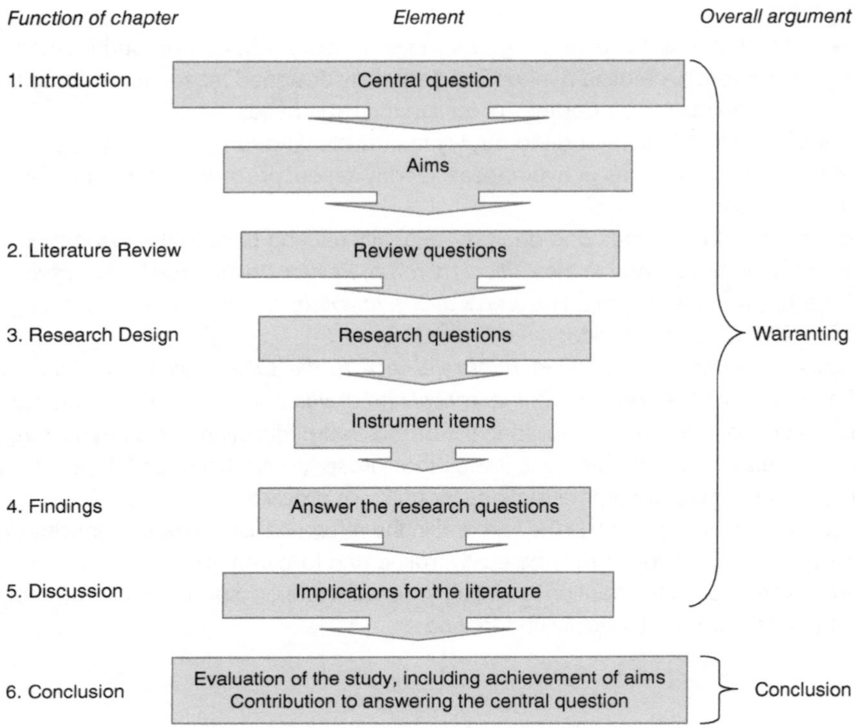

FIGURE 15.1 The logic of the overall argument in the core dissertation structure

sequencing of the written account are listed down the left-hand side, labelled according to their *function* in developing the overall argument. (You do not have to use functional titles in your dissertation. It is better for the development of the narrative to choose chapter names that reflect the content itself, e.g., 'Why are Noun Genders Difficult to Learn?' for a chapter reviewing the literature on that topic.) Down the centre of the diagram we have listed the element contained in each chapter, as it contributes to developing the logic of the overall argument. On the right-hand side we have indicated how everything written in the first five chapters contributes to the warranting for the claims made in the conclusion chapter. (Sometimes you will have more than one chapter for a component, in which case a larger number of chapters will provide the warranting.) Note how the arrowed boxes containing these key elements become progressively narrower, then broaden out again towards the conclusion. We use this depiction to signify how you may:

- begin with a general orientation towards a broad topic;
- select a small number of specific aims whose achievement can contribute to an understanding of that topic;

- identify a small number of review questions that represent one way of achieving the aims;
- select one or more research questions from amongst the many arising from the Critical Literature Reviews;
- focus tightly on a particular data set, collected and interrogated using particular approaches;
- critically consider how the answers to the research questions relate back to the literature already reviewed, and possibly also have implications to which you wish to draw attention for other literature; and
- reconnect with the general orientation by evaluating the achievement of the aims and the contribution made to addressing the topic.

Let us briefly introduce the sequence of elements in Figure 15.1, before examining them in detail. First, progressively narrowing the focus. The research topic is firmed up as a *central question*, expressed in general terms (as mentioned in Chapter 4). The dissertation as a whole will make some modest contribution towards answering it. The central question drives the investigation, which is designed to achieve specific *aims*. They concern conducting a small-scale empirical study in a particular context, informed by a specified theoretical orientation, and using a specified methodology and methods of data collection and analysis. To inform a decision about the research design best able to achieve these aims, *review questions* are identified, which drive the Critical Literature Reviews. They are undertaken to find out what is known from other authors' work. This information may offer pointers for the focus of the empirical research, any associated theoretical orientation and the methodological approach. An outcome of the Critical Literature Reviews is to identify detailed *research questions* that the empirical research will seek to answer. The research questions dictate the specification of the *instrument items* (e.g., specific questions in a survey or experimental stimuli) for the data collection. Responses to the instrument items are analysed to *answer the research questions*.

Second, progressively broadening the focus again. The findings are also interpreted and discussed by relating them to relevant literature already reviewed, so as to show how they are supported by others' work or offer a challenge to it. Implications of the findings may also be drawn for other literature domains that were not previously reviewed. The conclusion summarizes what has been found out and evaluates how well the research has been conducted, including *how far the aims have been achieved*. The *contribution* of the findings to *answering the central question* is asserted. So we come full circle:

- The investigation begins by posing the central question, signalling the journey towards a conclusion.
- The conclusion claims knowledge (which, for a doctoral dissertation, should be new knowledge) relevant to answering the central question.
- Between the two lies the warranting for the claims in the conclusion. It is built up through the Critical Literature Reviews, the empirical research and the relating of the findings to others' work.

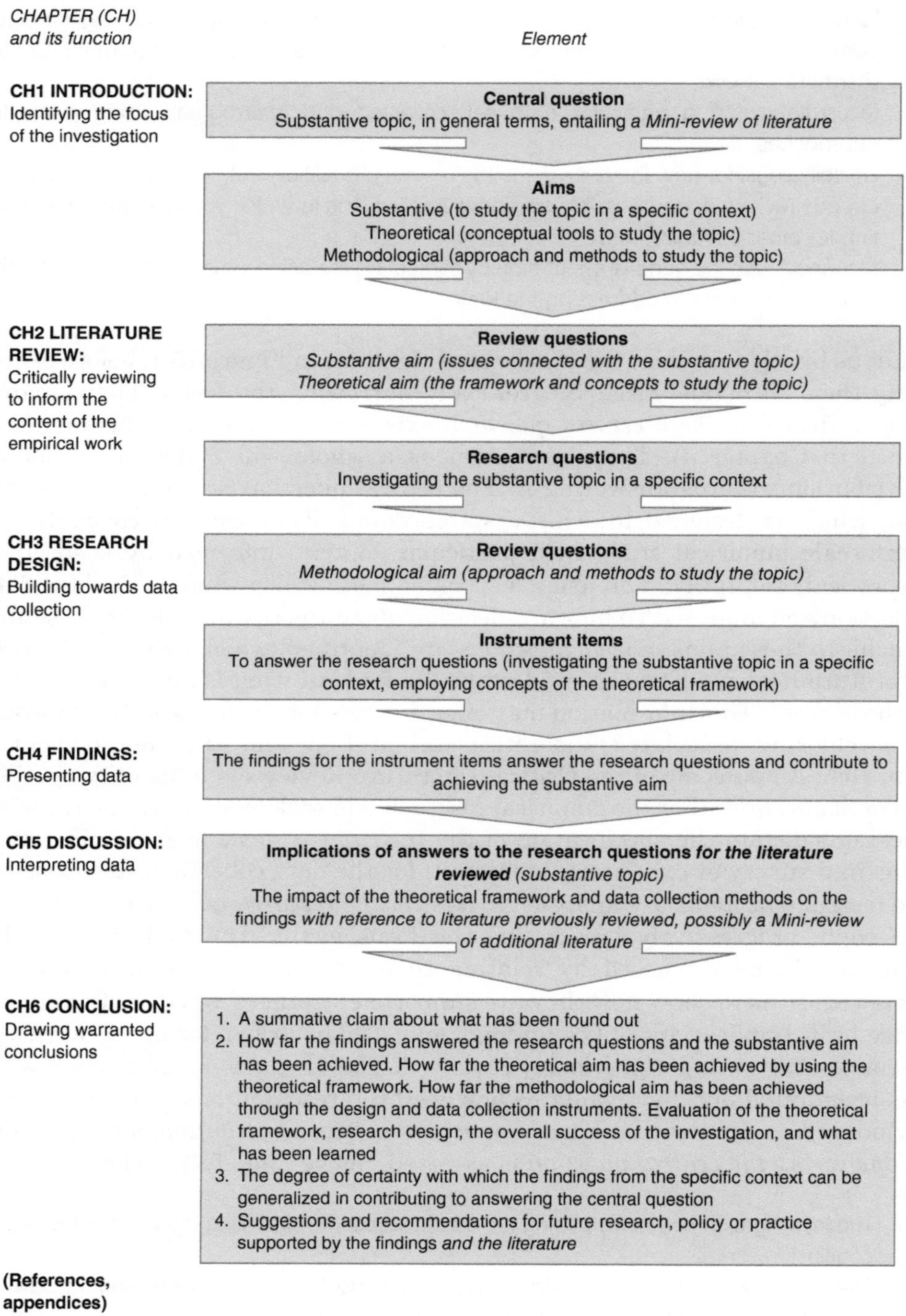

CHAPTER (CH)
and its function
Element
CH1 INTRODUCTION:
Identifying the focus of the investigation
Central question
Substantive topic, in general terms, entailing a Mini-review of literature
Aims
Substantive (to study the topic in a specific context)
Theoretical (conceptual tools to study the topic)
Methodological (approach and methods to study the topic)
CH2 LITERATURE REVIEW:
Critically reviewing to inform the content of the empirical work
Review questions
Substantive aim (issues connected with the substantive topic)
Theoretical aim (the framework and concepts to study the topic)
Research questions
Investigating the substantive topic in a specific context
CH3 RESEARCH DESIGN:
Building towards data collection
Review questions
Methodological aim (approach and methods to study the topic)
Instrument items
To answer the research questions (investigating the substantive topic in a specific context, employing concepts of the theoretical framework)
CH4 FINDINGS:
Presenting data
The findings for the instrument items answer the research questions and contribute to achieving the substantive aim
CH5 DISCUSSION:
Interpreting data
Implications of answers to the research questions for the literature reviewed (substantive topic)
The impact of the theoretical framework and data collection methods on the findings with reference to literature previously reviewed, possibly a Mini-review of additional literature
CH6 CONCLUSION:
Drawing warranted conclusions
1. A summative claim about what has been found out
2. How far the findings answered the research questions and the substantive aim has been achieved. How far the theoretical aim has been achieved by using the theoretical framework. How far the methodological aim has been achieved through the design and data collection instruments. Evaluation of the theoretical framework, research design, the overall success of the investigation, and what has been learned
3. The degree of certainty with which the findings from the specific context can be generalized in contributing to answering the central question
4. Suggestions and recommendations for future research, policy or practice supported by the findings and the literature
(References, appendices)

FIGURE 15.2 Developing the logic of the overall argument in the core dissertation structure

Figure 15.2 fills out the picture by dividing the development of the overall argument into six sequential steps. Each step will normally be written up in a particular chapter (though some steps may require more than one chapter). We have indicated in italic script where the Critical Literature Reviews, and also Mini-reviews, contribute towards the warranting for claims in the conclusion chapter.

We can now show, step-by-step, how to use the logical progression to bring together the research process and the overall argument in your written account. It demonstrates how planning, drafting and note-taking are of considerable support to the conceptualization of what can be a complex integration of ideas and procedures.

Step 1: identifying the focus of the enquiry

Start writing the first draft of your introductory chapter before you have done anything more than background reading, to help you clarify the focus of your investigation. Include your initial attempt at formulating your *central question*. Posing a central question is a potent way of giving direction to your thoughts. Formulating this overarching direction as a question implies that there is something problematic or unknown and significant within your area of research interest that your study can contribute to addressing.

Typically, postgraduate students wish primarily to address a substantive topic in their field of enquiry (rather than developing or testing theory, or trialling a new method of data collection or analysis). You will not know precisely what contribution your study will make yet, but you can anticipate obtaining findings that will contribute towards answering your central question. Articulating the central question constitutes the first stage in building up the warranting for claims in your eventual conclusion.

Initial reference can be made to the literature from the substantive topic area, based on a Critical Literature Mini-review that is informed by your background reading. This will help focus your search for specific review and research questions, while justifying the scientific or practical significance of the central question. Justify to your target audience why the focus of your investigation is important, by indicating how it can add to knowledge in the field of enquiry.

The central question demonstrates to your examiners that you are concerned with a topic of wider significance than simply your own small-scale investigation in a particular context. The central question is not specific to the context that you will be investigating. Rather, it provides your link from, and back to, the generalization and abstraction necessary to locate your work within the wider domain represented by the literature. For example, in Chapter 14 we gave an example Critical Review structure that might have been inspired by the central question *How can teachers be encouraged to remain committed to their job in developing countries?* This question could be answered in many different ways. In our example, the literature review element focused in on asking how school leaders can play a role. We would anticipate that the empirical research would focus further, to examine how leaders in specific schools fulfil that role.

Thus, your central question does not in itself indicate what your contribution to answering it will be. You need to sharpen your initial focus by identifying the three specific *aims* that your investigation is designed to achieve:

- Your *substantive aim* – precisely what you intend to find out about the substantive topic (e.g., determine factors affecting the effectiveness of some aspect of a practice in a specific context).
- Your *theoretical aim* – what concepts and, perhaps, over-arching theory you intend to use to achieve your substantive aim (e.g., employ a particular set of concepts as a framework for investigating your chosen aspect of practice in this specific context).
- Your *methodological aim* – how you are going to find out what you need to know in order to achieve your substantive aim (e.g., employ a particular methodological approach, research design, ethical standards, and methods of data collection and analysis to investigate your chosen aspect of practice in this specific context).

In attempting to achieve your three aims, you need to think through how you will address any issues or problems to which your effort may give rise. The relevant literature may inform your understanding of these issues. Achieving your substantive aim raises the issue of deciding exactly which aspects of your substantive topic to investigate in detail in the specific context for your investigation. Achieving your theoretical aim raises the issue of acknowledging the strengths and limitations of the theory or set of concepts you plan to employ, and the degree of applicability of your theoretical orientation to the empirical phenomenon. Achieving your methodological aim raises the issue of assessing the validity of the assumptions underlying your methodological approach, and the strengths, limitations and fitness-for-purpose of the methods you plan to employ.

The nature of the central question simultaneously affects what your aims are and reflects your intellectual project. To communicate your rationale effectively for the central question you have chosen, it is worth articulating what your intellectual project is and what your values are in relation to the topic you are investigating. For instance, if your interest is in improving in-service training for social workers, you may be pursuing knowledge-for-action from a positive value position towards this practice. However, if your interest is in finding out whether women and men interpret second-hand car advertisements differently, you may be pursuing knowledge-for-understanding from a relatively impartial value position.

Attempting to specify your substantive, theoretical and methodological aims in the first draft of the introductory chapter can help you to think through what you are going to do. The central question and aims can always be refined in a later draft, informed by your continuing reading and research design work.

Signposting for effective communication with your examiners

As a critical reader, you will have appreciated authors who communicate their messages clearly. A dissertation is a long piece of work, so your examiners may easily lose track of what you are doing, why, and where your work is leading to. It is in your interests to assist them, through regular signposting in your text. Keep in mind the question: what do the examiners need to know next? Provide them with clear indicators that enable them to make connections between one section or chapter and whatever follows. There is an old saying: 'First, tell them what you are going to tell them. Then tell them. Finally, tell them what you've told them.' Far from an invitation to be mechanically repetitive, this is an instruction: continually help your target readers to follow the development of your overall argument. At the end of the introduction and the end of each subsequent chapter, your conclusion can include a brief summary of what has been discussed or presented and (except for the last chapter) an indication of what will come in the next chapter. At the beginning of each chapter (except the introduction), outline very briefly what the chapter will cover.

The small amount of repetition incurred is more than compensated for by the value of keeping your critical readers fully in the picture. Further, you can offset direct repetition by using existing information as a building block for saying something new, e.g., 'In that A is the case, the next consideration is B,' or 'We established in the previous chapter that C is the case. We now turn to the question of why that might be so.' Any difficulty you experience with providing a succinct description of what you have said, or are going to say, may signal a need to sharpen your thinking or to refine your dissertation structure.

Step 2: critically reviewing literature to inform the content of the empirical work

You will recall that in Chapter 14 we discussed the role of formulating *review questions* as a means of focusing a self-contained Critical Literature Review. In such a review, you build up the warranting for the claims in your conclusion by providing an answer to each of your review questions. In the more extensive investigation that constitutes a dissertation, the review questions are a product of the broader agenda of the study. The initial choice of topic (framed by your central question) and your decisions about how you are going to investigate it (framed by your aims) play a major part in determining your review questions for your Critical Literature Reviews, since these reviews are designed to inform your empirical investigation.

One or more review questions will relate to issues connected with achieving your substantive aim through your empirical investigation. You will direct some of your critical reading and associated Critical Synopses and Critical Analyses towards answering each review question. The Critical Literature Review you conduct may form one or more sections in a literature review chapter. Each section will develop its own argument. The account of what you found in the literature provides the warranting for the claims in your section conclusion, answering the review question that drives it.

Similarly, you will probably pose one or more review questions about the theoretical orientation, related to your theoretical aim (e.g., what is meant by a particular set of concepts and how they may be employed as a framework for investigating your chosen aspect of the practice in this specific context). The Critical Literature Review generated in this way may also appear in the literature review chapter, since the theoretical orientation is often closely tied to understanding the literature in the substantive area of investigation. However, for clarity it is useful to have a dedicated section for the review questions about the theoretical orientation, and sometimes it makes sense to put them in a chapter of their own.

As you read and follow up references to further work, you should look out for any major 'landmark' texts that bear directly on your empirical investigation. These are important works that have shaped in a big way what is known about the topic. You can thereby ensure that your written review acknowledges and evaluates the ideas or evidence that they contain. The evaluation can take account of what others say about the landmark texts, but you should draw your own conclusion, based on the strength of the arguments that you identify in your own reading of them. Paying attention to landmark texts will help you to convince your examiners that you have conducted a thorough search and are aware of leading authors' work. As you assemble your various Critical Analyses and Critical Synopses, you will be able to identify themes that you can draw upon in developing answers to your review questions.

Your substantive and theoretical Critical Literature Reviews may valuably inform your empirical work. The answers to the review questions you have obtained give you a sound basis for formulating your more specific *research questions* (sometimes expressed as hypotheses), in the light of whatever the literature has revealed. Your data collection instruments will be designed to answer your research questions, themselves informed by the relevant literature.

Identifying your research questions in this way builds up the warranting within your overall argument a little further. You will be able to show your examiners that you have taken into account what is already known from others' work. For a doctoral dissertation, you can highlight how your study stands to develop significant new knowledge by pointing to the limits of what is already known, and showing that your work will reach beyond these limits. Reading critically and constructing the first draft of your literature review chapter (or chapters) before you finalize your research design puts you in a good position to ensure that your investigation builds on others' work and that you demonstrate this to your examiners.

Step 3: building towards data collection

The literature has an equally important part to play in informing the design of your empirical investigation. This time, the review question or questions you pose will concern:

- Methodology – the ontological assumptions (about the nature of the social world) and epistemological assumptions (about how we can have knowledge of it) that are framing your approach to empirical work (see Chapter 8).
- Your choice of methods, including their strengths, limitations and fitness-for-purpose as means of seeking answers to your research questions, and any ethical issues that these methods may raise (if your research involves people as participants) and how you will deal with them.

The methodological Critical Literature Review is likely to form a dedicated section in your research design chapter rather than in your earlier literature review chapter(s). Alternatively, you may present Mini-reviews of methodological literature distributed across your research design chapter, to justify each decision about instruments, procedure and ethical considerations, as they arise in the narrative. The literature you draw on will include, but need not be restricted to, research methods textbooks. Others' research may offer you a methodology to adopt or methods to emulate. Nor need you look only within your own substantive area for such inspiration, since many approaches are relatively generic and transferable.

As always, your written account must develop an argument that justifies your conclusion to the section. To draw warranted conclusions about your choice of methodology and methods, you will be critically evaluating others' accounts about conducting empirical research: methodological paradigms, data collection and analysis methods, sampling and piloting, and ethical issues. Your literature-backed conclusion will help to convince your examiners of the reasons why you have adopted your methodological approach, and why your chosen methods for data collection and analysis stand a strong chance of answering your research questions fully.

In the light of your earlier Critical Literature Review of relevant theory, you may now construct a theoretical framework of linked concepts appropriate for your methodological approach. This framework relates to the formulation of your research questions. These research questions, in turn, determine the detailed design of your data collection instruments, such as interview schedules or observation guides. Each item included in the instrument is designed to make some contribution to answering a research question. For example, an interview schedule might include questions on each factor identified in the literature as playing a role in organizational effectiveness, in order to answer the research question 'What do members of this organization believe influences the effectiveness of their practice?' The answer to each research question is intended to tell you something about the substantive topic in the specific context of your empirical work, which in turn relates, via your theoretical orientation, to your central question. Thus, decisions made about the design of the research instruments directly affect your ability to arrive at a convincing conclusion to your work as a whole.

Providing a step-by-step account of the empirical research procedures is essential for convincing your examiners that you knew what you were doing and why you were doing it. In principle, you should give enough information for someone else to be able to replicate your work accurately.

It is equally crucial to make explicit your procedures for checking, summarizing and analysing data, to pave the way for the presentation of your findings. Your examiners need convincing that the claims you are making on the basis of your analysis are well grounded in the procedures you have adopted. (If the data include quantifiable variables, it is necessary to explain which statistical procedures and tests you are conducting and why. Procedures for coding and analysing qualitative data are less standardized than for quantitative data, which adds to the importance of setting them out.)

Making your research design, rationale and procedures clear will together strengthen the warranting within your overall argument. You show your examiners how you chose your approach with care, took into account what is known about different approaches in making this choice, and thought through how you were going to conduct and analyse your empirical research.

Step 4: presenting data

The empirical data you gather and, consequently, your account of what you find, are essential to developing a convincing overall argument. They constitute the new evidence on which the warranting within the overall argument ultimately rests. The supporting evidence that the literature can offer is also important. But the core of the warranting in an account of an empirical investigation obviously lies in the empirical findings. Depending on the nature of your research questions and consequent data, you may divide your reporting into sections within the same (or more than one) chapter. The presentation of your findings must be structured so as to summarize the results that provide answers to your research questions. Together, the answers to your research questions contribute to the achievement of your substantive aim (identified in Step 1).

Note that reviews of the published literature have no place here. It is only you who can say what you have found. Relating your findings to the literature – an integral part of discussing them – is certainly important. But that is the *next* logical step in developing your overall argument (Step 5 below), and it can wait until after the findings have been presented.

Present then discuss or present-and-discuss?

One adaptation of our advice on presenting data before discussing it is to combine the account of your presentation of findings with your discussion of them in one or more 'findings and discussion' chapters. In this approach, the findings that answer a particular research question are *presented* and followed immediately by the relevant *discussion*. The sequence is repeated for the next research question, and so on. The logic is still 'present first, then discuss', but the present–discuss sequence is used in turn for each research question, rather than listing all the findings first and then engaging in all the discussion. Which structure to adopt will depend in part on the extent to which your raw results are as discrete in nature as the questions they are used to answer. Some data sets cannot be divided up at the reporting stage, and the global picture of what you found will need to precede any attempt to pick out patterns that address the research questions.

Not discuss-and-forget-to-present!

With a present-and-discuss structure, beware of failing to present all of your data because you are preoccupied with the discussion. In the logic of developing your overall argument, the findings are the sole source of evidence from your own empirical investigation. So the warranting for the claims in your eventual conclusion about the outcomes of your study, and their contribution to answering your central question, depends on this evidence. Your examiners are unlikely to be convinced if your account makes claims about how your findings are supported by or challenge what others have reported in the literature, but omits to supply the evidence of what you found.

Step 5: interpreting data

The warranting your findings offer for the claims in the conclusion to your overall argument can be considerably enhanced if you relate what you found to what others have found or, perhaps, did not think of looking for. Since all your research questions relate ultimately to your central question, it is necessary also to discuss the combined significance of your answers, taken together. In short, you need to use reference back to the literature in your earlier substantive Critical Literature Review to demonstrate the extent to which your findings are consistent with or challenge what is already known and not known about the topic.

Your empirical work may be small-scale but, in contributing towards an answer to your central question, your findings do add something to knowledge about the substantive topic, and maybe also to the accumulation of knowledge about related social phenomena and practices. You need to convince your examiners of the extent to which your findings may have wider significance for contexts other than the one you investigated empirically. The literature can help you demonstrate this significance. You may be able to show that other researchers have found similar things, that your findings fill a gap in knowledge about the topic, or even that your findings contradict what others have found and so raise questions about the convincingness of their research.

You may wish to reach beyond your own topic, and perhaps highlight the implications of your findings for literature in other areas that you have not already referred to. Incorporating a Critical Literature Mini-review at this point could enable you to do this (e.g., where your study was conducted in a particular kind of organizational setting, but the findings turn out to be relevant to other organizational settings, or generically to all organizations).

Equally, you will want to convince your examiners that while you have been rigorous in your data collection and analysis, you are also aware of the limitations of what you have done. For example, it is important to reflect self-critically on the impact of your theoretical framework on the findings. (For instance, this framework may have directed attention towards some aspects of the empirical phenomenon while downplaying other aspects that a different theoretical orientation might have picked up.) Similarly, it is important to reflect self-critically on how your findings may have been affected by the data collection and analysis methods. (Suppose that your data collection methods relied solely on informants' perceptions about their practice. A limitation would be the lack of any check on whether their perceptions matched what they actually did.) You may wish to make brief reference to relevant theoretical and methodological literature that you critically reviewed earlier and, by adding in a Critical Literature Mini-review, to additional literature (e.g., where your theoretical framework sensitized you to certain aspects of the phenomenon, but you now see that other concepts could draw greater attention in future research to other aspects that turned out to be important).

Acknowledging the likely effect of your theoretical orientation and methods on your findings may seem to undermine the warranting within your overall argument because you are admitting to limitations in your empirical work. But you actually *strengthen* your warranting because you demonstrate that you are realistic about what you have achieved, aware of the compromises you made, and appropriately cautious about the certainty and generalizability of what you have found.

Step 6: warranting for the claims in the conclusion of your overall argument

Your literature review and accounts of the empirical research design and of the data collected and analysed are all geared to developing the warranting within your overall argument. Now you are in a position to take the final step: pulling the different aspects of the study together in articulating a strong conclusion about how your investigation has contributed towards answering your central question.

We suggest you attend to four components that together make for a strong conclusion in a dissertation, each of which depends either directly or indirectly on your critical reading of the literature and your self-critical engagement with your own work. The components are:

1. A summative claim about the answers to your research questions and how they relate to the existing literature.
2. A set of self-critical reflections on what you have achieved, including what limitations you have identified and what you have learned from your experience of conducting research.
3. An evaluation of the extent to which the answers to your research questions contribute to answering your central question, in terms of both their certainty and their generalizability.
4. A look towards the future, to consider what subsequent research might usefully focus on and (if appropriate) how your own investigation might inform practice or policy.

Component 1

The summative claim reflects the conclusions to your findings and discussion chapter(s) and should briefly pick out the key claims and observations from the literature that informed the formulation of your research questions. In this way, you show your examiners that you have located your own findings appropriately within the wider context of research.

Component 2

The reflective component is not always particularly visible in published research but it is essential in work for assessment. Examiners must gain a clear idea of the learning process that you have gone through. You need to consider:

- To what extent have you achieved your three aims (substantive, theoretical and methodological)? You can gauge this by looking at the wording of your aims to see if there is anything that you were unable to achieve. Where you have fallen short in one or more of your aims, you need to explain why and make a frank assessment of how far this situation has compromised your study.

- What is your evaluation, now, of the theoretical framework and design of your empirical investigation? Did they enable you to find out and interpret what you hoped? Did the approach you took inhibit you from seeing the full impact of any important variable or factor? How might the research design be improved if you were to repeat the investigation (e.g., could additional concepts or a modified design give you a chance of developing more robust knowledge about your topic)?
- How do you assess your success in conducting the research? Although things may not have gone perfectly, there is no need to frame your account over-negatively. Your examiners are interested only in how much you have *learned* from anything that went wrong.

Component 3

There are two key evaluations to make, based on the two dimensions of variation amongst knowledge claims (introduced in Chapter 10). They are: your degree of certainty that your study has answered your research questions reliably and adequately; and the extent to which you believe that your findings can be generalized beyond the context in which you operated, to the broader contextual domain covered by your central question, or even beyond this domain.

The certainty that you express in your findings, having provided reliable and adequate answers to your research questions, is a product of the reflections you have just made on your approach and practice. To gain another perspective on the same issues, imagine that someone else is about to do a piece of research that will address the same research questions, using the same framework and approach as you did, and a data source (informants, text or whatever) that meets the same criteria as those that you specified. How certain are you that this new researcher would come up with the same results as you? Asking this question may help you to separate out features in your findings that you feel are robust and likely to be found by anyone, from others that you suspect are a product of some unintentional circumstance.

As regards to generalizability, the issue is the extent to which your findings reflect more general patterns, so that they can be judged representative of the wider domain encompassed by your central question (or even beyond this domain), either directly or at a more abstract level. Bear in mind that one social context is simultaneously like:

- *All other* social contexts (at a high level of abstraction, as where all social situations involve interaction between people – e.g., a school is like all social situations because it entails people who interact with each other).
- *Some other* social contexts (at a more concrete level, any setting shares some features with another setting of the same kind – e.g., different schools all contain learners).

- *No other* social context (at a very concrete level, the combined features of one setting differ from those of any other – e.g., no two schools are identical in all respects, not least because learners and teachers in any school are unique individuals).

Thus, you must assess whether details of your own research context affect the degree of generalization that it is reasonable to make. Examine the wording of your central question and research questions: identify how the narrow context of your research questions potentially maps onto the wider context of the central question, and where aspects of the wider context are most likely to fall outside of anything that your study has explored. You can identify what is a safe limit for your generalization by checking whether there are sufficient significant similarities between your context and these aspects of the wider context for you to generalize convincingly that far. (Or further, depending on the degree of significant similarity between your context, the wider context, and an even wider range of contexts beyond that.)

We discussed in Chapter 10 how, normally, it pays neither to be overconfident about the certainty of your conclusions nor to over-generalize. Modest claims are often the most plausible ones. Authors who admit to limitations in what they did and state that their results *might* indicate something more general, or that there *may* be applications of their findings to new contexts, are often more convincing than those who assert that they have definitely *proved* something of major general significance.

Component 4

The section where you focus on future research, policy and practice is important. Placing it at the end has strategic value, particularly if your investigation has been only partly successful. Since it looks forward, it enables you to end on a positive note, with new ideas. Note that suggestions for future research and recommendations for changes in practice or policy amount to claims about what should be done. To convince your readers that they should accept these claims, very briefly insert warranting for each claim by referring back to your data and to the literature you have previously reviewed.

The end of your conclusion chapter is the end of your narrative, but not the end of your piece of work nor, indeed, the end of the warranting within your overall argument. The reference list is the final point where your critical reading of the literature contributes to convincing your examiners. It enables them to follow up your literature sources, and its accuracy and completeness is indicative of the thoroughness of your investigation. Similarly, any appendices (such as examples of your research instruments) add to the warranting for the claims in your conclusion. So they must also be presented with care.

Applying your critical frame of mind

We have described in detail how specific areas of the literature are integral to developing a strong and coherent overall argument throughout a dissertation, exemplifying how this contribution works in a dissertation that uses the core structure. Other logics and associated structures are possible, and we look at some of them in the next chapter. But any structure has to meet the criteria for assessing the dissertation. So all structures will share some form of critical engagement with relevant literature, both to inform the empirical investigation and to show how the findings relate back to this literature, and maybe have implications for other literatures.

Making effective use of Critical Literature Reviews to support a larger enquiry requires thoughtful initial planning, continual monitoring and regular adjustment as the research process proceeds towards the final written dissertation. The earlier you get focus, start planning the structure of your written account and begin drafting sections of it, the more you take charge and harness the literature for your purposes, so making efficient use of your time. Habitually applying the critical frame of mind that you have been developing throughout your postgraduate studies, both to the literature you critically read and to the account that you self-critically write, will enable you to make this complex undertaking as straightforward as possible.

16

Critical Literature Reviews in Alternative Dissertation Structures

Keywords

exploratory investigation; inductive approach; research themes; warranting unit

This chapter extends our exploration of the contribution that engaging critically with the literature makes to a dissertation involving empirical research. You will recall that the core dissertation structure, detailed in the last chapter, employs a 'one-shot' approach: conducting the Critical Literature Reviews for the entire substantive topic, theoretical orientation and methodology just once, complemented by a Mini-review in the introduction and perhaps in the discussion of findings.

But some dissertations develop their narrative more inductively (e.g., starting with an empirical investigation and developing explanatory theory from it), and a single progression through those steps may not be appropriate. Instead, it is possible to engage with smaller amounts of literature, more frequently, as we will demonstrate. Recall though, that any structure you choose must enable you to develop a convincing overall argument. This means using literature to inform your empirical work, subsequently relating your findings back to the literature, and possibly pointing towards additional literature that could help illuminate the phenomenon further. The approach below is one way of ensuring that your empirical work never gets divorced from the literature on which it depends for strengthening its contribution to your overall argument – whatever your dissertation structure.

Building up the logic of your overall argument within 'multiple-shot' structures

The best way to conceptualize alternative structures to a dissertation is to separate out what happens at the beginning and end of the dissertation (Step 1: Introduction and Step 6: Conclusion) from what happens in the middle (Steps 2–5). It is this middle part, along with the rationale for the study presented in the introduction, that forms the warranting for the conclusion. In a 'multiple-shot' dissertation structure, instead of a single middle section, there are several, connected in some way. We will refer to each of these middle sections as a *warranting unit*. Between them, they link with the introduction to constitute the warranting for the dissertation as a whole. These warranting units can relate to each other in different ways.

In most respects, a warranting unit mirrors the structure of the set of warranting components in the core one-shot dissertation design (see Chapter 15):

- Step 2 – reviewing relevant literature, so as to demonstrate that your empirical focus entails developing significant new knowledge; leading to
- Step 3 – describing the design your investigation; resulting in
- Steps 4 and 5 – presenting and discussing your empirical findings, including their implications for the literature you reviewed earlier and possibly also for other additional literature.

But there are some minor differences, which should strike you as logical as we work through the detail. To see what they are, we simply open up, and modify the details of, the structure that we laid out in Figure 15.1. Where, there, we could infer that each label inside an arrow referred to the dissertation as a whole, now we will explicitly indicate which subsection of the dissertation is addressed within a particular warranting unit.

Figure 16.1 presents the basic, or generic, design of the warranting unit, which essentially acts as the template for the later variations. The introduction to the whole dissertation will have incorporated Step 1, including mention of the focus and content of each warranting unit. This is how you indicate that the content of the unit is directed towards achieving a particular subpart of the substantive, theoretical and methodological aims of the dissertation, with the ultimate capacity to contribute to answering the broad central question.

Steps 2–5 build up the warranting for the claims associated with the specific focus of that warranting unit. There is no Step 6, because that is in the final chapter of the dissertation. However, there is now an interim conclusion at the end of Step 5, which achieves two purposes. First, it reports what has been found out about the specific focus. Second, it points ahead to the next chapter by highlighting the implications of what has been found for the next

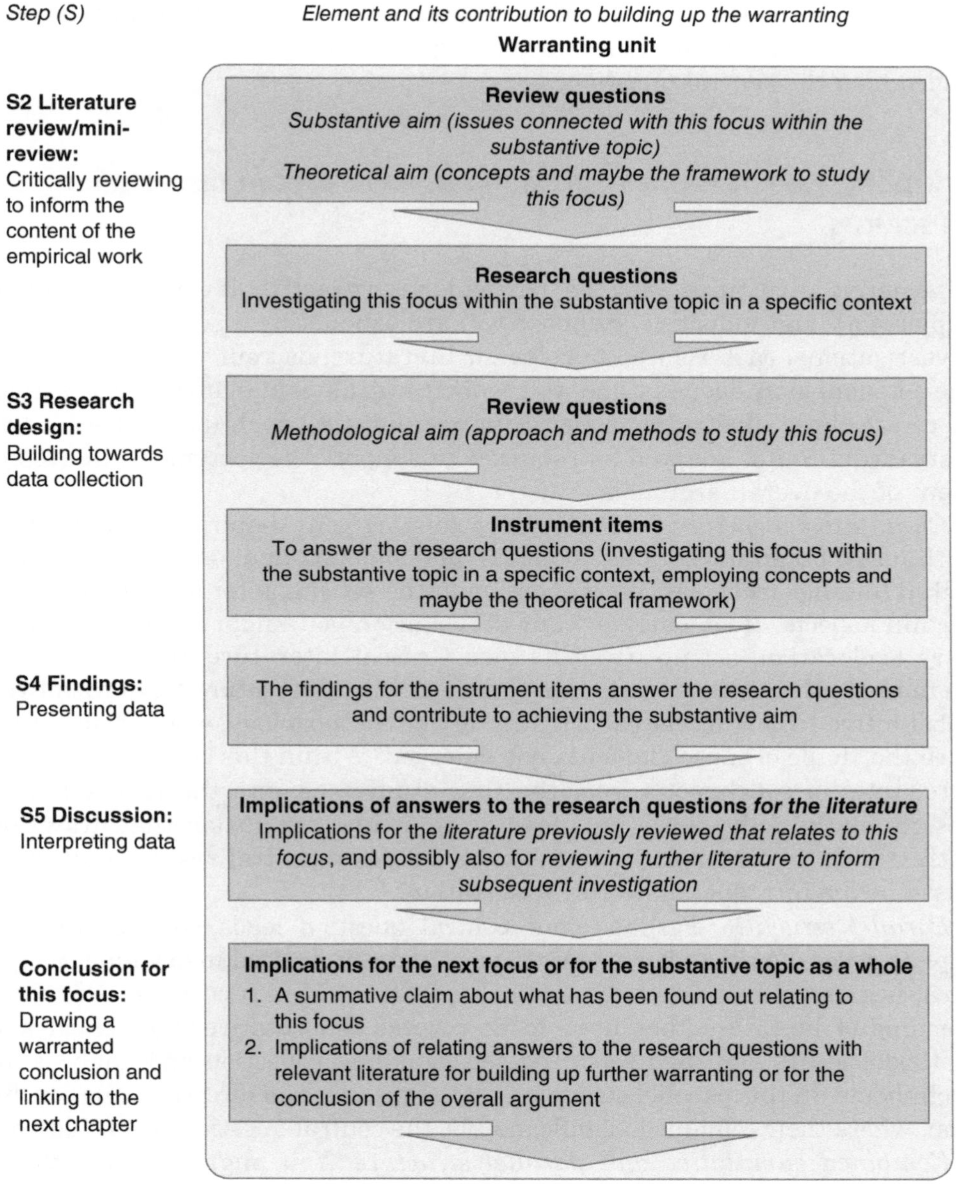

Step (S)
Element and its contribution to building up the warranting
Warranting unit
S2 Literature review/mini-review:
Critically reviewing to inform the content of the empirical work
Review questions
Substantive aim (issues connected with this focus within the substantive topic)
Theoretical aim (concepts and maybe the framework to study this focus)
Research questions
Investigating this focus within the substantive topic in a specific context
S3 Research design:
Building towards data collection
Review questions
Methodological aim (approach and methods to study this focus)
Instrument items
To answer the research questions (investigating this focus within the substantive topic in a specific context, employing concepts and maybe the theoretical framework)
S4 Findings:
Presenting data
The findings for the instrument items answer the research questions and contribute to achieving the substantive aim
S5 Discussion:
Interpreting data
Implications of answers to the research questions for the literature
Implications for the literature previously reviewed that relates to this focus, and possibly also for reviewing further literature to inform subsequent investigation
Conclusion for this focus:
Drawing a warranted conclusion and linking to the next chapter
Implications for the next focus or for the substantive topic as a whole
1. A summative claim about what has been found out relating to this focus
2. Implications of relating answers to the research questions with relevant literature for building up further warranting or for the conclusion of the overall argument

FIGURE 16.1 A basic warranting unit for building up part of the warranting for the overall argument

stages of the account. It may indicate the need to build up further warranting in the context of another element of the substantive topic, or signal the type of contribution being made towards the conclusion of the overall argument at the end of the dissertation. An interim conclusion does not, however, attempt to address the central question of the dissertation. Rather, in the final chapter, all of the warranting units are drawn together to support integrated claims addressing the central question.

Adapting two or more warranting units to create dissertation structures

Alternative structures may be particularly attractive if your research is exploratory and inductive. Suppose you are conducting a series of empirical investigations, each related to relevant literature, as your understanding of the phenomenon deepens and you work towards explanatory theorization. Here are three illustrative structuring possibilities, each using at least two warranting units, adapted as required to support the incremental development of the overall argument.

Cumulative structure. You may need to start your empirical investigation with just a broad initial idea about the phenomenon and, only in the light of initial findings from, say, an immersion in the setting, later focus in depth on certain aspects. If so, early in your dissertation you might report a preliminary exploration, set up using its own Critical Literature Mini-reviews. A more in-depth coverage, with appropriate Critical Literature Reviews for the substantive topic, theoretical orientation and methodology, would come later, once the shape of these elements has emerged. Within this cumulative structure, interim conclusions from the first study feed into the rationale and design for the follow-up study, leading to a final conclusion that draws on both studies to contribute towards answering the central research question posed in the introduction to the dissertation.

Parallel structure. Perhaps your central question leads you naturally to explore several quite independent themes, and you proceed to examine each in turn, beginning each one with Critical Literature Mini-reviews for the three domains of literature that need to be covered (substantive, theoretical and methodological), and then reporting separate data collection and analysis for each theme. In this parallel structure, all the themes lead directly to the conclusion, where their combined significance for the central question is considered.

Combined cumulative and parallel structure. You might begin with an exploratory empirical investigation. From the results you surface several different themes of interest, each of which you pursue independently, bringing the implications of all the themes together in the conclusion.

Figure 16.2 summarizes the three illustrative structures described above. There are plenty of other possibilities. You can build on these ideas to work out a structure for your dissertation that will enable you to develop a convincing overall argument. Your aim in building your dissertation structure around adapted warranting units is always to deploy information from the literature appropriately and sufficiently to meet the assessment criteria employed by your examiners. Let us exemplify in more detail how you could do this through the cumulative, parallel and combined structures.

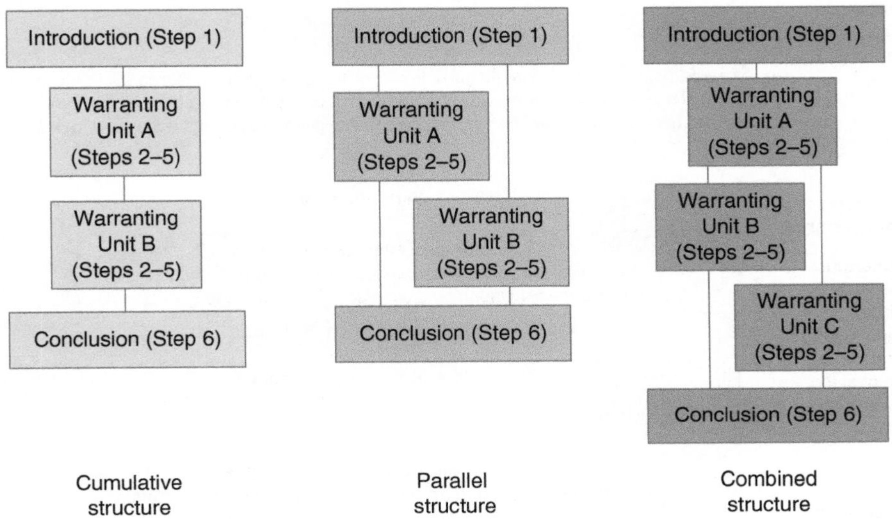

FIGURE 16.2 Location of warranting units in three potential dissertation structures

Creating a cumulative exploratory-main study structure for a dissertation

A typical basis for this structure is when you begin by conducting exploratory empirical research so that you can experience how the substantive topic plays out in particular contexts. This experience, written up entirely within one chapter, sensitizes you to particular substantive, theoretical or methodological issues. It thus informs your decision about which aspects of the topic and setting to study in depth, which theoretical ideas could form the most insightful framework for understanding them, and which methods promise to generate the richest data. The larger main study is divided into several chapters. Figure 16.3a flows into Figure 16.3b, the two together charting the details of this two-stage cumulative structure.

Note how the two adaptations of the basic warranting unit contribute sequentially as complementary 'building blocks' for developing the warranting of the overall argument. Most important for doctoral dissertations: the incremental engagement with the literature (as indicated by *italic* font in Figure 16.3a and Figure 16.3b) enables you to demonstrate that your work has been informed by the literature even at the exploratory stage, and that it does reach beyond what is already known to contribute significant new knowledge about your topic.

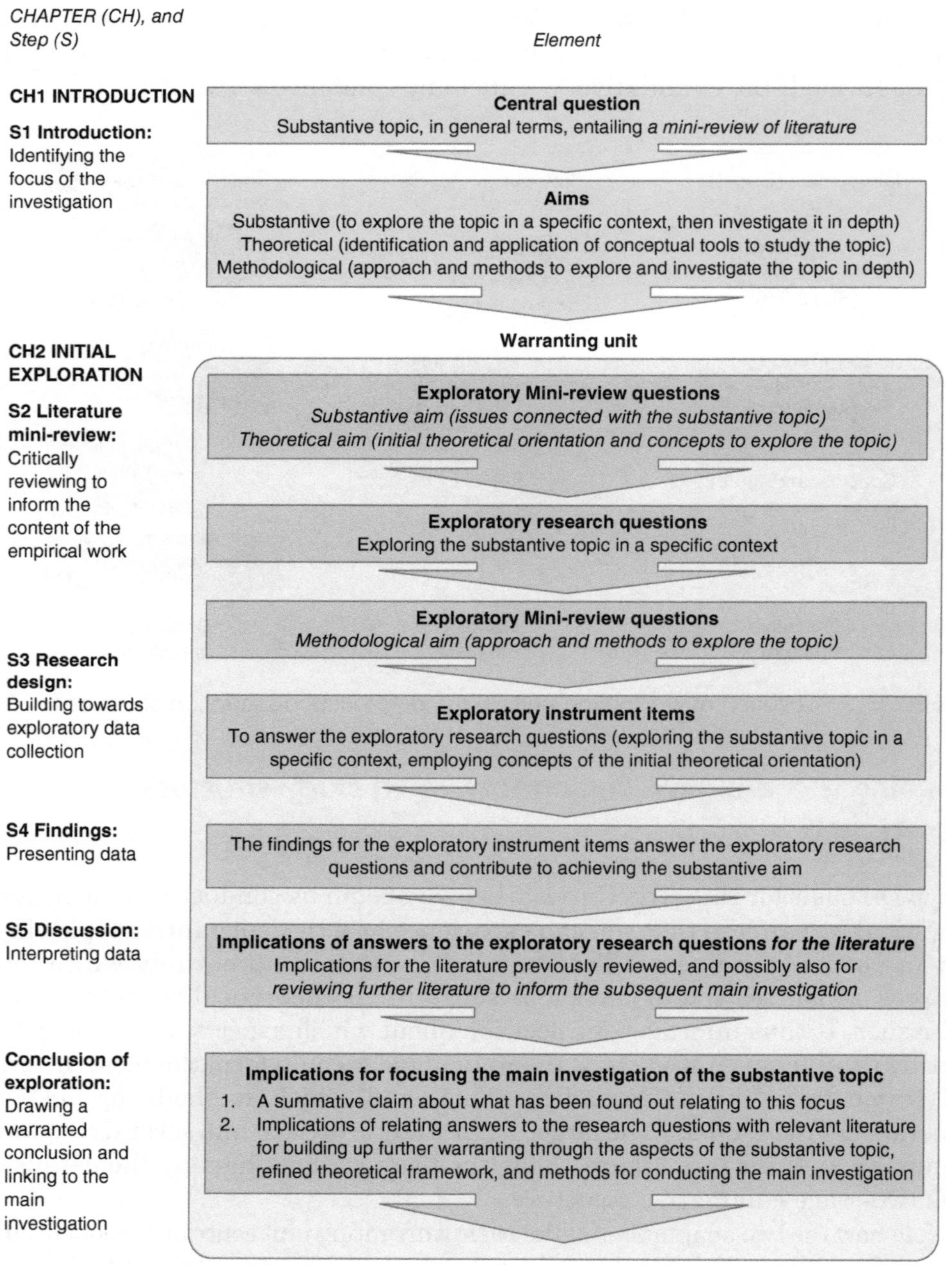

CHAPTER (CH), and Step (S)
Element
CH1 INTRODUCTION
S1 Introduction: Identifying the focus of the investigation
Central question
Substantive topic, in general terms, entailing a mini-review of literature
Aims
Substantive (to explore the topic in a specific context, then investigate it in depth)
Theoretical (identification and application of conceptual tools to study the topic)
Methodological (approach and methods to explore and investigate the topic in depth)
Warranting unit
CH2 INITIAL EXPLORATION
S2 Literature mini-review: Critically reviewing to inform the content of the empirical work
Exploratory Mini-review questions
Substantive aim (issues connected with the substantive topic)
Theoretical aim (initial theoretical orientation and concepts to explore the topic)
Exploratory research questions
Exploring the substantive topic in a specific context
Exploratory Mini-review questions
Methodological aim (approach and methods to explore the topic)
S3 Research design: Building towards exploratory data collection
Exploratory instrument items
To answer the exploratory research questions (exploring the substantive topic in a specific context, employing concepts of the initial theoretical orientation)
S4 Findings: Presenting data
The findings for the exploratory instrument items answer the exploratory research questions and contribute to achieving the substantive aim
S5 Discussion: Interpreting data
Implications of answers to the exploratory research questions for the literature
Implications for the literature previously reviewed, and possibly also for reviewing further literature to inform the subsequent main investigation
Conclusion of exploration: Drawing a warranted conclusion and linking to the main investigation
Implications for focusing the main investigation of the substantive topic
1. A summative claim about what has been found out relating to this focus
2. Implications of relating answers to the research questions with relevant literature for building up further warranting through the aspects of the substantive topic, refined theoretical framework, and methods for conducting the main investigation

FIGURE 16.3A The exploratory stage of a cumulative two-stage dissertation structure

CHAPTER (CH), and Step (S)	*Element* **Warranting unit**
CH3 LITERATURE REVIEW **S2 Literature review:** Critically reviewing to inform the content of the empirical work	**Main investigation review questions** *Substantive aim (selected issues connected with the substantive topic)* *Theoretical aim (refined theoretical framework and concepts to study the topic in depth)*
	Main investigation research questions Investigating selected aspects of the substantive topic in a specific context
CH4 EMPIRICAL STUDY **S3 Research design:** Building towards in-depth data collection	**Main investigation review questions** *Methodological aim (methods to study the topic in depth)*
	Main investigation instrument items To answer the main investigation research questions (exploring selected aspects of the substantive topic in a specific context, employing the refined theoretical framework)
CH5 RESULTS **S4 Findings:** Presenting data	The findings for the exploratory instrument items answer the main investigation research questions and contribute to achieving the substantive aim
CH6 DISCUSSION **S5 Discussion:** Interpreting data Interim conclusion	**Implications of answers to the main investigation research questions *for the literature reviewed*** *(substantive topic)* The impact of the exploratory and main investigation theoretical framework and data collection methods on the findings *with reference to literature previously reviewed, possibly a Mini-review of additional literature*
CH7 CONCLUSION **S6 Conclusion:** Drawing warranted conclusions	1. A summative claim about what has been found out from the initial exploration plus the main investigation that was informed by it 2. How far the findings from the initial exploration plus the main investigation answered the exploratory and main investigation research questions and the substantive aim has been achieved. How far the theoretical aim has been achieved by using the initial theoretical orientation and refined theoretical framework. How far the methodological aim has been achieved through the two-stage design and the data collection instruments. Evaluation of the theoretical framework, research design, the overall success of the investigation, and what has been learned 3. The degree of certainty with which the findings from the specific context can be generalized in contributing to answering the central question 4. Suggestions and recommendations for future research, policy or practice supported by the findings *and the literature*
(References, appendices)	

FIGURE 16.3B The main investigation stage of a cumulative two-stage dissertation structure

Creating a structure for investigating independent themes in a dissertation

Suppose now that your research strategy is to study several distinctive aspects of your substantive topic, perhaps investigating diverse themes that are of equal status, rather than building on each other. Figure 16.4 depicts

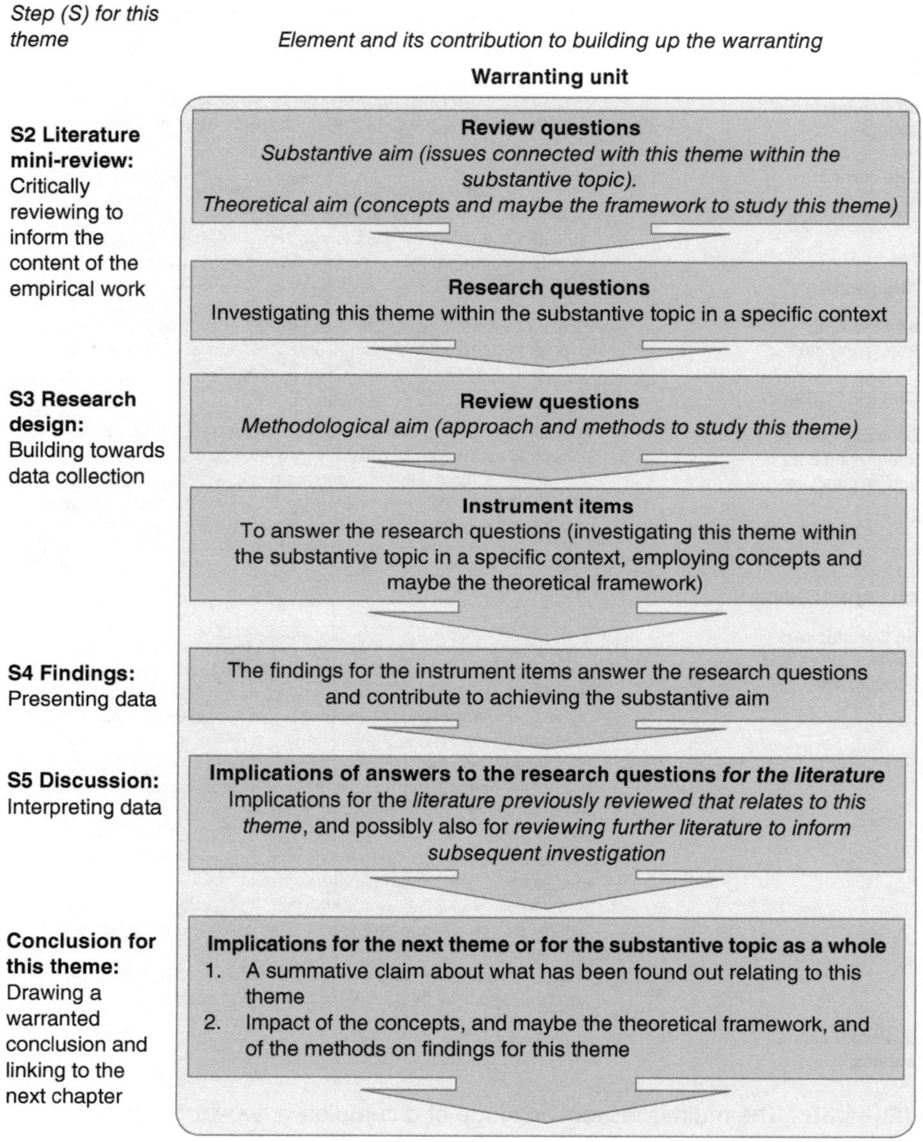

FIGURE 16.4 One of several independent themes in a dissertation structure

the unit for one theme. You will notice how this thematic adaptation closely follows the logic of the basic warranting unit, informing the empirical work focused on the particular theme through a mini-review of the most relevant literature, linking the findings to this and possibly additional literature, and assessing the impact of the theme's conceptual lens and methods on the findings. Figure 16.5 shows how you can incorporate this theme as the first of several independent themes within your structure for the whole dissertation.

CHAPTER (CH) and Step (S)	*Element*
CH1 INTRODUCTION **S1 Introduction:** Identifying the focus of the investigation	**Central question** Substantive topic, in general terms, entailing *a mini-review of literature* ↓ **Aims** Substantive (to investigate four aspects of the topic through themes A, B, C and D) Theoretical (identification and application of conceptual tools to study the four themes) Methodological (approach and methods to explore and investigate the four themes) ↓
CH2 THEME A: S2–5 **CH3 THEME B: S2–5** **CH4 THEME C: S2–5** **CH5 THEME D: S2–5**	**Elements for Theme A** (as detailed in Figure 16.4), then **Theme B, C, D** in turn. Each theme entails a *Mini-review of literature* ↓
CH6 CONCLUSION: Drawing warranted conclusions	• A summative claim about what has been found out from investigating Theme, A, B, C and D • How far the findings from the four thematic investigations answered their respective research questions and the substantive aim has been achieved. How far the theoretical aim has been achieved by using the theoretical framework for each theme within the overall theoretical orientation. How far the methodological aim has been achieved through the design and data collection instruments for each theme. Evaluation of the theoretical orientation, research design, the overall success of the investigation, and what has been learned • The degree of certainty with which the findings from the specific context can be generalized in contributing to answering the central question • Suggestions and recommendations for future research, policy or practice supported by the findings *and the literature*
(References, appendices)	

FIGURE 16.5 Incorporating several independent themes into a dissertation structure

Thus, to build up the warranting of your overall argument, theme by contributing theme, you could repeat this adapted warranting unit for each theme in turn, each one occupying a chapter of the dissertation. The remainder of your dissertation structure would be the introduction, coming before the first theme, and the conclusion, coming after the last. Notice how the introduction features the same elements as in the introduction for the core dissertation structure (Figure 15.2 in the previous chapter) and the cumulative two-stage structure (Figure 16.3a and b above), adapting them where required. Similarly, the conclusion covers the same four components, adapted to fit the thematic approach, as these other structures. So you could think of the introduction and conclusion as adaptable 'units', between which you insert one or more adapted warranting units.

Creating a combined cumulative and parallel dissertation structure

Suppose you undertake an initial exploratory investigation, from which you identify two independent themes. You then investigate each theme empirically, and bring them together in the conclusion. The dissertation structure could comprise:

- the introductory unit for the whole dissertation, heralding the structure to follow (an adaptation of the introduction in Figure 16.3a);
- an exploratory warranting unit, whose conclusion identifies the two independent themes (an adaptation of the exploratory warranting unit in Figure 16.3a);
- a thematic warranting unit, whose conclusion includes implications for the substantive topic as a whole and a link to the next theme (an adaptation of the warranting unit for a single theme in Figure 16.4);
- a second thematic warranting unit, whose conclusion includes implications for the substantive topic as a whole (another adaptation of the warranting unit in Figure 16.4);
- a conclusion unit for the whole dissertation, which includes a summative claim about what has been found out from the exploratory investigation and the subsequent investigation of the two independent themes (an adaptation of the conclusion in Figure 16.5).

Adapting introductory, warranting and conclusion units for your own structure

From these illustrations, you should now have a sense of the potential for creating a range of structures that employ multiple warranting units in different combinations, each contributing towards the warranting of your overall argument. The key requirement across all these structures is to follow the principle of engaging critically with the most relevant literature before and after each piece of empirical work to ensure that the significance and novelty of your findings are fully demonstrated to your examiners.

Our advice can do no more than act as a guide for you to learn-by-doing by structuring your own dissertation, but we can also offer some props to help you along the way. That is the focus of the next chapter.

17

Tools for Structuring a Dissertation

Keywords

abstract; dissertation structure; Dissertation Logic Check Template; Linkage Tracker Test

We offer here three tools to help you with developing an overall argument in both the research process and the written dissertation that reports it. They relate directly to the discussion in the previous two chapters. First, we offer a template that you (and your supervisor) could use to track the developing logic in your overall argument as you plan your investigation and write your dissertation. It is based on the core dissertation structure, but we briefly highlight how it may be adapted for alternative structures. Second, we describe an outline for the core dissertation structure, reflecting the six steps outlined in Chapter 15 for integrating Critical Literature Reviews into the development of an overall argument. Finally, we suggest a way of applying a simple test to your written account, whichever dissertation structure you choose, to check for flaws in the logic of your argument and for any material that may be irrelevant to it.

Checking the logic of your developing argument

Table 17.1 is the Dissertation Logic Check Template for the core structure. It is a means of ensuring that you gain focus early on, so that you build up the logic of your research effort – and hence the written account – as you go along. You and your supervisor can also use it to check that you have not left out any steps in the logic or links between the steps. If you wish to use (or adapt) the template for your dissertation, we recommend that you download the electronic version from the SAGE website: https://study.sagepub.com/wallaceandwray3e. The electronic version is a file in Microsoft Word, in which each cell will expand to fit the amount of text you write. You can edit the file if you want to change the order or content of any template items to suit your dissertation structure.

TABLE 17.1 Tracking the development of your overall argument within a core dissertation structure

Template: Developing a logical argument throughout a dissertation (core structure)

Element of logic	**Content in this dissertation**
Establishing the substantive and theoretical focus and significance, and the methodological approach	
Title (incorporating keywords from the central question)	Title:
1: Introduction	
Central question (a broad problematic issue in the substantive area)	Central question:
Substantive aim (a specified topic within the substantive area, in a particular context)	Substantive aim:
Theoretical aim (the conceptual orientation framing investigation of the substantive topic)	Theoretical aim:
Methodological aim (the methodological stance, design and methods for addressing the substantive topic)	Methodological aim:
Identifying, evaluating and building on the most relevant existing knowledge	
2: Literature Review	
Review questions for the substantive aim (issues related to the substantive topic)	Review question(s), substantive aim:
	In summary, the answer to each review question, substantive aim:
Review questions for the theoretical aim (selecting the theoretical framework, defining concepts)	Review question(s), theoretical aim:
	In summary, the answer to each review question, theoretical aim:

(Continued)

TABLE 17.1 *(Continued)*

Template: Developing a logical argument throughout a dissertation (core structure)

Element of logic	Content in this dissertation
Building towards the sample and focus of the data collection instruments	
3: Research Design	
Review question for the methodological aim (issues relating to the methodology and methods)	Review question(s), methodological aim:
	In summary, the answer to each review question, methodological aim:
Research questions for achieving the substantive aim (informed by answers to the review questions)	Research questions:
Sample: relevant to the substantive aim (sources of empirical evidence to answer the research questions)	Sample (e.g., sites, informants, texts, observations):
	Why this sample is being chosen and how it can contribute to answering the research questions:
Focusing the data collection instruments	
Data collection instruments: relevant to the substantive aim (also reflecting theoretical aim)	Instruments (e.g., online survey, observation schedule):
	Any instruments or raw data to be included in appendices, as supporting evidence of the design:
	In summary, how the items within instruments are designed to obtain answers to specific research questions:
	In summary, how these items employ concepts of the theoretical framework:
Focusing the presentation of the findings	
4: Findings	
Empirical findings: relevant to the substantive aim (order of presentation, linkage with research questions)	In summary, how the presentation of findings is organized (e.g., findings relating to each research question in turn):
	In summary, the way that the presentation of the findings has been organized is signalled to readers:
	In summary, the answer that particular findings give to each research question:

Template: Developing a logical argument throughout a dissertation (core structure)

Element of logic	Content in this dissertation
Focusing the discussion of the findings	
5: Discussion of Findings	
For the substantive aim, theoretical aim (synthesizing findings, implications for the literature demonstrating their significance)	In summary, the contribution that answers to the research questions makes to achieving the substantive aim:
	In summary, implications of answers to the research questions for the substantive, and possibly theoretical, literature reviewed:
	In summary, any implications of answers to the research questions for other relevant literature domains:
Theoretical aim, methodological aim: (how the research approach may affect the findings)	Impact of the strengths and limitations of the theoretical framework on the findings:
	Impact of the strengths and limitations of the methods on the findings:
Articulating and evaluating the contribution of the research to the substantive and theoretical focus	
6: Conclusion	
Knowledge gained	Summative claim stating what knowledge the research has generated about the substantive topic:
Evaluating the achievement of the substantive aim, theoretical aim, methodological aim, success of the research, what was learned	In summary, how far the research questions have been answered and the substantive aim achieved:
	In summary, how far the theoretical aim has been achieved by using the theoretical framework to guide investigation of substantive topic:
	In summary, how far the methodological aim has been achieved through the research design and data collection instruments:
	Overall evaluation of the research, ways in which the design might have been improved:
	Degree of certainty about how far findings from the context investigated can be generalized in contributing to answering the central question:

(Continued)

TABLE 17.1 *(Continued)*

Template: Developing a logical argument throughout a dissertation (core structure)	
Element of logic	**Content in this dissertation**
Implications for research, possibly policy and practice	List of any recommendations for researchers, policy-makers, practitioners supported by evidence from the findings and literature:
Signposting to highlight the logic of the overall argument developed	
1. Is it stated at the end of the introductory chapter how the argument will be developed in other chapters?	
2. Is there an introduction to each of the other chapters indicating what will be covered in each section?	
3. Is it stated at the end of each other chapter (not conclusion) how the overall argument will be taken forward?	
4. Are all references to literature in the text fully and accurately presented in the reference list to enable readers to find them?	
5. Does the labelling of appendices make clear their contribution to the development of the overall argument?	

Reading through the template for the most common dissertation structure, item by item, will give you a sense of how, as also depicted in Figure 15.1, the focus narrows towards the specifics of the research design and then broadens out again as its implications and applications are considered. The logical flow is clear. Establishing the central question and aims enables the literature review questions to be identified. The Critical Literature Reviews can then be focused around answering the review questions, so identifying where the gaps in knowledge are, and, in the methodological Review, helping to determine the best methods and instruments for data collection.

You can treat the template as an electronic 'working document', filling in and revising individual items as you go along. You can use the partially completed template as a prompting device, helping you to keep track of how Critical Literature Reviews or Mini-reviews and all the other parts of your work are making their contribution to the development of your overall argument.

To illustrate how the template can be used as a working document from the outset of dissertation research using the core structure, we provide in Table 17.2 the first few completed items of a template – those that can typically be drafted early on. Our illustration is based on a study that pursues the intellectual project of knowledge-for-action. The substantive topic is how women who work as administrators in British universities might face and overcome barriers to their career progression. The normative purpose is to inform practice in order to improve the extent to which women administrators can achieve their full potential.

TABLE 17.2 Illustration of a part-completed Dissertation Logic Check Template (core structure)

Element of logic	Content in this dissertation
Establishing the substantive and theoretical focus and significance, and the methodological approach	
Title (incorporating keywords from the central question)	Title: *Factors Affecting the Aspirations to Senior Administrative Responsibility, and the Strategies for Career Progression, of Women Administrators in British Universities.*
1: Introduction	
Central question (a broad problematic issue in the substantive area)	Central question: *What barriers may inhibit women administrators in universities from aspiring to, and progressing in their career towards, achieving a senior administrative position, and how may these barriers be overcome?*
Substantive aim (a specified topic within the substantive area, in a particular context)	Substantive aim: *To investigate facilitating factors and ways in which they supported the career progression strategies of women who have overcome any barriers to achieving senior administrative positions in British universities.*
Theoretical aim (the conceptual orientation framing investigation of the substantive topic)	Theoretical aim: *To develop a framework focusing on the interaction between facilitating factors, associated mechanisms of operation, and career progression strategies identified in the literature on professional women's careers, and apply it to map the experiences of women who are senior administrators in British universities.*
Methodological aim (the methodological stance, design and methods for addressing the substantive topic)	Methodological aim: *To employ a social constructionist approach for the design of a small-scale qualitative investigation which will gather, through interviews, the perceptions of female senior administrators in British universities about the contribution of facilitating factors on their career progression strategies that enabled them to overcome any barriers to achieving these positions.*

(Continued)

TABLE 17.2 *(Continued)*

Element of logic	Content in this dissertation
Identifying, evaluating and building on the most relevant existing knowledge	
2: Literature Review	
Review questions for the substantive aim (issues related to the substantive topic)	Review question(s), substantive aim: 1. *What does the literature reviewed suggest is the range of strategies for career progression adopted by women who aspire to become senior administrators or managers in general, and in the education sector in particular?* 2. *What does the literature reviewed suggest are the facilitatory factors that support women's aspirations to become senior administrators or managers, and how do these factors support their career progression strategies, including overcoming any barriers they face in achieving these aspirations?* 3. *To what extent are these factors and strategies applicable to the aspirations and career progression of women administrators in British universities?*
	In summary, the answer to each review question, substantive aim
Review questions for the theoretical aim (selecting the theoretical framework, defining concepts)	Review question(s), theoretical aim: 1. *What conceptualizations have been employed to characterize women's professional career progression strategies, and to characterize factors and their mechanisms of operation that facilitate women's career progression towards senior administrative or management positions?*
	In summary, the answer to each review question, theoretical aim
Building towards the sample and focus of the data collection instruments	
3: Research Design	
Review question for the methodological aim (issues relating to the methodology and methods)	Review question(s), methodological aim: 1. *What are the strengths and limitations of interviewing as a method for gathering data on informants' perceptions?*
	In summary, the answer to each review question, methodological aim

The items completed at the start ensure that the Critical Literature Reviews have manageable foci flowing directly from the central question and aims, and that the answers to the review questions can inform the design of the empirical work. Once the first drafts of the literature reviews are done, a summary answer to each review question can be inserted, informing the development of the research design, and so on.

Adapting the Template for alternative structures

The Dissertation Logic Check Template is just a device for helping you structure your thinking. Its power lies in prompting you to justify the reasoning for your many decisions as you conduct and write up your dissertation research. The Template is readily adaptable for alternative dissertation structures, since the items it contains simply make up the logic for the development of the overall argument within any structure.

The ideas we offered in the previous chapter for creating alternative dissertation structures were built round adaptations of the basic warranting unit. Our aim was to ensure that any specific empirical focus is informed by relevant literature and implications of the findings are related to the literature to demonstrate their significance and any implications for other foci. In Table 17.3 we have adapted the Logic Check Template to the shape of the basic warranting unit, so that it can be easily adapted and incorporated in alternative dissertation structures. You can download the electronic version from the SAGE website: https://study.sagepub.com/wallaceandwray3e. Then, to suit your alternative dissertation structure, you can paste the content into your own Logic Check structure, edit the entries, and so forth. It fits into the flow of the Logic Check in the same way as adapting the basic warranting unit and inserting it into the flow of the dissertation structure, discussed in Chapter 16.

TABLE 17.3 Illustrative adaptation of the basic warranting unit for incorporating into a Logic Check

Template: Developing a logical argument in steps (S) in a dissertation (warranting unit)

Identifying, evaluating and building on the most relevant existing knowledge	
S2: Literature Review (this focus)	
Review questions for the substantive aim (issues related to this focus within the substantive topic)	Review question(s), substantive aim:
	In summary, the answer to each review question, substantive aim:
Review questions for the theoretical aim (concepts and maybe the framework to study this focus)	Review question(s), theoretical aim:
	In summary, the answer to each review question, theoretical aim:

(Continued)

TABLE 17.3 *(Continued)*

Template: Developing a logical argument in steps (S) in a dissertation (warranting unit)

Building towards the sample and focus of the data collection instruments	
S3: Research Design (this focus)	
Review questions for the methodological aim (issues relating to the methodology and methods for this focus)	Review question(s), methodological aim:
	In summary, the answer to each review question, methodological aim:
Research questions for this focus within the substantive aim (informed by answers to the review questions)	Research questions:
Sample: relevant to this focus within the substantive aim (sources of empirical evidence to answer the research questions)	Sample (e.g., sites, informants, texts, observations):
	Why this sample is being chosen and how it can contribute to answering the research questions:
Focusing the data collection instruments	
Data collection instruments: relevant to this focus within the substantive aim (also reflecting the theoretical aim)	Instruments (e.g., online survey, observation schedule):
	Any instruments or raw data to be included in appendices, as supporting evidence of the design for this focus:
	In summary, how the items within instruments are designed to obtain answers to specific research questions:
	In summary, how these items employ the concepts of the theoretical framework:
Focusing the presentation of the findings	
S4: Findings (this focus)	
Empirical findings relevant to this focus within the substantive aim (order of presentation, linkage with research questions)	In summary, how the presentation of the findings is organized (e.g., findings relating to each research question in turn):
	In summary, the way the presentation of the findings has been organized is signalled to readers:
	In summary, the answer that particular findings give to each research question:

Template: Developing a logical argument in steps (S) in a dissertation (warranting unit)

Focusing the discussion of the findings	
S5: Discussion of Findings (this focus)	
For the substantive aim, theoretical aim as relevant to this focus: (synthesizing findings, implications for the literature demonstrating their significance)	In summary, contribution that answers to the research questions make to achieving the substantive aim:
	In summary, implications of answers to the research questions for the substantive, and possibly theoretical, literature reviewed:
	In summary, any implications of answers to the research questions for other relevant literature domains:
Theoretical aim, methodological aim, as relevant to this focus (how the research approach may affect the findings)	Impact of the strengths and limitations of theoretical framework on the findings:
	Impact of the strengths and limitations of the methods on the findings:
Articulating and evaluating the contribution of the research to the substantive and theoretical focus	
Conclusion (this focus, linking to the next chapter)	
For this focus: knowledge gained	Summative claim stating what knowledge the research has generated about this focus within the substantive topic
	In summary, how far the research questions for this focus have been answered and a contribution to the substantive aim achieved
Implications for the next focus or conclusion chapter	How the findings for this focus and their implications for literature inform the next focus or contribute to the conclusion of the overall argument

In the cumulative two-stage dissertation structure that we depicted in Figures 16.3a and b, you could use both the full Dissertation Logic Check Template (core structure) (in Table 17.1 above) for the dissertation as a whole, and the warranting unit version (Table 17.3) for the exploratory study that is embedded in its Chapter 2 (Figure 16.3a). The focus for the inserted template could read 'initial exploration'. In this way, the results of the initial exploration would feed into the logic of the main study. The same approach could be used for other structures, as with the separate investigation of multiple independent themes (see Figure 16.5).

Outline of the core structure for a dissertation

While stressing the potential for structuring a dissertation in different ways, our main focus throughout Part Three is on the 'one-shot' core structure, introduced in Chapter 15 and forming the basis of our template in Table 17.1. We offer here a detailed outline of the content for each part of the written account within this structure, indicating the likely location of the main text components. We highlight in *italic* script the various places where Critical Literature Reviews may be located or referred back to. (You should, of course, also check the regulations of your institution for indications of what must be included and where.)

Title

- Containing keywords that reflect the central question you are seeking to answer, expressed in general terms.

Abstract

- A brief summary (around 200 words) of the purpose of the study, empirical work and your conclusions (see the section later in this chapter for guidance on how to write the abstract).

Acknowledgements

- Any acknowledgement you wish to make of the support of individuals (e.g., your supervisor, your family) and of the cooperation of informants.

Chapter 1: Introduction

- A statement of purpose – to contribute to answering a central question expressed in general terms, typically about a substantive topic in your field of enquiry.
- A statement of the more specific aims of your research – substantive, theoretical and methodological.
- A justification of the significance of the central question, *with brief reference to relevant literature.*
- A statement of your value position in relation to this topic, as it shapes the focus of your enquiry.
- A summary of the broad issues (or problems) that will need to be addressed in order to achieve your three aims (above), *giving brief reference to relevant literature*:
  - substantive (indicating why it may not be straightforward to decide which aspects of the substantive topic identified in the central question should be investigated in detail);

  - theoretical (indicating why the choice of theoretical framework may not be straightforward);
  - methodological (indicating why the choice of methodology and methods may not be straightforward).
- A brief description of the context of your enquiry. If you are investigating practice in a country other than the one in which you are studying, you may wish to outline the national context as it relates to your central question, possibly with *reference to relevant literature*. Doing this will familiarize your examiners with the context and enable them to appreciate any significant differences between this context and those which they know well.
- A brief final section in which you outline the rest of the study – signposting the content of the remaining chapters, and how these chapters develop your argument about the contribution your investigation makes to answering your central question.

Chapter 2: Literature Review

- A chapter introduction signposting what will be covered in each section.
- *A Critical Literature Review addressing review questions relating to your substantive aim and associated issues*, leading to a summary conclusion of your position, as determined by the answers you obtained.
- *A Critical Literature Review addressing a review question (or questions) relating to your theoretical aim and associated issues*, leading to a summary conclusion about the nature of the framework that you will need to guide your empirical investigation (and whether you will be adopting or adapting an existing framework, or developing your own).
- A brief chapter conclusion in which you identify one or more detailed research questions (alternatively expressed as hypotheses to be tested) in the light of the answers obtained to your review questions.
- A signpost stating how the Research Design chapter will take the next step towards seeking answers to your research questions.

Chapter 3: Research Design

- A chapter introduction setting out what you are going to cover in each section, indicating how you will employ your theoretical framework to address the research questions through your research design.
- The theoretical framework that you are using to help you understand and analyse the substantive topic relating to your central question.
- *A Critical Literature Review of the literature addressing a review question (or questions) relating to your methodological aim and associated issues*, considering how other researchers have approached these issues and have investigated similar substantive topics, leading to a summary conclusion of your position, as determined by the answers you obtained.
- An account of your methodology and methods, including as appropriate:
  - a justification for the methodological paradigm within which you are working;
  - your detailed methods of data collection and your justification for using them;
  - specification of the sample of informants and your rationale for selecting them from the wider population;

  - a summary description of your data collection instruments indicating how research questions (or hypotheses) about the substantive topic are addressed, and your rationale for using the instruments chosen;
  - a summary of the data collection effort (e.g., piloting, the number of interviews or the number of individuals surveyed);
  - a summary of how the data are to be analysed (e.g., statistical methods, use of matrices for qualitative data);
  - ethical factors taken into account, and how (e.g., confidentiality of interviews);
  - the timetable for the research process (e.g., timing of first and second rounds of interviews).
- A chapter conclusion reflecting on the strengths and limitations of your design (e.g., reliability, internal and external validity, sample size relative to population size), and indicating that you will evaluate the design in the concluding chapter in the light of your experience with implementing it.
- A signpost stating how the findings chapter will present the result of implementing this design as the means of answering your research questions.

Chapter 4: Findings

- A chapter introduction where you set out the ground to be covered in each section.
- A summary of all the findings, as relevant to answering each research question (or hypothesis) in turn, possibly supported by tables and matrices, diagrams and quotations from informants.
- A concluding summary of key findings and emerging issues or themes that you have identified.
- A signpost stating how these issues or themes will be taken up in the discussion chapter.

Chapter 5: Discussion

- A chapter introduction, setting out the ground to be covered in each section.
- A discussion of your findings and the answers they give to your research questions, including the implications *for the literature on the substantive topic that you critically reviewed earlier.*
- A brief reflection on how your theoretical framework may have impacted on the findings, *referring to theoretical literature you critically reviewed earlier.*
- A brief reflection on how your choice of data collection methods may have impacted on the findings, *referring to methodological literature you critically reviewed earlier.*
- As appropriate, a discussion of the implications of your findings *for other relevant literature domains.*
- A chapter conclusion summarizing how the findings support or challenge what other authors have reported in the literature on the substantive topic and your evaluation of the possible impact of your theoretical framework and data collection methods on what you found (and possibly did not find because you did not look for it).
- A signpost stating how you will draw conclusions about the contribution of your findings to answering your central question in the Conclusion chapter.

Chapter 6: Conclusion

- A chapter introduction where you set out the ground to be covered in each section.
- A summative claim about the answers obtained to your research questions and how they relate to the literature, *referring back briefly to your Critical Literature Reviews.*
- Self-critical reflections on the extent to which you have achieved your substantive, theoretical and methodological aims, limitations of your work that you have identified, what you have learned from the experience of researching and how the research design could have been improved.
- An evaluation of the extent to which the answers to your research questions contribute to answering your central question, in terms of both the degree of certainty and generalizability.
- A look towards the future, to consider what subsequent research might usefully focus on, and (if appropriate) how your own investigation might inform practice or policy. Any recommendations should be backed by very brief reference to your evidence and *literature on the substantive topic.*
- A final statement asserting, in summary, the contribution of your study to answering the central question posed in the introductory chapter and reflected in the title of the dissertation.

Reference List

- Should contain all works to which reference is made in the text, but not background material to which you have not made direct reference.
- Is presented in author alphabetical order and in the required format.

Appendices

- For example, research instruments, letters to informants, examples of raw data.
- Labelled in a way that helps the reader identify the material and relate it to one or more particular locations in the main text (where there should be reference directly to it).

Adapting the structure

Although our outline has six chapters, labelled according to their function, your dissertation could have more, or fewer, as appropriate for the story you wish to tell and the way you structure the account; and you can give them content-related titles, rather than functional ones, if you wish. In all cases, simply ensure that each chapter makes its distinctive contribution to the developing logic of your overall argument, with its own chapter introduction, chapter conclusion and signposting. Where research is composed of several independent data sets (or substantially different analyses of the same data set), as with a thematic investigation, each one may need to be justified and reported

(Continued)

(Continued)

separately. This can be achieved by repeating the structure for the Chapters 3 to 5 in the outline above for successive (sets of) research questions. Such repetition will work best if either each set of research questions derives from the answers to the previous set, or each new account picks up on one of an original set of research questions identified at the end of the Chapter 2 in the outline. If necessary, the Chapter 2 itself can also be part of the repeated process, so that more than one Critical Literature Review is presented, as appropriate to the changing focus of the progressing investigation.

Tracking the logical flow of your overall argument

The structure outlined above provides a framework that encourages you to develop a logical overall argument through your dissertation, ensuring that the structure you have chosen helps you to meet the dissertation assessment criteria as fully as possible. Every part of a defensible account of empirical research should link logically together, from the title, with its keywords indicating the focus of the study, through to the reference list and any appendices. The 'Linkage Tracker Test' (below) prompts you to look for these links in your written text and to detect any gaps. It is worth applying the Test to everything you draft as you go through the research process, and also to the complete draft of the dissertation, as you prepare it for submission.

The 'Linkage Tracker Test' to check the developing logic of your overall argument

The Linkage Tracker Test assesses the relevance of any piece of your text to the story you are telling. How well do all the parts of the written account of your investigation link together? As critical readers of your work, supervisors and examiners are likely to notice any digressions and any claims that have not been adequately backed up. To apply the Linkage Tracker Test to your draft written work, select any piece of the text (this includes tables, figures, references and appendices). Then ask yourself two questions:

1. Why is this material here?
2. How does this material contribute to the development of my overall argument?

The answers should be clear to you and to your reader. If not, how can you make them so? Is the material in the right place? Would removing it help you to sustain a tighter focus?

Constructing an effective abstract for your dissertation

Although your examiners are obliged to read your entire dissertation, no one else is. So if you want others to engage with your work, you need to signal why it would be worth their while. It is the abstract that will best 'sell' your research. It is a snapshot that can draw in, or put off, potential readers. Since a dissertation is a long text, the abstract is usually not quite as short as the equivalent for a published paper. But it is going to be few words to capture everything you have said in the complete account. You need a clear structure to construct an effective abstract. In particular, it is important to recognize the difference in both form and function between an abstract and an introduction. The latter only sets the scene. The former has a great deal more work to do.

The structure we recommend reflects the approach in this book. As an abstract writer, you need to put yourself in the position of your potential readers, understanding what would motivate them to look at your abstract, and what would help them decide whether to read the full dissertation. Accordingly, we recommend that you adopt a logical flow, as laid out in Table 17.4. This way, you ensure you cover all the important information, and you have control over how you use your word allowance. You can easily see if one aspect of your

TABLE 17.4 Logical flow for composing the dissertation abstract

Focus question	Orientation of your text
Why might someone want to read this?	Make clear in the first sentence what topic and issues you are addressing. Maybe begin with 'The central question addressed is …'.
Why is this an important question to ask?	Locate your work within the existing research literature – very succinctly. The reader needs only a sense of what sort of previous research is relevant to understanding yours, e.g. 'With particular reference to the critical discourse theory of Fairclough and Wodak, …'; or 'Answering this question entails revisiting March and Olsen's (1976) *garbage can* model of decision-making, in the light of 21st century management models …'. Keep in mind that your abstract may be read in isolation, by people who do not have access to the bibliography. Nevertheless, it is worth giving the date of a key landmark text, particularly if likely to be familiar to readers.
What do they need to know about my aims in writing it?	Indicate your intellectual project – that is, what motivates your investigation (see Chapter 9). For example, you might write: 'The study is motivated by the need for improvement in …'; or 'Developing new insights into this phenomenon will shed light on …'; or 'The purpose of the study was to test training materials for …'.

(Continued)

TABLE 17.4 *(Continued)*

Focus question	Orientation of your text
What did I do?	Provide the core elements of the method and the main findings. You do not have to give all the detail. Keep the account organized, remembering its purpose in giving the reader a clear impression of what you did, e.g., 'Interviews were conducted with …'; 'Using a series of experiments that measured …'; 'Texts were gathered from … and analysed for …'.
What are my main claims?	There is only space for your *main* claims and not for much background or justification. If readers want to know how you came to draw these conclusions, or how reliable they are, they will need to look at the full text. Your job here is to give the headlines only, e.g., 'Overall, nurses were more likely than doctors to attribute low performance to under-resourcing, while doctors blamed poor management'.
How might readers find this useful?	Indicate the potential for generalization beyond your own study. Your readers are interested in how your work might inform their own world of investigation. For example, 'It can be inferred from these results, that all teenagers from ethnic minority groups are …'; or 'It remains unclear whether these findings would hold for other populations of care home residents because …'.

account is getting too big. In particular, this structure will help you avoid using up words with an unnecessary introductory passage, or too much fine detail about aspects of your study design.

In Chapter 18 you can find some brief comments on writing abstracts for other purposes, particularly a conference, since the requirements are somewhat different.

The structured dissertation as a foundation for your next steps

Your dissertation is destined for assessment, but you may also share your research in other forums. For many postgraduates a significant event is the viva voce, oral examination or public defence, in which your examiners ask probing questions about the work. As sceptical but fair critical readers, your examiners want to be in a position to pass your dissertation. The structured approach to reading and writing that we have introduced in this book offers you more than just a logically organized, soundly argued account that locates your research effectively within the broader research literature.

It also provides you with clarity about what you did and why, and what the opportunities and risks were of the approach you took. This sort of insightful understanding of your own work is vital for convincing examiners in an oral examination that you are capable of crossing the boundary into professional academic research.

Meanwhile, it is likely that you will be presenting accounts of your research at conferences and in journal articles. While the fundamental principles are the same, there are differences in how you must organize your material and present your knowledge of the research literature in these other contexts. We offer some guidance in the final chapter.

18

Using the Literature in Research Papers and Oral Presentations

Keywords

abstracts; academic career; conference presentations; journal articles; oral presentations; research papers

At some point you may want to write about your research for an academic journal or present it at an external conference. We concentrate in this chapter on presenting to the wider scholarly community, but what we say also applies to reports and presentations prepared for your progression and assessment as a student.

It is clearly impossible to condense a dissertation-sized project into an 8,000-word paper or 20 minute oral presentation. Working out what to include and what to leave out derives from developing your sense of audience, a core element in self-critical writing. While your dissertation itself may be read by other scholars, you stand to inform, and perhaps influence, many more academics and students by getting your work published and by presenting it at conferences.

Most members of this wider audience will be unknown to you. Yet you need to develop a sense of their needs and expectations. They are likely to expect a concise presentation of your argument, either about your dissertation as a whole, or some part of it (for example, a thematic account of certain findings). They will want a few 'take-home' messages in your conclusion. The literature you have critically read will underpin the warranting for the claims made in your conclusion. Your task in structuring your article or presentation is therefore to build a focused account, developing a convincing argument within the space or time allowed.

Developing your overall argument in a written research article

You might wish to write an academic journal article reporting your empirical investigation, your literature review, or a related theoretical or methodological issue. In all cases, reference to the academic literature will have to be briefer than in the dissertation, and must be tightly focused on the precise purpose of the paper. You cannot simply use a chunk of review from your dissertation without reworking it.

The logic of the overall argument in an academic journal article

The *logic* of the overall argument in a data-based journal article (Figure 18.1) is also the mechanism for working out the structure of your paper. As with Figure 15.2, the Critical Literature Review components are italicized. A comparison of Figures 15.2 and 18.1 shows how selective the shorter report is. Key features of the logic in Figure 18.1 include:

- Your central question may or may not be the same as that for your dissertation. Choose the question that best equips you as the writer, and therefore your readers, to maintain a clear focus and structure for the paper in its own right. It is enough to tell the reader that your report reflects a small part of something bigger.
- In this example, the aims are substantive: they relate to what was done and found out, rather than to the theoretical context or the methodology (as would be appropriate for a theoretical or methodological paper).
- The Review Questions section is the main place where you provide your critical evaluation of the literature. We have restricted the coverage to the substantive area. You must decide which questions to cover, and which literature to refer to. These questions need not be identical to those in your dissertation, nor need the coverage of literature be as broad. Go for what is appropriate for this paper.
- Whereas in the full dissertation there are separate Critical Literature Reviews that engage with theory and methodology, there is not space for them in a shorter report (unless it is focused on them directly). It is normally enough to state what theoretical framework and methodology you adopted, with brief references to the literature to demonstrate the origins of those ideas.
- The details of the research instruments are in brackets in our structure because space limits what you can include. Options include putting these details in an appendix, if space permits, or giving a brief description with one or two examples. Consider what the reader minimally needs, for understanding how you focused your data collection.

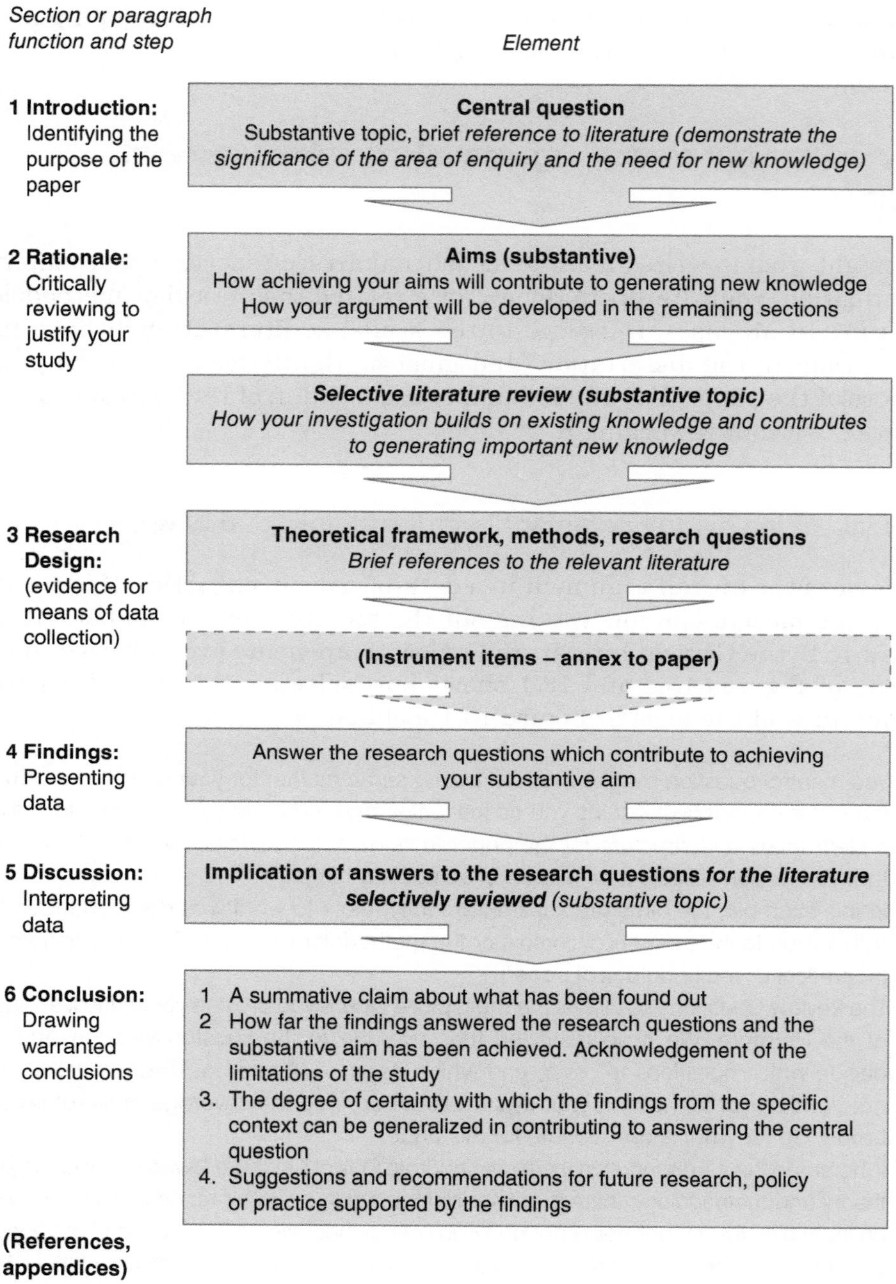

Section or paragraph function and step
Element
1 Introduction: Identifying the purpose of the paper
Central question
Substantive topic, brief reference to literature (demonstrate the significance of the area of enquiry and the need for new knowledge)
2 Rationale: Critically reviewing to justify your study
Aims (substantive)
How achieving your aims will contribute to generating new knowledge
How your argument will be developed in the remaining sections
Selective literature review (substantive topic)
How your investigation builds on existing knowledge and contributes to generating important new knowledge
3 Research Design: (evidence for means of data collection)
Theoretical framework, methods, research questions
Brief references to the relevant literature
(Instrument items – annex to paper)
4 Findings: Presenting data
Answer the research questions which contribute to achieving your substantive aim
5 Discussion: Interpreting data
Implication of answers to the research questions for the literature selectively reviewed (substantive topic)
6 Conclusion: Drawing warranted conclusions
1 A summative claim about what has been found out
2 How far the findings answered the research questions and the substantive aim has been achieved. Acknowledgement of the limitations of the study
3. The degree of certainty with which the findings from the specific context can be generalized in contributing to answering the central question
4. Suggestions and recommendations for future research, policy or practice supported by the findings
(References, appendices)

FIGURE 18.1 The logic of the overall argument in a paper reporting your research

- As with the dissertation, the final components of the structure provide answers to the questions raised earlier. First, the Research Questions driving the investigation are answered, and then the answers to those questions are related back to the literature that was reviewed, to show how your work has contributed to resolving issues you identified in your critical evaluations. Keep tightly focused on just the questions addressed in this report.
- The purpose of the Conclusion is to give the reader take-home messages about what you have achieved in the research. Use a clear structure that relates to the sequence of issues covered.

Incorporating literature into the written structure of an academic journal article

Here is our recommended outline for structuring a paper reporting your research. As with the dissertation, it follows the logical structure but it is not identical. Again, we indicate in *italic* script where you may wish to incorporate selected literature in support of your overall argument. We have also suggested the minimum and maximum number of words to aim for in the main sections in a paper which totals around 8,000 words including references and any appendices. You may wish to give the sections different titles. But do include them all, so you maintain the basis for developing every component of your overall argument. This outline is very adaptable (e.g., you might wish to combine the findings and discussion sections).

Title

- Containing keywords that reflect the central question you are seeking to answer, expressed in general terms.

Abstract

- Brief summary of the content of the paper and your argument (around 100 words). (See later for a note on writing the abstract.)

Introduction (500–1,000 words)

- Statement of purpose – to contribute to answering a central question about a substantive topic in your field of enquiry.
- Justification of the significance of your area of enquiry and identification of a significant need for new knowledge which your research will help to address, *with very brief reference to the most relevant literature.*

- Statement of your value position in relation to this topic, in so far as it shapes the research to be reported.
- Statement of the relevant substantive aims of your research.
- Signpost indicating how, in the remaining sections of the paper, you will develop your argument to contribute towards answering the central question.

Literature Review (1,000–2,000 words)

- *A highly selective review of relevant literature relating to your substantive topic to demonstrate what is already known about it, the limits of what is known, and how your investigation will build on what is known and extend its limits by generating new important knowledge.*

Research Design and Methods (500–1,000 words)

- The theoretical orientation or framework for helping you understand and analyse the substantive topic relating to your central question, *with very brief reference to the most relevant literature.*
- An account of your methodology and methods, *with very brief reference to the most relevant literature*, including as appropriate:
  - a justification for your methodological approach;
  - methods of data collection and your justification for using them;
  - specification of the sample of informants and your rationale for selecting them from the wider population;
  - a short note on your data collection instruments indicating how research questions (or hypotheses) about the substantive topic are addressed (and signposting that one or more of the instruments are in an appendix at the end of the paper, if that is the case);
  - a summary of the data collection effort (e.g., piloting, the number of interviews or the number of individuals surveyed);
  - a summary of how the data were analysed (e.g., statistical methods, use of matrices for qualitative data);
  - any ethical factors taken into account, and how (e.g., confidentiality of interviews);
  - the timetable for the research process (e.g., timing of first and second rounds of interviews).

Findings (1,500–2,500 words)

- A summary of your relevant findings for each research question in turn, possibly supported by tables and matrices, diagrams and quotations from informants.

Discussion (1,000–2,000 words)

- A discussion of your findings and any emerging issues, indicating the answers they give to your research questions, including the implications *for the literature on the substantive topic that you critically reviewed earlier.*

Conclusion (500–1,500 words)

- A summative claim about the answers obtained to your research questions and how they contribute significant new knowledge, *referring back very briefly to the selected literature you critically reviewed earlier.*
- Self-critical reflection on the limitations of your study, including the extent to which you have achieved your substantive aims.
- An evaluation of the extent to which the answers to your research questions contribute to answering your central question, in terms of both the degree of certainty and generalizability.
- A look towards the future, to consider what subsequent research and associated theorizing might usefully focus upon, and (if appropriate) how your investigation might inform practice or policy. Any recommendations should be backed by very brief reference to your evidence and *the most relevant literature on the substantive topic.*

References

- Containing all and only works to which reference is made in the text.
- Presented in author alphabetical order and in the required format.

(Appendix)

- An option for including one or more instruments for data collection in order to provide evidence of how you attempted to answer your research questions.

Developing your overall argument in an oral presentation

Although oral presentations are sometimes prepared independently of a written paper, often there is an associated written version. We certainly do not advocate preparing a written paper and reading it out (this is not an effective approach to oral presentations). However, you will find it helpful to draw on the logic of a written paper (see Figure 18.1) when preparing an oral presentation. This will facilitate writing up the paper for publication, such as in a volume of conference proceedings. More generally, the underlying logic of a written paper helps anchor an oral presentation, where there is not time to give all components a full airing.

When we listen to someone talk about their research, we do not have the same needs and priorities as when we read about it.

- Readers can revisit difficult ideas, slow down and speed up their intake, skim over information they already know, and stop to think about new ideas and look up words and concepts. Listeners cannot, so the speaker must judge how fast to introduce and develop ideas, and which terms to explain, and must build in opportunities for listeners to take in new ideas and their potential implications.
- Readers often navigate a text in a non-linear order, checking how something said in one place relates to things said later or earlier. Listeners are reliant on the speaker providing signposts about the overall structure of the paper and how the components relate to each other.

In short, a successful oral presenter understands the needs and expectations of the particular audience. It is worth some thought and checking who is likely to attend and how much they might know about your topic.

Regarding the research literature, we saw above that readers of a research report expect to see a substantive critical account of the existing literature, including a reference list, as a contextualization for and justification of the claims being made. However, the complexity of critical accounts of the literature can create a problem for listeners. Furthermore, at conferences dedicated to a particular topic, most listeners will be familiar with the literature, and they would rather hear what is new, than what they already know.

This is a situation in which the twin skills of *critical reading* and *self-critical writing* (or in this case *self-critical preparation for speaking*) work very well together. Your audience will most appreciate a very concise, focused presentation of one or two key issues arising from the literature that reflect your critical thinking and show how it has inspired your own research. So *inspire and interest* them by being selective, and moving on to what they really want to hear about – your work.

Importantly, this approach applies not only when you use the literature to contextualize an account of your own research, but also when the entire presentation is about the literature. Even then, the listeners will gain most from a sharp account along the lines of 'Overall the literature seems to favour X, but there is an interesting question arising from it, which is Y. So I want to just focus on Y and demonstrate how the claims about Y do not quite add up.'

We advocate presenting just one of the ideas from your dissertation, providing a broad-brush contextualization that invites your listener to take for granted that you know more about the literature than you are going to tell them (though you would tell them in a written version). Just how much scope this gives in an oral presentation is clear when we take the logical structure of a research report (Figure 18.1) and see how that translates into what to include in a presentation.

The structure of an oral presentation

Title

- Containing keywords reflecting the central question you are seeking to answer. Your title determines how carefully your abstract is read, so over-clever or misleading titles can work against you.

Abstract

- Your abstract is the main way to attract your audience. (See below for a note on how to compose it.)

Introduction

- Get straight into the content of the paper by presenting your central question. As with a written report, it need not be the same central question that drives the entire project and dissertation.
- Present your aims for the work reported, not the entire dissertation.
- Locate your presentation in relation to a significant need for new knowledge, *mentioning the kind of literature, and at most one or two names associated with it, to which it relates.*
- Outline the structure of your presentation, so your listeners have a sense of where you are going.

No formal Literature Review?

- *Your audience will expect you to know the literature and to have critically engaged with it, so this element of the logic is essential. However, avoid having a long literature review section. Rather, identify one key issue arising from the literature, with indicative quotations from two or three main sources.*

Theory, methods, instruments

- While the theory, methodology and instruments sections must be part of the logical structure of your presentation, you may well not have time to say much about them. Speakers commonly say 'I adopted this methodology. If you want to know why, ask me at the end.'

Findings and discussion

- The findings and discussion sections are usefully combined in an oral presentation. This is the part your audience is likely to be most interested in. With limited time, you have a strong responsibility to guide them through your data effectively. Avoid just describing your findings. Show how they help answer your research questions. Be disciplined about not including aspects of the data irrelevant to your current purpose, however interesting they are.
- It is a good idea to include a self-critical reflection on the limitations of your study, particularly the extent to which you have achieved your substantive aims, so as to head off any potential criticisms from the audience in the questions section at the end.

Conclusion

- It is important in an oral presentation to finish with a clear summary of what you asked and what you found, to ensure the audience has inferred the underlying logical structure, even though you have not given equal time in your presentation to all of its components.

Handout?

- Handouts will be necessary if you are presenting information that is too detailed to be seen on the screen, such as text data or complex diagrams. Otherwise handouts are usually optional. They do ensure your audience has an accurate record of what you said, increasing the likelihood that they will cite your work. For this purpose, you can choose to compose an abstract different from the one appearing in the conference documentation. Think: what will be most useful to my audience?

- If you are providing a handout anyway, include references to the works you mention.

Remember that any time given over to questions and comments from the audience at the end of your slot can be used to make good any aspects of the logical structure that you did not cover to the audience's satisfaction. This enables you to take more risks with what you say, knowing you can provide extra detail later. It also means you need to be prepared to answer questions on a range of issues relevant to your larger project.

Note that the same logical structure can work with more than one order of presentation. Where conferences offer only very short slots, consider options that allow you to present your most important messages first, and fill in the rest of the information afterwards. So the logic of your overall argument is to first give the claims in the conclusion, and then the warranting that makes these claims convincing.

When you attend others' oral presentations, critically assess what they do, to get ideas about what does and does not work – paying special attention to the literature review aspect of their work. Certain features underpin all good presentations. In particular, a clear structure helps your listeners to feel confident that they will follow what you say.

Creating your abstract for an academic journal article or presentation

In Chapter 17 we suggested an approach for compiling the abstract for your dissertation. Abstracts for journal articles and presentations are usually much shorter – perhaps only 100–200 words. A journal article abstract follows the same structure as the dissertation one, so you can use Table 17.4 as your guide. The main challenge is deciding what detail to leave out. Recall how, in Chapter 3, we recommended that you, as a critical reader, engage with journal article abstracts. Readers accept that not all information can be captured there, and use an abstract as a tool to decide if they should continue reading. Your primary aim, then, is to indicate the potential points of contact between your work and the target audience's purposes in reading the research literature. The first question on their mind, as on yours as a critical reader, is *Why am I reading this?* (Critical Synopsis Question A). They will be looking for a correspondence between their needs and some element of your central question, review questions, methodological or theoretical aims or research questions. So be explicit, by including keywords capturing the core ideas. You can also use the middle column of Table 18.1 (as applicable) for indications on what to prioritize.

TABLE 18.1 Logical flow for composing a conference abstract

Focus question	Orientation of the text	How this addresses reviewers and attendees
Why might this be of interest to people at the conference?	Make clear in the first sentence what topic and issues you are addressing. Maybe begin with 'The central question addressed is …'	• Reviewers need to know that your presentation is relevant to the conference themes • Attendees need to know why they would find your paper relevant and interesting
Why is this an important question to ask?	Locate your work within the existing research literature just enough to show what sort of previous research is relevant, e.g., 'With particular reference to the critical discourse theory of Fairclough and Wodak …'; or 'March's (1976) *garbage can* model of decision-making is revisited in the light of 21st century management models …'. There is no space for references, but it is worth giving the date of a central work	• Reviewers are judging whether you are familiar with the context of your work, or just doing something that is isolated and hence not likely to be useful to others • Attendees are looking for points of contact between your work and theirs, so they know they will understand what you are doing and see the relevance to their own work
What did I do?	Say what method you used, and move on, e.g., 'Interviews were conducted to …'; 'Using a series of experiments that measured …'; 'Texts were gathered from … and analysed for …'	• Reviewers are gauging whether your methods were reliable. In a presentation you won't have time to describe them in the detail necessary for the audience to judge their quality. Reviewers are gatekeepers of research quality and want to ensure you don't mislead your audience • Attendees want to know if your method is like theirs (e.g., what ideas they might get for their own work) or whether you will be reporting a type of data they believe is interesting and valid

(Continued)

TABLE 18.1 *(Continued)*

Focus question	Orientation of the text	How this addresses reviewers and attendees
What are my main claims? (Sometimes you can replace this section with a list of hypotheses or research questions, so people have to attend to find out the results)	Give the headlines only, e.g., 'Overall, nurses were more likely than doctors to attribute low performance to under-resourcing, while doctors blamed poor management'	• Reviewers are trying to establish whether your claims seem plausible given your aims and method • Attendees are looking for the hook – will this be an interesting presentation? Here you try to sell your work as worth attending because of what it can tell them about something in the world
How might readers find this useful?	Suggest the potential for generalization beyond your own study to other contexts which might be similar in significant ways, e.g., 'It can be inferred from these results, that all teenagers from ethnic minority groups are …'; or 'It remains unclear whether these findings would hold for other populations of care home residents because …'	• Reviewers are trying to judge whether your findings are likely to be relevant to attendees. If they can't find evidence of generalizability, they won't see much point in your presenting the work to others • Attendees are always looking for that hook from your work into theirs. If your work can't generalize to a domain of their interest they won't bother coming

Conference abstracts are different, because they address two very distinct types of reader at once:

- The reviewers who decide whether to accept your presentation for the conference.
- The conference attendees who decide whether to attend your presentation.

If you pitch the abstract wrongly you might fail to get into the conference or, if you get in, find that you fail to attract an audience, because you did not capture people's interest. So you need a structure that can help you be successful in both regards. Table 18.1 mimics the structure of Table 17.4, but there are two differences. First, not all the focus questions are the same. Second, we have added comments on addressing the two readerships.

The beginning of the end, or the end of the beginning?

For many postgraduate students, getting a pass for their dissertation heralds the beginning of an academic career. If you are in this group, you will find that critical reading and self-critical writing skills are highly transferable, and that they offer a sound starting point for continuing to develop your critical frame of mind through good academic practice.

Many academic activities benefit from critical reading. They include supervising students, mentoring post-doctoral researchers and colleagues, and peer-reviewing journal articles, research funding applications and conference abstracts. Self-critical writing, meanwhile, helps ensure that everything you write, from books and journal articles to lecture materials and comments on students' work, is crafted for its purpose and audience, so you have the impact you seek.

Whether as an academic or in some other job or profession that draws on your critical reading and writing skills, the challenge is to remain alert to what you are trying to achieve, and how the skills and knowledge you have accumulated can be best used to achieve it. Over to you.

Glossary

abstract a. A short summary of an academic journal article, dissertation or other research report, placed at the beginning of the text to provide readers with key information about the content.

b. A prospective description of a conference presentation, submitted in order to be allotted a presentation slot, and usually circulated to attendees to help them decide whether to attend the presentation.

abstraction A mechanism for generalization, whereby specific details of any given context are ignored so as to capture similarities across a broader range of contexts.

academic journal article A publication that contains original research by the author(s). It usually appears in a specific volume (sometimes volume and part) with a year date, though electronic-only journals do not always adhere to that practice. Journal articles are usually subject to peer review before acceptance, which entails critical feedback from academic experts aimed at improving the quality of the paper.

argument In this book, the combination of a conclusion containing one or more claims, and the warranting for it, based on some form of evidence.

assumptions Underlying ideas, often not explicit, that shape the thinking of the researcher or reader.

central question A question about the social world that any given study can make a contribution to answering. Central questions unite researchers into groups within and across disciplines. Example: How can vulnerable children be supported through their early years?

certainty A continuum, from believing that a claim is definitely the case, to that it might be the case. Authors control how vulnerable their work is to criticism by selecting the level of certainty appropriate to the reliability of their research design and findings.

Comparative Critical Summary A short text drawing on the answers to the Critical Synopsis questions for two or more research articles, to compare their capacity to answer the reviewer's review question.

concepts Abstract ideas that capture features of the social world through language, enabling researchers to examine and compare them.

conclusion (component of argument) The set of claims made by a researcher, the reliability of which is determined by the strength of the warranting.

conclusion (of dissertation) The final chapter or section, in which answers to the central question are offered, drawing on the warranting of the previous chapters. Reflections on the reliability of the research are given, to indicate the appropriate level of certainty. Comments on the potential for generalization beyond the scope of the research are included.

Critical Analysis Questions A set of ten questions applied to a frontline research text, to generate material for a Critical Review of a text.

Critical Literature Review An account of multiple published texts that scrutinizes the authors' claims and the warranting for them, as relevant to the reviewer's own review question(s).

Critical Literature Mini-review A short Critical Literature Review that goes into more depth than a Comparative Critical Summary, but covers a smaller range of texts than a full Critical Literature Review. It can form part of a warranting unit, or help to link a transition in the narrative.

Critical reading Reading research accounts with insight and scepticism, willing to be convinced but requiring warranting for the claims made.

Critical Summary A short text presenting an insightful evaluation of one research article, based on the Critical Synopsis Questions.

Critical Synopsis Questions Five basic questions to ask when reading a text without conducting an in-depth analysis.

data-driven literature Research reports of an empirical, rather than theoretical or methodological, enquiry.

dissertation A long text written for assessment or examination in a university that reports the candidate's own empirical, theoretical, practice-based or literature-based research. Dissertations need to conform to the specific length and formatting requirements of the institution. In some countries, a long dissertation is called a thesis.

Dissertation Logic Check Template An editable document that can be used to develop the logic of a dissertation project and track incremental writing-up, as the project proceeds.

evidence Information that indicates whether a claim is valid. Along with reasoning, evidence forms a major element of warranting. Sources of evidence include findings from the literature or research.

generalization A continuum based on the capacity for a specific claim to apply beyond the context that generated it. Authors control how vulnerable their work is to criticism, by selecting the level of generalization appropriate to the similarity between their own research context and other contexts. Generalization typically entails an increasing level of abstraction, as details local to specific contexts are set aside.

ideologies Beliefs, ideas and principles connected systematically to generate a rationale for social, political or economic policy and behaviour.

intellectual project The researchers' purpose, based on what they are trying to achieve. The main intellectual projects are knowledge-for-understanding, knowledge-for-critical evaluation, knowledge-for-action, and training.

knowledge-for-action An intellectual project focused on improving how things are done.

knowledge-for-critical evaluation An intellectual project focused on exposing problems with what is currently done.

knowledge-for-understanding An intellectual project focused on examining some phenomenon from a relatively impartial standpoint.

labels In this book, a loose group of concepts with a narrow focus, such as *criminal activity* to capture *burglary*, *theft*, *conspiracy* and *deception*.

Linkage Tracker Test A tool that helps you check that everything included in your narrative needs to be there.

metaphor A word or phrase used to characterize a phenomenon, although it is not literally true. In academic research it can be a device for conceptualizing a complex phenomenon in simple terms. The metaphor highlights certain features of the phenomenon while ignoring others. It offers a means to explore the phenomenon in new ways.

methodological aim What you plan to do, in order to achieve your substantive aim (e.g., what research design you will use, how you will collect and analyse your data).

model In this book, a tightly grouped set of concepts with a narrow focus, that are associated in a manner that creates a coherent element of theory (e.g., a cause-and-effect relationship). Models are often presented graphically.

opinion A viewpoint that generates claims, but without adequate warranting.

oral presentation An assessed component, or a conference or workshop presentation, usually given by the researcher about his or her own work. Typically, oral presentations are supported by a visual display, such as PowerPoint, and often by a printed handout.

perspective In this book, a loose group of concepts with a broad focus. Thus, a *cultural perspective* might focus on shared beliefs, values and codes of behaviour.

policy literature Texts produced by policy-makers or their advisers and shaped by their assumptions and beliefs, often political. These texts may draw on a range of resources, including the findings of academic research, to develop a case for making a change with onward impact on practices.

practice knowledge Knowledge derived from undertaking professional or other relevant activity, rather than only observing or questioning others. Thus, it includes 'know-how' skills and deeply embedded instincts based on experience.

practice literature Texts that comment on or give recommendations for how an activity can or should be done.

research knowledge A description of observed patterns arising from systematic empirical investigation.

research question A question that determines the design and conduct of part or all of an empirical investigation. Research questions are inspired by the puzzles or significant needs for new knowledge identified in the critical literature review. They are answered in the discussion after the findings have been reported.

research report Any written account of research. In this book, the term is used to refer to reports of original, empirical research – where data have been analysed in order to address a question – in contrast to literature reviews or textbooks.

review question In this book, it is a question that determines the scope and focus of part or all of a Critical Literature Review. Review questions are inspired by identifying ways of developing answers to the central question. They are answered in the discussion at the end of the literature review chapter(s) or section(s).

self-critical writing Academic writing where the author consciously attempts to take account of the needs and expectations of critical readers in order to convince them of the author's argument. The author habitually interrogates his or her own writing from the perspective of the target audience, to check how well the argument is communicated, and whether it is likely to be convincing to this audience.

signposting Indications in the narrative of the relationship between parts of the whole text, particularly stating what a chapter will cover, or has covered, and how it relates to what has come before and will follow.

substantive aim The intended achievement of a contribution to significant new knowledge about the topic.

task-driven reading Reading for a particular purpose, particularly answering review questions, as opposed to general background reading.

theoretical aim The intended use of theory to achieve understanding of the phenomenon under examination. In a theory-focused piece of work, the theoretical aim may include the development of new theory.

theoretical knowledge One of the three kinds of knowledge claim. It explains a phenomenon in conceptual terms, with reference, often, to models and perspectives.

theoretical literature Academic writing, the primary goal of which is to offer new conceptualizations, models and theories about aspects of the social world.

theories In this book, a tightly linked set of concepts sufficiently broadly focused to be relevant to several domains. The concepts, which may already be combined into models, are associated in some way that can offer explanations, or make predictions.

thesis A substantial written text, usually for a doctorate. In some countries it is known as a doctoral dissertation.

training Practical advice, tuition and application, aimed at changing practice.

warranting The reason(s) for accepting a claim. It can be based on empirical evidence, explanation or reasoning based on theory, personal experience and practice knowledge.

warranting unit A component of the larger text that provides warranting for an interim conclusion.

Appendix 1

'One word or two? Psycholinguistic and sociolinguistic interpretations of meaning in a civil court case', by Alison Wray and John J. Staczek [abridged version of the article in *The International Journal of Speech, Language and the Law* (2005), 12(1): 1–18, published by the University of Birmingham Press].

Abstract

What relative weighting should be given, in a court case, to psycholinguistic and sociolinguistic explanations of an alleged offence? We review the case of an African-American Plaintiff, who claimed that her receipt at work of a framed document with the title 'Temporary Coon Ass Certificate', from a white male supervisory-level employee in the same company, constituted racial discrimination in the workplace. Dialect research conducted by JJS, as expert witness for the prosecution, demonstrated that the dialectal use of 'coonass' (as it is more commonly spelled) to refer to Cajuns (white settlers of French descent) was restricted to the states of Louisiana and south-eastern Texas. It was argued by the prosecution to be unreasonable to expect someone from another part of the United States to know the meaning of the word. The jury found in favour of the Plaintiff. The prosecution case rested upon the premise that when a word is unknown, it will be interpreted by breaking it down into smaller units, in this case 'coon' and 'ass', both derogatory terms, the former strongly racist. We explore the psycholinguistic rationale for this assumption, and its converse, that when a word is well-known to an individual, (s)he may fail to see how it is constructed.

Introduction

This paper discusses a 1996–7 case of alleged racial harassment in the workplace, based upon a perceived use of language in an offensive manner. The African-American Plaintiff filed the action, alleging that her employer, the US

Department of Energy, created a hostile work environment. The case was heard in the United States District Court for the District of Columbia.

The Plaintiff claimed that, on returning from vacation, she found in her desk drawer a framed certificate with the title 'Temporary Coon Ass Certificate' and her name printed on it. The document was signed by a white Department of Energy employee based at a workshop in east Texas, the site of a recent team visit that the Plaintiff had been unable to attend. The Plaintiff, upon receiving the certificate, 'immediately experienced emotions of shock, outrage and fury, and felt the certificate and the statements contained therein constituted a serious racial slur' (communication from the clerk of the Plaintiff's attorney to JJS, as expert witness for the Plaintiff, 7 August 1996). The Plaintiff sought internal remedies in the form of sanctions against the sender and alleged that: 'the Defendant condoned the hostile environment by failing to discipline the sender or take other remedial action' (ibid.). In September 1997, the jury found in favour of the Plaintiff and awarded some $120,000 in compensatory damages against the US Department of Energy.

The Plaintiff was not the only Department of Energy employee to receive such a certificate, and was one of two African Americans in this round of certificate distributions. In court testimony, the sender stated that he had picked up a bulk load of certificates in 1985 at the World's Fair in New Orleans.

Q You've given out 'Coonass Certificate' [*sic*] just like the one you gave to [the Plaintiff] for 10 or 11 year [*sic*], it that right?

A That's correct, sir.

Q And what you did, I gather, is you got a package of 'Coonass Certificates' from a restaurant, is that right?

A Yes, sir ... I picked them up, brought them to the site. I made changes to them, basically about where they came from, took 'Plantation House' off, and at that point in time I put 'Tex-Oma-Complex' on the bottom of them.

(Trial Transcript: cross-examination of Defense witness by Plaintiff's attorney, 21 August 1997, p. 37.)

Since acquiring the certificates, he had issued them regularly, with the implicit approval of his supervisors:

Q And the supervisors you've had over that 11-year period that you've been giving out the 'Coonass Certificate,' has any of your supervisors said to you, 'Don't give out these Coonass Certificates'?

A No, sir.

Q Have any of them said the 'Coonass Certificate' is racially offensive?

A No, sir.

(Trial Transcript: cross-examination of Defense witness by Plaintiff's attorney, 21 August 1997, pp. 39–40.)

Certificates were issued after site visits made by teams from other company offices. The meaning of the term 'coonass' as 'white Cajun' (see below) was allegedly explained during the visits. The Plaintiff was sent a certificate in error, since her name appeared on the list of attendees even though she did not participate in the visit.

Interpreting 'coonass'

We shall examine, below, sociolinguistic and psycholinguistic factors that play a role in the interpretation of a word's meaning. First, however, we examine the printed evidence, since dictionaries are in general, and certainly were in this case, viewed as a key source of authoritative information.

The term 'coonass' (non-hyphenated) appears in two dictionary sources: *The Historical Dictionary of American Slang (HDAS)* and *Dictionary of American Regional English (DARE)*. Its primary meaning is given as a term for Louisiana Cajuns. Although the term 'Cajun' is historically complex with regard to racial group and social status, Cajuns are classically defined as the white descendants of settlers in Acadia, a former French colony of eastern Canada, who were deported by the British, or relocated voluntarily, to the south-western territories, including Louisiana, in the mid-eighteenth century (*American Heritage Dictionary of the English Language (AHDEL),* 1992: 9). DARE attests that the usage of 'coonass' is confined to Louisiana and south-eastern Texas, though it is also known to regional speakers in Mississippi, Arkansas and Alabama. Research to determine this regional distribution was based on formal interviews with informants in the South.

In addition to the core definition, however, the following specific entries are notable:

- 'Coonass is still a pejorative for any low-life individual, especially Negroes' (DARE informant, File eKY).
- 'The term "coonass" ... may have been a racial allusion suggesting a Cajun-black genetic mixture' (HDAS informant, Dormon, 1983: 87).

The combined evidence above suggests that 'coonass' has two meanings, the second alluding to, if not actually referring to, African ancestry. However, the status of the latter entries is questionable, as we shall see presently. Unequivocal, though, is the offensive meaning of the separate terms 'coon' and 'ass'. A wide range of standard and specialist dictionaries give as one meaning of 'coon', 'a Negro', and indicate that it is a slang and derogatory term. Its origin is consistently reported as a shortened form of 'raccoon', itself a word of Algonkian Indian origin. 'Ass' is identified in HDAS as a US version of British 'arse', the buttocks or rump. As such, it is considered a 'vulgarism' (HDAS). AHDEL gives the definition as 'a vain, self-important, silly, or aggressively stupid person', based on a primary meaning of 'donkey'.

What sort of quality of evidence is obtained from dictionaries, though? In the course of questioning, the expert witness for the defendant made a number of observations regarding the validity of dictionary definitions:

> ' ... these dictionaries are only as good as the people they're talking to ... These are not definitions. These are recorded testimonies of what people think these things mean.'
>
> (Trial Transcript: direct examination of expert witness for the Defense, 22 August 1997, p. 44.)

Referring to the DARE and HDAS:

> 'Those two dictionaries are based on interviews with people, asking them what regional or slang terms mean to them. The reason for that is because these terms are not – have no standard accepted meaning.'
>
> (Trial Transcript: cross-examination of expert witness for the Defense, 22 August 1997, p. 60.)

As the observations of this expert witness indicate, care needs to be taken with dictionary entries where there is no evidence of general consensus within a speech community, or where there are grounds for doubting the validity of the statement that the dictionary cites. Specifically with regard to the two attestations, above, that 'coonass' can imply African ancestry, it is possible that the claimed extension of the term to black people is a post hoc rationalization based on folk etymology. In actual fact, the consensus across dictionaries, including both HDAS and DARE, is that 'coonass' has an etymology in which 'coon' does not figure at all, being, rather, the corruption of the French '*connasse*', a vulgarism used as an insult.

Dictionaries, then, can offer valuable insights into the historical origin and at least some current perceptions of a word's meaning. However, there is more to meaning than this. The instructions to the expert witness for the prosecution were to ascertain 'not the specific meaning of "Coonass" within Cajun circles, but ... what the words "Coon" and "Ass" generally mean, how they are generally intended and received, and the hurtful potential of these words' (Memorandum from the clerk of the Plaintiff's attorney to expert witness for the Plaintiff). Dictionaries can give only limited insight into these matters, since they are unable to comment on meanings of words *in use*, that is, in relation to (a) the text in which they occur, (b) their role in a particular communicative act, or (c) the social context that might determine why a speaker/writer chooses one term over another, and how a hearer/reader interprets it.

Sociolinguistic considerations

Language, whether oral or written, exists within a context of use. Both speakers and hearers bring to their understanding of a word or phrase a knowledge founded on a socialization, education and experience that may be totally or partially shared, or not shared at all. The term 'coonass' is clearly dialectal and, as such, certain questions follow:

- How is the word likely to be interpreted by an individual who does not come from, and has not lived in, the region in which the word is customarily used?
- What contextual and other considerations might come into play when such a person is interpreting the term?

Regarding the first question, the Plaintiff, an African-American woman living and working in Washington D.C., was neither from the dialect area in which the term 'coonass' was in use (Louisiana and south-eastern Texas), nor from one of the 'dialect contact areas' (Mississippi, Arkansas and Alabama). Dialect contact areas are locations where, usually because of geographical proximity and/or cultural or commercial links, dialect forms might often be heard, even if not used by the local population. Should the Plaintiff, then, reasonably be expected to have known what 'coonass' meant? During cross-examination, the expert witness for the defendant stated:

> ' ... it's not unreasonable to think that people – not only people in South Louisiana and East Texas – would be familiar with the term ... People all over the place know this.'
>
> (Trial Transcript: cross-examination of expert witness for the Defense by Plaintiff's attorney, 22 August 1997, pp. 49–50.)

That is, this expert witness considered unfamiliarity to be the exception rather than the rule. In contrast, the view of the expert witness for the Plaintiff was that the term as a reference to a Cajun could not be expected to have widespread recognition across the United States.

How can this difference of opinion be interpreted? The expert witness for the Plaintiff had carried out some informal and random sampling of African

Americans and White Americans in the Washington D.C. area, to determine their understanding of the term 'coonass'. He found that almost all of those questioned perceived a racial overtone in the term and viewed it as offensive and disrespectful.

In contrast, the expert witness for the Defense was himself a South Louisianan of French Acadian descent – that is, of Cajun ancestry. He then, originated from, and resided well within, the dialect area in which the term was in use and he was, as a result, highly familiar with it. This fact is apposite because the issue was whether a member of a speech community is able to assess the extent to which people who are not members of that speech community share its lexical inventory. In other words, how aware are dialect speakers about (a) which words in their vocabulary are dialectal, and (b) how widely known they are beyond the immediate area? If we do not perceive the need for remedial action, we are unlikely to undertake it. It is, consequently, significant that the expert witness for the Defense stated:

> 'Frankly, I didn't look for definitions of "coonass" because I know what it means.'
>
> (Trial Transcript: cross-examination of expert witness for the Defense, 22 August 1997, p. 43.)

Turning now to the second question, words do not operate in isolation. They are interpreted in relation to other words with which they occur and also the situational and social context in which they are used. We may reasonably conjecture that had the Plaintiff not been African-American, she would probably have reacted to receiving the certificate with bafflement rather than distress. Even taking into account the generalized understanding of 'ass' as a derogatory term, the fact that the Plaintiff's case was one of racial harassment indicates that she reacted predominantly to seeing the word 'coon'. Indeed, in court she stated:

> 'When I pulled [the certificate] out, the first thing I saw was "coon". I didn't see "temporary". I didn't see "ass". All I could see was "coon" ... I was shocked. I was outraged.'
>
> (Trial Transcript: direct examination of the Plaintiff by Plaintiff's attorney, 20 August 1997, p. 36.)

Thus, her own ethnic identity formed part of the context within which her reading of the words 'coonass' caused offence. The contention of the prosecution was that the sender should have been aware of, and sensitive to, the possibility that these context parameters could lead to an interpretation of the phrase as offensive. In other words, even though he had no reason to anticipate that *anyone* would receive a certificate without having had the term explained to them during their visit, nor that if anyone did do so, they would be African-American, the potential for the phrase to cause offence should have been taken into account when he decided to send the certificates.

An examination of the certificate itself, however, reveals some counterbalancing factors. Firstly, it is to be signed by 'a certified coonass', implying that if an insult is intended, even in jest, that insult falls first, and more heavily, on the sender than the recipient. More than that, it indicates that the certificate represents a gesture of inclusion, not exclusion, that is, it is welcoming the recipient into membership of a group, not labelling him or her as a member of an outsider group. Secondly, the smaller print on the certificate indicates that the sentiments in the definition of a 'certified coonass' are predominantly positive – that is, the description is complimentary. Thirdly, several words co-occurring with 'coonass' in the text ('boudin', 'crackins', 'crawfish etouffee' and 'gumbo') are clearly dialectal and their presence arguably heightens the impression that 'coonass' itself might be.

Psycholinguistic considerations

Wray (2002) begins her book *Formulaic Language and the Lexicon* with the following anecdote:

> In a series of advertisements on British TV early in 1993 by the breakfast cereal manufacturer Kellogg, people were asked what they thought Rice Krispies were made of, and expressed surprise at discovering the answer was rice. Somehow they had internalized this household brand name without ever analysing it into its component parts. (p. 3)

Why should this happen? She proposes that: '... overlooking the internal composition of names is a far more common phenomenon than we might at first think ... [and] it is actually very useful that we can choose the level at which we stop breaking down a chunk of language into its constituent parts' (pp. 3–4). In the course of her book, Wray draws on an extensive critical examination of the research literature to demonstrate that the internal composition of phrases and polymorphemic words is, indeed, often overlooked, and also develops a psychological model of how we learn and store lexical material, that accounts for why it comes about (see later).

In the trial, the expert witness for the Defense was asked whether he viewed 'coonass' as a single word or two words. In reply, he compared it to the word 'firefly': '"firefly" is not "fire" or "fly"; it's a "firefly". It's an expression used together' (Trial Transcript: direct examination of the expert witness for the Defense, 22 August 1997, p. 14). In the case of 'firefly' there is, of course, a clear hint as to why it gained its name, that relates to its component parts. However, internally complex words and multiword phrases often have an apparent etymology that is misleading, with subcomponents that do not represent what they seem to. Thus, the 'ladybird' or 'ladybug' is so-called not because it is female or resembles a lady, but because it was traditionally a creature of 'Our Lady', the Virgin Mary (compare German 'Marienkäfer', 'Mary's beetle'). A 'penknife' is not a knife that is the size or shape of a writing implement, but a knife originally designed for sharpening quills ('pen' = 'feather').

What of 'coonass', then? If we set aside the single proposal, discussed earlier, that the term takes the form it does because it first referred to black Cajuns, and if we follow instead the more reliable etymology from French, then 'coonass' is no more made up, historically, of 'coon' and 'ass' than 'carpet' is made up of 'car' and 'pet' or 'browsing' is made up of 'brow' and 'sing'. We must recognize a direct link, within the dialect area of its use, between a French word for a part of the body and a consistently applied derogatory term for an immigrant group of French settlers from Canada and their descendants. Any association with African-Americans is after the event and imposed by outsiders.

But does that make the externally imposed, albeit historically false, interpretation any less real to those who make it? More appositely here, does the 'innocent' etymology of a word or phrase excuse insensitivity on the part of its contemporary users? In order to assess this issue, we need to return to Wray's proposal that words and phrases are not always broken down into their smallest components. She identifies several interrelating reasons why that might occur. One is well-exemplified above: in many cases an apparently polymorphemic word does not, in fact, break down into components that help one work out the meaning. The same applies to phrases, from the clearly irregular 'by and large' through to many multiword expressions whose internal oddity we could easily overlook (e.g., 'perfect stranger'; 'broad daylight'; 'in order to'). In these instances, there will be no benefit in examining the word or phrase too closely. However, that cannot be the root of the issue, for how would the user *know* that the word or phrase was partly or entirely non-compositional, unless by attempting to do that analysis?

Wray's explanation is that when we encounter new words and phrases, we only break them down to the point where we can attribute a reliable and useful meaning, and then we stop. She terms this strategy *needs only analysis* (Wray, 2002: 130–2). Needs only analysis suggests that people who have been raised in Louisiana or southeast Texas will, having encountered the term 'coonass' and having accepted without question that it refers to a Cajun, have had no reason to engage in further analysis of it. This could go some way to explaining how the sender of the 'coonass' certificate apparently failed to anticipate the possibility of a misunderstanding. Furthermore, it could account for why the expert witness for the Defense felt that he did not need to look the phrase up: 'because I know what it means', and why he described the racial interpretations as 'not standard meanings' (Trial Transcript: cross-examination of the expert witness for the Defense, 22 August 1997, p. 44).

In contrast, someone who does not know the word has an additional 'need', and will therefore engage with more analysis, by breaking down the incomprehensible whole into comprehensible parts, naturally using the 'word' break as the morphological boundary. The result is two words with independent meanings: 'coon' and 'ass'. The decoding that is required by a person encountering 'coonass' for the first time is minimal: no more than the recognition that there are two components, both derogatory, implying that their combination must also be so.

What of the sender? Although he may never have needed to break down 'coonass' into its components to derive meaning, nevertheless, he would presumably only need to have once caught sight of the word 'coon' on its own on the certificate to have noticed, and quite differently computed, its meaning as a separate item. Yet he appeared never to have made the connection between 'coon' and 'coonass':

Q You're familiar with the term 'coon', aren't you?

A Yes, sir, I am.

Q You understand that that has a racially-derogatory meaning?

A Yes, sir, I do.

Q And you knew that the term 'coon' has a racially-derogative meaning to African Americans at the time that you prepared the certificate that's been marked as Plaintiff's Exhibit Number 1, isn't that true?

A That's correct.

(Trial Transcript: cross-examination of Defense witness by Plaintiff's attorney, 21 August 1997, p. 40.)

His claim is particularly striking in view of the fact that he had actually handed a certificate to another African-American employee, yet still did not see a connection between 'coonass' and 'coon' (Trial Transcript: cross-examination of Defense witness by Plaintiff's attorney, 21 August 1997, p. 42). This makes most sense from the perspective of *needs only analysis*, and would be a case of 'constituent blindness' brought about by the strong and consistent association of a specific meaning with the composite word 'coonass'. More accurately, it would be 'pseudo-constituent blindness' since 'coon' and 'ass' are not, historically or actually for the dialect speakers, constituents of the whole. For such individuals to see 'coon' and 'ass' in 'coonass' is – a word break notwithstanding – comparable to a standard English speaker noticing 'sea' and 'son' in 'season'.

Conclusion

So, what does a word mean? We operate within, and across, speech communities. Whatever we may intend by a word, we must be constantly aware of how it is, or could be, received by others. Nevertheless, we may, for good psycholinguistic reasons, be blind to the internal construction of a word or phrase in our own language variety. Meanwhile, that same internal construction may be all too plain to those unfamiliar with the item. The user of the construction may discover the other possible interpretations only by chance. Is it then reasonable for a court to expect that a word with strong local cultural associations will always be recognized as potentially ambiguous, even though, within its own realm of application, it is not?

The judge and jury are put into a difficult situation in such cases, assuming that they take both parties to have made an innocent interpretation of the disputed term. The Judge, in his summing up, stated:

> [T]o determine ... whether the Temporary Coon Ass Certificate was racially offensive, you should consider [the sender's] intent to discriminate or not to discriminate against blacks, the subjective effect of the forwarding of the certificate on [the Plaintiff], and the impact it would have had on any reasonable person in [the Plaintiff's] position.
>
> (Trial Transcript: summary of the Judge, 25 August 1997, p. 19.)

The Judge allows for the possibility that while the sender's intent was non-discriminatory, the impact on the Plaintiff was nevertheless one of deliberate discrimination. Achieving a ruling therefore entailed deciding which of the two was more justified in their blindness to the other's perception. For linguistic awareness cuts both ways: the sender might have been expected to have an awareness of non-dialect users' interpretations of 'coonass', but, similarly, the recipient might have been expected to spot, from the various indicators, that she was reading an unfamiliar dialect term.

This linguistic awareness, we have argued, may rest on more than the words themselves. The Plaintiff's initial sight of the certificate, when the word 'coon' was all she saw, may have blinded her to the possibility that 'coonass' meant something other than 'coon' + 'ass'. Meanwhile, the sender did not deny familiarity with the word 'coon' and its racist meaning, only any awareness that 'coonass' might be construed by a person who did not know the term, as containing the word 'coon'. We propose that her constituent awareness, and his constituent blindness, are entirely natural consequences of linguistic processing.

Just how a court should handle such psycholinguistic considerations is another matter. They could clearly have some bearing on the issue of intent but it could still be argued that, however explicable the oversight might be in psycholinguistic terms, it is part of the educational level required of a manager or supervisor that he or she will be language-aware in relation to differences between linguistic varieties used, and encountered, in the workplace. At the very least, the outcome of this case suggests that individuals in a socially responsible position are expected to appreciate the singularity of their own dialect or slang forms to a sufficient extent that they will refrain from using them with people likely to be unfamiliar with – or to misconstrue – their meaning.

References

American Heritage Dictionary of the English Language (3rd edn). (1992) Boston: Houghton Mifflin Co.

Dictionary of American Regional English. Volume 1. (1985) Cambridge, MA: The Belknap Press of Harvard University Press.

Dormon, J.H. (1983) *The People Called Cajuns: An Introduction to an Ethnohistory.* Lafayette, LA: The Center for Louisiana Studies.

Historical Dictionary of American Slang. Volume 1: A–G. (1994) New York: Random House.

United States District Court for the District of Columbia (1997) Transcript of Trial (Civil Action No. 96–401) Before the Honorable Harold H. Greene, United States Judge and a Jury, August.

Wray, A. (2002) *Formulaic Language and the Lexicon.* Cambridge: Cambridge University Press.

Appendix 2

'Sharing leadership of schools through teamwork: a justifiable risk?', by Mike Wallace [abridged version of the article in *Educational Management and Administration* (2001), 29(2): 153–67, published by SAGE].

Abstract

This paper develops the empirically backed normative argument that ideally school leadership should be shared among staff, but the extent of sharing that is justifiable in practice depends on diverse contexts of schools, and consequent risks – especially for headteachers – that may inhere in the endeavour to share leadership. Findings are discussed of research into senior management teams (SMTs) in British primary schools showing how the headteachers variably shared leadership by setting parameters for teamwork according to a differing mix of belief in a management hierarchy and in equal contribution of team members. A model is put forward which links interaction between headteachers and other SMT members according to their belief in a management hierarchy and in equal contribution with different levels of team synergy. A contingent approach to sharing school leadership is justified on the basis of this model and implications for training are identified.

Sharing leadership – in principle

The purpose of this paper is to develop the normative argument that school leadership should ideally be extensively shared but, because school leaders do not live in an ideal world, the extent of sharing which is justifiable in practice depends on empirical factors. In other words, championing of shared leadership draws on principles which are contingent on the situation, not absolute. Specifically, I wish to explore empirical factors connected with the contexts of schools and consequent risks – especially for headteachers – that may inhere in their endeavour to share leadership. Findings will be discussed from research into senior management teams (SMTs) in British primary schools, whose role is to support the headteacher in leading and managing the institution. Typically, they consist of the headteacher, deputy head and other teachers with the most substantial management responsibility. Team members are variably involved in making policy and routine management decisions on behalf of other staff, whose views are represented in some measure. The term 'management' in the label 'management team' therefore refers both to leadership (setting the direction for the organization) and to management activity (orchestrating its day-to-day running). A combined cultural and political perspective was employed to investigate how the 'culture of teamwork' expressed in SMTs embodied contradictory beliefs and values. These beliefs and values reflected the wider social and political context, which impacted reciprocally on team members' use of power, and affected the extent to which leadership was shared between team members.

Several principles have been advanced to support the claim that school leadership should be shared relatively equally amongst staff. Most centre on staff entitlement. First, staff are entitled to contribute to decisions which affect their work and to be empowered to collaborate in creating an excellent institution. Shared leadership is morally just (Starratt, 1995; Sergiovanni, 1996) in a democratic country where individual rights are accorded high priority. Second, since staff give their professional lives to their school, they are entitled to enjoy the comradeship that working with colleagues can engender. Participating in shared leadership has intrinsic value, potentially, as a fulfilling experience for all involved (Nias et al., 1989; Wallace and Hall, 1994). Third, staff are entitled to gain this experience to further their professional development and career aspirations. It offers individual team members a potent opportunity for workplace learning, whereby they may improve their performance in their present role and prepare for promotion. A fourth principle looks to staff obligations as student educators. Adult working relationships in schools play a symbolic part in fostering children's social development. As role models, staff have a responsibility to express in their working relationships the kind of cooperative behaviour they wish their students to emulate.

A fifth principle focuses on valued leadership outcomes rather than the process. Shared leadership is potentially more effective than headteachers acting alone. Staff are interdependent: every member has a contribution to make as leadership tasks can be fulfilled only with and through other people. Achieving extensive ownership of policy decisions is therefore necessary if staff are to work together to implement them. Empowerment through mutual commitment and support enables staff to achieve more together than they could as individuals (Starratt, 1995; Wallace and Hall, 1994). In these circumstances, they can achieve an optimum degree of *synergy*, which may be defined as group members combining their individual energies to the best of their ability in order to achieve shared goals. Advocates assume that staff will adhere to these principles if given the chance: those offered their entitlement will take it up; they will act as good role models for students; and they will collaborate and generate synergy.

Prescription versus practice

Such ideas are embedded in normative theories of educational leadership from which prescriptions for practice are derived (Starratt, 1995; Sergiovanni, 1996), informing the school restructuring movement in North America (Pounder, 1998) and advocated for the UK by a few commentators (Southworth, 1998). They commonly refer to notions of transformational leadership and organization-wide learning originating with the world of business (e.g., Senge, 1990; Conger and Kanungo, 1998). Principals (headteachers) are urged to promote transformation of the staff culture through articulating a vision of a desirable future state for the institution; garnering colleagues' support for it; and empowering them to realize this shared vision through developing management structures and procedures emphasizing professional dialogue, teamworking and mutual support. How principals should behave, according to these theories, reflects assumptions about the real world of schools which include:

1. Principals possess freedom to determine their vision, their strategy for inspiring colleagues to share it, and the means for implementing it through their practice.
2. It is possible to engineer change in a teacher culture with predictable results.
3. Elements of the teacher culture are mutually compatible and individual interests are reconcilable, facilitating transformation that results in unity of purpose.
4. Empowerment of teachers leads to their actions to realize the vision proffered by principals.

Should these assumptions prove unrealistic, it follows that the principles on which the normative theory rests must be compromised if it is to have prescriptive value. That transformational leadership is deemed exceptional enough in North American schools and industries to merit books and training programmes promoting it suggests that the assumptions behind transformational leadership do not obtain in North America. Their applicability to the UK is even more questionable.

First, British headteachers have lost their freedom to be visionaries because of central government reforms. 'National standards for headship' (Teacher Training Agency, 1998: 4) require that 'the headteacher provides vision, leadership and direction for the school and ensures that it is managed and organized to meet its aims and targets'. The content of these aims and targets is largely determined by a central government engaged in a nationwide school target-setting exercise and imposing what, when and how literacy and numeracy must be taught in primary schools. Headteachers are expected both to articulate and gain colleagues' support for government ministers' educational vision and to ensure its implementation.

Second, research on schools implies that the teacher culture is not directly manipulable through leadership, though it is open to change (e.g., Nias et al., 1989). Attempts to stimulate cultural development may precipitate cultural change in unforeseen and undesired directions (Wallace, 1999). Hargreaves (1994) found that attempts in North America to foster a collaborative teacher culture merely engendered 'contrived collegiality' – a poor substitute for the genuinely collaborative culture which he argues may arise spontaneously.

Third, teacher cultures frequently contain incompatible elements: contradictory beliefs and values coexisting in tension. An earlier study of secondary school SMTs (Wallace and Hall, 1994) showed how their culture of teamwork encompassed two contradictory sets of beliefs and values. SMT members believed in a *management hierarchy* topped by headteachers, since they are in charge of running the school under supervision from the governing body, and have a unique ability to affect colleagues' careers through their contribution to staff selection and development. The sense of hierarchy was reinforced by the system of graded posts for staff, representing differential status, salary and responsibility levels. Senior staff are entitled to oversee the work of junior colleagues for whose work they are responsible. At the same time, team members believed in the ability of all their number to make an *equal contribution* to teamwork, being entitled to have an equal say in working towards consensual decisions whatever their status in the management hierarchy. Headteachers were hierarchically superior as creators, developers and leaders of their SMTs, but also were team members whose opinion carried equal weight with that of colleagues.

Fourth, empowerment of other staff does not guarantee that they will take up this entitlement in a manner acceptable to headteachers. Research shows that a significant minority of SMT members remain uncommitted to teamwork (e.g., Weindling and Earley, 1987; Wallace and Hall, 1994). Even where commitment is uniform, SMT members other than the headteacher may use power accompanying their team membership to act in ways that lie outside the limits of practices that accord with the headteacher's 'comfort zone' (the range of others' acceptable behaviours).

Under the structure of authority in British schools, the decision over how far to share leadership has long lain with headteachers. Research over recent decades suggests that perhaps the majority actually behaved more in accordance with the 'headmaster tradition' born of nineteenth-century public schools (Grace, 1995). Many primary heads identified closely with 'their' school, confining shared leadership to empowering colleagues to deliver their agenda (Hall and Southworth, 1997). In a hands-off political climate, headteachers enjoyed considerable agency, empowered to adopt their idiosyncratic construction of headship, often entailing restricted sharing of leadership which cast their colleagues exclusively in the role of followers. However, research also suggests there was limited followership, teachers publicly toeing headteachers' official line in the 'zone of policy' (Lortie, 1969) while, behind the classroom door in the 'zone of practice', they also possessed sufficient agency discreetly to do their own thing.

Central government education reforms have changed all that. Local administration has been largely replaced by additional central government authority to direct educational essentials like curriculum and to determine standards through legislation and financial incentives, complemented by devolution of authority to headteachers (within centrally determined limits) over inessentials like the operating budget. The most compelling reason for sharing leadership is now less a matter of principle than of pragmatism in a hostile environment. Headteachers must share leadership and their colleagues must deliver. The former are ever more dependent on the latter to contribute their specialist expertise in implementing mandated reforms, to feed this expertise into the leadership process as they gain experience with new practices, and to assist with monitoring implementation.

Headteachers now have less room to manoeuvre. Their notion of headship is increasingly constructed for them by external forces, and they can no longer afford *not* to accept the risk of sharing leadership in some degree. Yet an ironic consequence of central government strategy is to render sharing leadership as risky for headteachers as it is necessary. While they still enjoy exclusive authority to decide how far to share leadership, they are also held uniquely accountable for the outcomes of their decision. Reforms designed to strengthen external accountability, like national assessment of pupil learning and regular inspection of schools (both involving publication of results), have increased the vulnerability of the very headteachers on whom central government ministers depend to implement reforms. Headteachers alone are charged with legal responsibility for running the school within the oversight of the governing body. The accountability measures have increased the likelihood that headteachers will be publicly vilified if evidence is revealed of failure to implement central government reforms or to reach stipulated targets for educational standards.

Headteachers are confronted by a heightened dilemma: their greater dependence on colleagues disposes them towards sharing leadership. In a context of unprecedented accountability, however, they may be inhibited from sharing because it could backfire should empowered colleagues act in ways that generate poor standards of pupil achievement, alienate parents and governors, or incur inspectors' criticism. If this is the reality of schooling, how far should headteachers be expected to risk sharing leadership, since it could negatively affect their reputation, colleagues' work and ultimately children's education? If the risk of ineffective leadership can be reduced by limiting the amount of sharing, is it justifiable for headteachers to adopt a contingency approach, varying the degree of sharing as the situation evolves?

The case of primary school SMTs

The remainder of the paper seeks a tentative answer to these questions by considering evidence on the operation of primary school SMTs. First, relevant aspects of the research design and the combined cultural and political perspective framing the investigation are outlined. Second, findings are reported showing how the headteachers variably shared leadership by setting parameters for teamwork according to a differing mix of belief in a management hierarchy and in equal contribution of team members. Third, a model is put forward which links different levels of team synergy with interaction between headteachers and other SMT members, according to their belief in a management hierarchy and in equal contribution. Finally, a contingent approach to sharing school leadership is justified on the basis of this model and implications for training are identified.

The research, funded by the Economic and Social Research Council, investigated SMTs in large primary schools. (For a full account, see Wallace and Huckman, 1999.) Institutions with over 300 students were selected because SMTs in them would probably constitute a subset of the teaching staff. A key criterion for selecting SMTs was members' unified professed commitment to a team approach. Headteachers at potential sites were contacted and individual SMT members' stated commitment confirmed during a preliminary visit. Focused, interpretive case studies of four SMTs (labelled as Winton, Pinehill, Kingsrise and Waverley) were undertaken over the 1995/96 academic year. Data sources comprised 58 semi-structured interviews (eight with headteachers, 20 with other members of the SMTs, 26 with a sample of other staff, and four with chairs of school governing bodies); non-participant observation of twelve SMT meetings and ten other meetings where SMT members were present; and a small document archive. Research questions for the case studies were derived from a literature review, the previous study of secondary school SMTs and an initial postal questionnaire survey of headteachers, to which interview questions related. Fieldnotes were taken during case-study observations and tape-recorded interviews. Summary tapes were prepared and transcribed with reference to fieldnotes, schedules and documents. Data analysis entailed compiling interview summaries that fed into site summaries, forming the basis for cross-site analysis. Tables were constructed to display findings, the data set was scanned to explore the contextual complexity of specific interactions and explanatory models were developed.

The cultural and political perspective guiding the research integrates concepts about teacher professional cultures and micropolitics. It focuses on the reciprocal relationship between culture and power: cultural determinants of differential uses of power and uses of power to shape culture (Wallace, 1999). Culture informs deployment of power which, recursively, contributes to the maintenance or evolution of this culture. A simple definition of *culture* is 'the way we do things around here' (Bower, 1966): beliefs and values about education, leadership and relationships common to some or all staff in a school. A *culture of teamwork* may develop among SMT members which comprises shared beliefs, values and norms of behaviour about how they work together. As indicated above, a pivotal feature of the culture in the case studies was the interplay between uses of power according to belief in the management hierarchy and in the entitlement of all team members to make an equal contribution to the SMT. The uneasy coexistence of these beliefs is a consequence of the flow of wider social and political forces for cultural change and continuity going back to the headmaster tradition (based on belief in a strict hierarchy); the subsequent upsurge of demands from teachers to share in leadership (reflecting belief in equal rights as colleagues to participate in schools located within a democracy); and the new 'managerialist' belief in public sector managers' right to manage (Whitty et al., 1998), to achieve goals set by their political bosses (reasserting belief in hierarchy but with headteachers now in the middle of the chain of command).

Following Giddens (1984), a definition of *power* as 'transformative capacity' – use of resources to achieve interests – is employed. This conception was selected to encompass interactions which vary between synergistic, where staff pull together to achieve the same goal, and conflictual, where they pursue incompatible goals. Power may be divided (Bacharach and Lawler, 1980) into *authority* – use of resources legitimated by beliefs and values about status, including the right to apply sanctions; and *influence* – informal use of resources without recourse to sanctions linked to authority (although other sanctions may be available). Headteachers' conditions of service give them exclusive authority over other staff, but teachers may wield influence in seeking to support or undermine headteachers. The latter have recourse to authority and influence to promote a particular culture of teamwork within the SMT but cannot guarantee it will happen. Controlling other staff is, for headteachers, more a matter of *delimitation* – allowing for different behaviour within the boundaries of their comfort zone – than of establishing directive control. Changing beliefs about the redistribution of authority and influence between headteachers, their colleagues and other stakeholders reflect the impact of externally imposed reforms which delimit the agency of headteachers and other staff along quite narrowly defined boundaries. Headteachers may have created their SMTs, but not under conditions entirely of their own choosing.

A balancing act

The four headteachers had authority to decide, according to their professional beliefs and values, whether to adopt a team approach to leadership and how far to share leadership within it. SMT operation at Winton was relatively egalitarian, with a strong emphasis on equal contribution by all members to a wide variety of team tasks. In the other three schools it was more hierarchical, with deputies being more involved than other members in a narrower range of tasks. The headteachers enjoyed very different degrees of freedom to choose their team mates. The headteacher at Pinehill was newly appointed from elsewhere and inherited other members of the SMT. The headteachers of Kingsrise, Waverley and Winton had been in post for some years. They had both created their SMT and played a major part in selecting all team colleagues when vacancies had arisen, so had been able to appoint colleagues who subscribed to their conception of teamwork.

Elements of a management hierarchy were intrinsic to headteachers' design of the team structures. The spread of individual management responsibilities among team members gave them joint oversight of other staff (Table 1). Senior teachers were either responsible for a group of classes (e.g., the junior department) or for a specialism (e.g., students with special needs). The extent to which headteachers shared leadership depended on the balance they sought between expressing belief in the management hierarchy and in equal contribution of team members in the SMT's operation. The headteacher at Winton had created a small team to facilitate extensive sharing consistent with her belief in promoting an equal contribution by all members, who could take initiatives and engage fully in debate. The hierarchical approach that she had rejected as tokenism, where a headteacher would merely seek support for his or her agenda, was close to that embraced by the other headteachers – who opted for larger teams.

TABLE 1 Case-study SMT membership

Status level of SMT members	Winton (4 members)	Pinehill (6 members)	Kingsrise (7 members)	Waverley (5 members)
Headteacher	1	1	1	1
Deputy Head	2	1	1	1
Senior Teacher	1	4	5	3

How limited headteachers' power can be to set parameters for SMT operation when inheriting a team was demonstrated at Pinehill. The new headteacher attempted to impose his authority to introduce a more hierarchical mode of operation on other members of the existing team. The previous headteacher and deputy had been absent for long periods and other members of the SMT had enjoyed the opportunity to make a relatively equal contribution to teamwork. Several would not, initially, accept the more restricted contribution the new headteacher allowed them. Department leaders used influence by offering minimal compliance to the headteacher while complaining to other teachers behind his back, generating a widespread perception of a disunited team.

Varying the balance between equal and hierarchical sharing

Different degrees of sharing were expressed through several aspects of the teams' practice. First, the extent and boundaries of team tasks diverged. At Winton, the headteacher encouraged all other SMT members to participate fully in most leadership tasks, extending to developing policy proposals. At Pinehill, team tasks excluded curriculum matters (which were addressed by a parallel group consisting of the headteacher, deputy head and a teacher designated as curriculum leader). Monitoring implementation of decisions extending to classroom observation was being developed through training for the headteacher and deputies at Winton. The headteachers of the other schools had accepted that this potentially threatening level of internal monitoring was a task for them alone. They were not sole determinants of the limits of SMT practice. Reticence among SMT colleagues to monitor the performance of other staff reflected their allegiance to the wider staff professional culture, which accorded individuals considerable classroom autonomy. These SMT members had used influence to voice their unease and realize their interest in avoiding an unwelcome task. The notion of a management hierarchy suited them here: they could argue it was not their job, as junior members, to monitor colleagues.

Second, the headteachers variably empowered team colleagues to contribute to tasks they did share. While the headteacher at Winton encouraged SMT colleagues to take initiatives within broad boundaries (such as piloting a system for improving student discipline), the other headteachers confined sharing to consulting team colleagues on their prespecified agenda. Where all members participated in making team decisions, the norm was universal that a working consensus must be achieved. Debate leading to a decision at Winton, however, commonly comprised 'open consultation' where all members were encouraged equally to offer ideas. The other headteachers tended to opt for a more hierarchical approach of 'bounded consultation', where they put forward their proposed decision and sought colleagues' comments before taking it to a meeting with other staff. Pooling information to build an overview was a feature of the four teams, but the flow of information and opinion was multidirectional at Winton and channelled more unidirectionally in the other SMTs towards what the headteacher wished to know.

Third, there was varied appreciation of individual members' complementary knowledge and skills. SMT members at Winton were aware of the complementarity of their expertise connected with their individual management responsibility, and of contrasting skills linked to personalities which were required to balance creative thinking with getting tasks completed. Awareness of complementarity in the other teams was restricted largely to knowledge connected with the hierarchical distribution of individual management responsibilities, suggesting that their contribution to the team did not run as deep.

While the team approach at Winton expressed belief in equal contribution of SMT members most fully, expression of belief in a management hierarchy was not only enshrined in the structure but was also reflected at times in the team's practice. Observation of Winton SMT meetings indicated that members other than the headteacher expressed their belief in the management hierarchy by ensuring that their contribution stayed inside the implicit boundaries set by her. They would check voluntarily that she was comfortable with the course of action they were advocating. The culture of teamwork shared throughout this team included the norm that the headteacher had authority as formal leader within the management hierarchy to pull rank, but only for contingent situations where equal contribution did not result in consensus. The flexibility with which all team members were able to switch between the two contradictory beliefs as circumstances changed was one foundation of synergy for this SMT. Unified commitment to combining individual energies in pursuit of a shared goal was not jeopardized when the prevalent norm of equal contribution was temporarily replaced by reversion to hierarchical operation. Team colleagues' willingness to switch in this way reduced the risk for the headteacher of losing control that relatively equal sharing can bring. The culture of teamwork here was sophisticated enough for contradictory beliefs and values to coexist without conflict, mutually empowering all members.

Sharing leadership though teamwork

The headteacher at Winton shared most leadership tasks, shared them with all her SMT colleagues, and did so relatively equally. While the other headteachers empowered their team colleagues to make a more restricted contribution as equals (especially to debate and some decisions), they shared fewer leadership tasks, shared less with more junior colleagues, and shared tasks unequally with all other members. The agency of all four headteachers was similarly delimited by national contextual factors connected with central government reforms, but differently by school level factors – notably the opportunity to create their team and choose its membership. The headteachers retained sufficient agency to employ their authority in orchestrating alternative approaches to sharing leadership within the SMT, dependent on their contrasting balance of belief in a management hierarchy and in equal contribution. Their team colleagues likewise had agency to use influence in making a supportive or resistant response to headteachers according to the balance of their own adherence to these contradictory beliefs and values. The agency of headteachers and their colleagues may have been more tightly delimited by reforms but it was still significant. The new central government promotion of a management hierarchy had yet to eliminate adherence to more egalitarian norms whose origin predates the reform era.

Figure 1 is a model explaining what occurred within the agency of the headteachers and other SMT members. It compares norms relating to belief in a management hierarchy and in equal contribution to which the headteacher subscribes (the left and right hand columns) with the equivalent norms to which other SMT members subscribe (the upper and lower rows). Each cell depicts the combination of norms held by the headteacher and other SMT members. (For simplicity, it is assumed that all other SMT members share allegiance to the same norm at any time.) The *upper left cell* represents the situation at Kingsrise and Waverley, whose headteachers adopted a strongly hierarchical team approach which their SMT colleagues accepted. Interaction was harmonious since there was congruence between norms followed by all members. The headteachers took a low risk of loss of control by restricting other members' contribution. The potential for SMT-wide synergy was also only moderate because the range of shared tasks over which their energies could be combined was limited. Other members were not encouraged to take initiatives or to contribute their ideas, beyond responding to the headteachers' proposals.

The *lower right cell* represents the situation at Winton, where the headteacher encouraged other members to make an equal contribution and they were willing to do so. Here the potential for SMT synergy was high because all members were involved in a wide range of tasks and were encouraged to contribute all of which they were capable, including taking their own initiatives. The risk of the headteacher losing control remained low only as long as other members sought outcomes within the headteacher's comfort zone and were willing to compromise if necessary to achieve this situation.

		Headteacher	
	Norms	*Management hierarchy*	*Equal contribution*
Other SMT members	*Management hierarchy*	**Moderate SMT synergy** • Headteacher operates hierarchically, • other members accept headteacher's seniority, • other members contribute few ideas, • working consensus achieved, • outcomes acceptable to headteacher.	**Low SMT synergy (disengagement)** • Headteacher encourages other members to make an equal contribution, • other members prefer headteacher to operate hierarchically, • other members contribute few ideas, • willingness to compromise in favour of headteacher, • outcomes acceptable to headteacher.
	Equal contribution	**No SMT synergy (open conflict)** • Headteacher operates hierarchically, • other members do not accept headteacher's seniority, • other members contribute few ideas, • no consensus achievable, • outcomes not acceptable to headteacher.	**High SMT synergy** • Headteacher encourages other members to make an equal contribution, • other members wish to make an equal contribution, • all members contribute many ideas, • outcomes acceptable to headteacher.

FIGURE 1 Modelling interaction between the headteacher and other SMT members

Interaction is harmonious in both cells where there is congruence between the norms followed by all members, but the level of synergy is potentially greater where all involved can make an equal contribution. The solid arrow linking the *upper left and lower right cells* indicates how a team may sustain harmonious interaction and reap as much synergy as is possible at any time through all members working towards making an equal contribution. If the contingency arises where one or more other members advocate action lying outside the headteacher's comfort zone, harmony may be sustained if they can accept the headteacher withdrawing a decision from the team and making it unilaterally, as the team leader who is externally accountable for the work of the SMT. The key to smooth operation and maximizing synergy is for both headteacher and other SMT members to be flexible enough to switch together temporarily, for such contingencies, from adherence to the norm of equal contribution to the norm of a management hierarchy.

The remaining two cells depict how synergy may be compromised through disjunction between norms followed by the headteacher and other SMT members. The *lower left cell* covers situations where the headteacher operates hierarchically by pulling rank according to his or her position in the management hierarchy. But other members do not accept this move, because it transgresses their belief in their entitlement to make an equal contribution. Conflict may ensue, as at Pinehill after the arrival of the new headteacher when other members found his strongly hierarchical approach to leadership unacceptable. The *upper right cell* covers situations where the headteacher encourages colleague members to make an equal contribution, but they act according to their subordinate position in the management hierarchy. The result is disengagement of other members, as they withhold from making the contribution fostered by the headteacher. Such a situation arose in the more hierarchical SMTs where headteachers encouraged other team members to participate in monitoring other staff but they declined the invitation, implying it was the headteacher's task as top manager.

From practice to prescription: a contingent approach to sharing leadership

This model indicates how different approaches to sharing leadership in the case-study SMTs proved significant for the degree of synergy attainable. While the arguments put forward earlier for the principle of sharing school leadership widely and equally are persuasive as far as they go, they fail to take into account two features of the real world, at least in Britain: the risk that sharing will result in ineffective leadership which is unacceptable because of its negative impact on students' education; and the strict hierarchy of accountability where the headteacher may have to answer for empowering colleagues to make an equal contribution if things are deemed to have gone wrong. The research implies that prescriptions for school leadership should be informed by evidence, and so rest on principles that are context-sensitive: the approach advocated will therefore be contingent on circumstances. For the UK, evidence-based principles might be:

1. School leadership should be shared widely and equally to maximize the potential benefit for children's education and for teachers' job satisfaction and professional growth.
2. Headteachers have responsibility for promoting shared leadership but the right, because of their unique accountability for doing so, to delimit the boundaries of sharing and to have the final say where there is disagreement over leadership decisions.
3. Other teachers have the right to participate in school leadership but the responsibility, because of the headteacher's unique accountability for their work, to ensure that they operate within the boundaries set, including letting the headteacher have the final say where there is disagreement over leadership decisions.

These principles would justify British headteachers working towards the most extensive, equal sharing of leadership possible to maximize potential for synergy, while allowing for contingent reversal to hierarchical operation to minimize the risk of disaster. Such a context-dependent prescription runs counter to the more generic prescriptions portrayed in North American normative theories like transformational leadership and organizational learning, whose applicability to the UK environment was questioned earlier. Arguably, such theories beg for elaboration and refinement to reduce their cultural relativity, so that they embrace more of the complexities of leadership in different real world situations and have wider applicability between contexts.

Finally, school leadership training and informal learning support should include raising participants' awareness of their contradictory beliefs and values. Assistance could be offered with learning to live with this contradiction and to switch between alternative beliefs and values as contingencies arise. Rather than offering simplistic advice (until recently, in Britain, pushing towards context-free equal sharing of leadership), headteachers could be advised to adopt a contingent approach, depending on an ongoing situational analysis.

The approach to training and shared leadership practice suggested here flies in the face of most training in the UK and elsewhere, which tends to reduce the complexity of leadership to a single formula for action. This research shows that real life is not so straightforward and the sooner training catches up with this complexity, the better. It is ironic that another UK reform – preparatory training for aspiring headteachers, introduced in 1997 – is cast so much in terms of hierarchy, reversing trainers' equally simplistic earlier orientation. The central government project of 'modernizing' the teaching profession, reflecting a hierarchical approach to leadership in the service of New Labour educational goals, may be challenged: it inhibits headteachers and their colleagues from sharing leadership in ways that maximize everyone's potential contribution. An approach to sharing leadership which works towards equal contribution, with an occasional regression to hierarchy, may be where the synergy lies that could really make a difference to the quality of school leadership, and so help raise educational standards. Yet the training syllabus focuses closely on the headteacher as directive top manager (Teacher Training Agency, 1998). Sharing leadership through an SMT scarcely makes it onto the new training agenda. Where is the justice in that?

References

Bacharach, S. and Lawler, E. (1980) *Power and Politics in Organizations.* San Francisco: Jossey–Bass.

Bower, M. (1966) *The Will to Manage.* New York: McGraw–Hill.

Conger, J. and Kanungo, R. (1998) *Charismatic Leadership in Organizations*. Thousand Oaks, CA: SAGE.

Giddens, A. (1984) *The Constitution of Society*. Cambridge: Polity Press.

Grace, G. (1995) *School Leadership: Beyond Educational Management*. London: Falmer.

Hall, V. and Southworth, G. (1997) 'Headship: state of the art review', *School Leadership and Management*, 12(2): 151–70.

Hargreaves, A. (1994) *Changing Teachers, Changing Times: Teachers' Work and Culture in the Post-Modern Age*. London: Cassell.

Lortie, D. (1969) 'The balance of control and autonomy in elementary school teaching', in A. Etzioni (ed.), *The Semi-Professions and Their Organization*. New York: Free Press.

Nias, J., Southworth, G. and Yeomans, R. (1989) *Staff Relationships in the Primary School: A Study of Organizational Cultures*. London: Cassell.

Pounder, D. (ed.) (1998) *Restructuring Schools for Collaboration*. Albany, NY: State University of New York Press.

Senge, P. (1990) *The Fifth Discipline: The Art and Practice of the Learning Organization*. London: Century Business.

Sergiovanni, T. (1996) *Moral Leadership: Getting to the Heart of School Improvement*. San Francisco: Jossey–Bass.

Southworth, G. (1998) *Leading Improving Primary Schools: The Work of Headteachers and Deputy Heads*. London: Falmer Press.

Starratt, R. (1995) *Leaders with Vision: The Quest for School Renewal*. Thousand Oaks, CA: Corwin Press.

Teacher Training Agency (1998) *National Standards for Headteachers*. London: TTA.

Wallace, M. (1999) 'Combining cultural and political perspectives: the best of both conceptual worlds?', in T. Bush, L. Bell, R. Bolam, R. Glatter and P. Ribbins (eds), *Redefining Educational Management: Policy, Practice and Research*. London: Paul Chapman.

Wallace, M. and Hall, V. (1994) *Inside the SMT: Teamwork in Secondary School Management*. London: Paul Chapman.

Wallace, M. and Huckman, L. (1999) *Senior Management Teams in Primary Schools: The Quest for Synergy*. London: Routledge.

Weindling, D. and Earley, P. (1987) *Secondary Headship: The First Years*. Windsor: NFER-Nelson.

Whitty, G., Power, S. and Halpin, D. (1998) *Devolution and Choice in Education*. Buckingham: Open University Press.

Index